The Hemmings Book of

DODGES

ISBN 1-591150-09-4
Library of Congress Card Number: 2002107917

One of a series of Hemmings Motor News Collector-Car Books. Other books in the series include:
The Hemmings Book of Postwar American Independents; The Hemmings Book of Buicks; The Hemmings Motor News Book of Cadillacs; The Hemmings Book of Postwar Chevrolets; The Hemmings Motor News Book of Corvettes; The Hemmings Motor News Book of Chrysler Performance Cars; The Hemmings Book of Prewar Chryslers; The Hemmings Book of Prewar Fords; The Hemmings Motor News Book of Postwar Fords; The Hemmings Book of Mustangs; The Hemmings Motor News Book of Hudsons; The Hemmings Book of Lincolns; The Hemmings Book of Mercurys; The Hemmings Book of Nashes; The Hemmings Book of Oldsmobiles; The Hemmings Motor News Book of Packards; The Hemmings Book of Pickup Trucks; The Hemmings Book of Plymouths; The Hemmings Motor News Book of Pontiacs; The Hemmings Motor News Book of Studebakers.

Copyright 2002 by and published by Hemmings Motor News, a division of American City Business Journals, Inc., also publishers of Special Interest Autos, Hemmings Rods & Performance, and Hemmings Collector Car Almanac. All rights reserved. With the exception of quoting brief passages for the purpose of review, reproduction in whole or in part is forbidden without written permission from the Publisher of Hemmings Motor News, P.O. Box 256, Bennington, VT 05201.

Hemmings Motor News
Collector Car Publications and Marketplaces
1-800-CAR-HERE (227-4373)
www.hemmings.com

Some words and brand names, for example model names, mentioned herein are the property of the trademark holder and are used by the publisher for identification purposes only.

The Hemmings Book of

DODGES

President and Publisher
James C. Menneto

Editor
Richard A. Lentinello

Designer
Nancy Bianco

Front cover: 1962 Dodge Lancer 770. Photograph by Don Spiro
Back cover: 1937 Dodge convertible sedan. Photograph by Bud Juneau

This book compiles driveReports which have appeared in *Hemmings Motor News*'s *Special Interest Autos* magazine (SIA) over the past 30 years. The editors at *Hemmings Motor News* express their gratitude to the following writers, photographers, and artists who made this book possible through their many fine contributions to *Special Interest Autos* magazine:

Harry Bradley	Bob Hovorka	Douglas Mellor
Arch Brown	Bud Juneau	Roy Query
Richard Carpenter	John Katz	Don Spiro
David Gooley	Michael Lamm	Jim Tanji
Ken Gross	Vince Manocchi	Russell von Sauers
Robert Gross	John Matras	Josiah Work

We are also grateful to David Brownell, Michael Lamm, and Rich Taylor, the editors under whose guidance these driveReports were written and published. We thank Chrysler Corp., Dodge Division and Motor Trend for graciously contributing photographs to *Special Interest Autos* magazine and this book.

CONTENTS

Special Interest Autos (SIA) magazine's back issues are referred to in this book by issue number. If in stock, copies may be purchased directly from Hemmings Motor News at 800-227-4373, ext. 550 or at www.hemmings.com/gifts.

1930 DODGE DD6

The First Dodge from Chrysler

By Arch Brown
Photos by Jim Tanji

NEWSPAPER advertisements, radio commercials and even the trade journals in January 1930 carried the word that four new lines of cars were being featured in the showrooms of Dodge Brothers dealers.

And so they were, but it was all a little misleading. Two of the four, models DA6 and the Senior Six, were carry-over series, unchanged from 1929. The Chrysler Corporation's Dodge Division had produced several thousand more cars than it had sold in 1929, and there are indications that the company also had on hand the component parts of a good many additional units. Obviously, the inventory had to be liquidated.

It was the other two cars, models DD6 and DCS, unveiled just after the first of the year, that were the true 1930 models—as well as the first Chrysler-designed automobiles to wear the Dodge Brothers badge. The DD6, represented by our driveReport car, was a sprightly six bearing a strong family resemblance to both the De Soto and the smaller Chryslers. The DD8, on the other hand, was the first eight-cylinder car ever pro-

duced by Dodge (see sidebar, page 11).

The Dodge brothers, John and Horace, had gotten their start—as had so many others in the 1890s—in the bicycle business. Moving on to greener pastures in 1901, they opened a machine shop in Detroit, where they built engines for Oldsmobile. Later, expanding their operation, they made both transmissions and engines for the fledgling Ford Motor Company.

As Ford prospered and grew, the Dodges became rich. They also became increasingly apprehensive about their own future, despite the fact that John Dodge had been a Ford vice president since 1906, for Henry Ford's operation was becoming increasingly self-sufficient.

By mid-1914 the Dodges had ceased to be suppliers of Ford components, and John Dodge had resigned his position at Ford. The brothers still held a large

block of Ford stock, which they eventually—in 1919—sold to Henry Ford for $25 million, a good deal less than its actual worth.

But meanwhile, late in 1914, the Dodge Brothers automobile was introduced. So well known and highly respected were Horace and John that dealers were waiting in line for the chance to secure a Dodge Brothers franchise, and the car was an instant success. Entering a crowded field, the new automobile zoomed to third place in the industry by the end of its first full year of production—an astonishing record!

In a sense that first Dodge Brothers car was like a grown-up Model T Ford. Horace Dodge—who was primarily the engineer, while his brother attended to the business end of the enterprise—knew the Model T well, both its strengths and its shortcomings. So the new Dodge was built to be every bit as sturdy and very nearly as simple as the Ford, but a little larger, rather more comfortable, a lot more powerful (35 horsepower to the Ford's 20) and more than half-again as costly. At $785, it

4 Originally published in Special Interest Autos #76, Jul.-Aug. 1983

Dodge's 1930 line was the first to bear Chrysler's stamp in styling and engineering. Appearance was much more contemporary than previous Dodge Brothers cars. **Above:** Dropping of the "Brothers" appellation in the name is emphasized by new radiator script.

was still a bargain, particularly since it had a real, three-speed gearshift in place of the Ford's pedal-operated, two-speed planetary transmission.

By 1920 the Dodge Brothers car was the industry's second-best seller, behind only Ford and well ahead of the industry's other volume leaders, Chevrolet, Buick and Overland. But before that year was out the brothers Dodge were dead, John of pneumonia in January and Horace 11 months later—of a broken heart, some said.

The two widows turned to Frederick Haynes, a veteran associate of their late husbands, and Haynes ran the company in competent, if unspectacular fashion. But neither of the ladies had any real interest in the automobile business. Nor, it soon became obvious, did their sons. Accordingly, in 1925 the enterprise was sold to Dillon, Read and Company, a New York banking house. The price was $146 million, the largest such transaction ever recorded up to that time, and surely sufficient to keep the widows in the fashion to which they had happily become accustomed.

In retrospect it would appear that Dillon, Read's primary interest in acquiring Dodge may have been a stock promotion in which they promptly netted some $14

million. But whatever their intent, it soon became obvious that the bankers had little expertise in the automobile game. At a time when moderately priced six-cylinder cars from competing firms were enjoying ever-increasing popularity, Dodge stuck stubbornly to its four. Quality suffered somewhat, too, and by the 1928 season—which, coincidentally, saw the introduction of the firm's first six-cylinder cars—Dodge had fallen to thirteenth place in sales.

At that point, Clarence Dillon and his associates were ready to bail out.

Enter Walter P. Chrysler. He had wanted to buy Dodge earlier on, and having failed to do so he had developed the De Soto to fill that particular slot in his product lineup (see *SIA* #59). But on July 31, 1928, the deal was consummated at last; the Dodge Brothers organization became a division of the Chrysler Corporation.

Apart from the formation of the Chrysler Corporation itself, the acquisition of Dodge was undoubtedly the single most important act of Walter Chrysler's astonishing career. Overnight, he had doubled his dealer network, multiplied his production capacity several times over, and acquired one of the best foundries in the business—all of which

were vital factors in Chrysler's expansion plans. That his five-year-old company had absorbed an organization considerably larger than itself perturbed Walter Chrysler not in the least, although the purchase was seen on Wall Street as an act of sheer folly.

Obviously, at that late date a new, Chrysler-engineered Dodge for 1929 was out of the question. The three Dodge Brothers series, known as the Standard, Victory and Senior sixes, though essentially unchanged, had already been re-christened as "1929" models, and their production was continued.

These were very good cars, by the way—sturdy, in the Dodge Brothers tradition. But Dodge had never, up to that point, been noted for its styling, and these models, with the possible exception of the smallest series, were downright homely. Immediately, steps were taken to adapt Chrysler styling to the Dodge chassis, and in January 1929 two handsome new cars appeared. The DA6 replaced the previous Victory model, and its companion was a gracefully redesigned Senior Six. The Standard series, which had been priced head-to-head with the De Soto, was torpedoed.

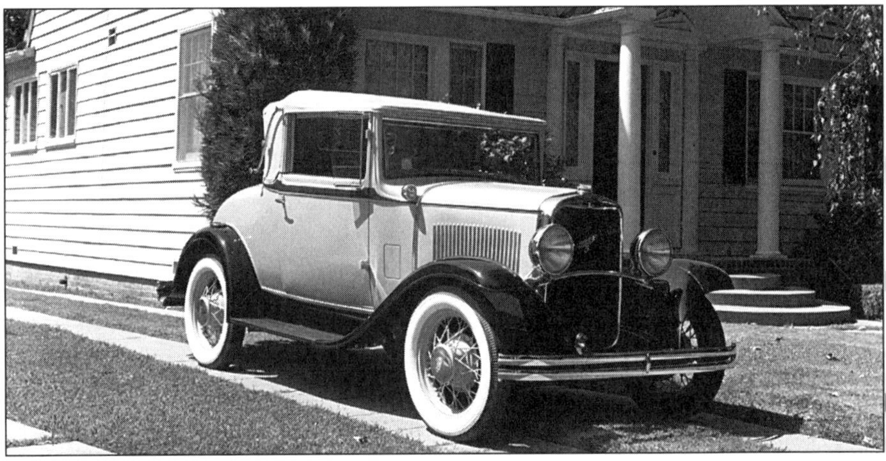

Right: *DriveReport car is rarest of the DD6 line, with just 620 examples produced during the 1930 model year.* ***Below:*** *Fold-out windshield was standard equipment to satisfy fresh-air fiends.* ***Below right:*** *Rumble seat passengers had no choice. They were subjected to an infinite amount of fresh air.*

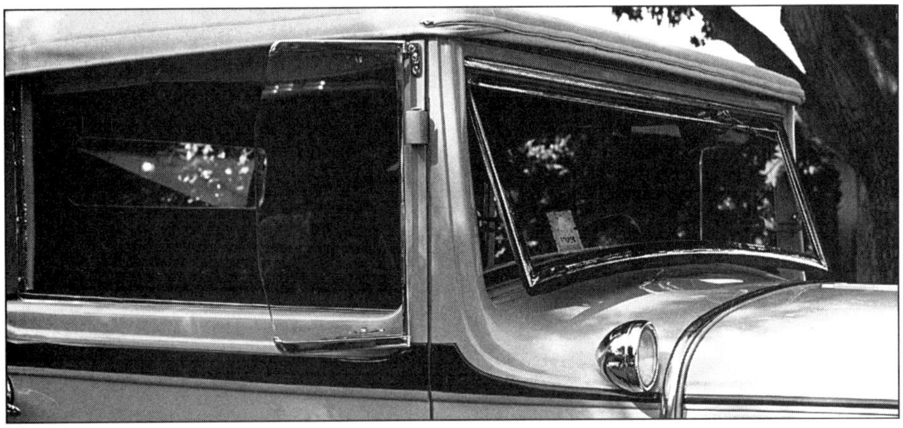

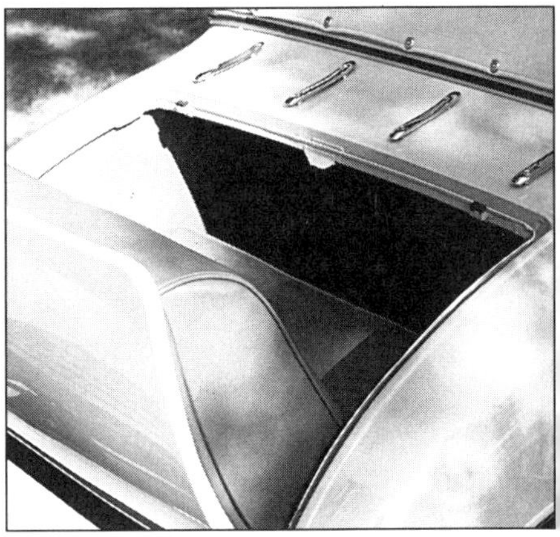

But of course it made no sense for the Chrysler Corporation to continue the manufacture of two such distinctly different lines of cars. An integrated product line would permit the concentration of the company's engineering talent, and make possible some important manufacturing economies as well.

The DD6 and DC8 series were the first Dodge cars to reflect that approach. An examination of their specifications (see sidebar below) will reveal how closely they were related to their corporate siblings from the De Soto and Chrysler Divisions. And it was with these cars that the phasing out of the Dodge Brothers name was begun. By the end of 1930, company advertisements referred to them simply as Dodge cars, though the familiar Dodge Brothers logo, with its six-pointed star, was retained for a few more years.

These new, Chrysler-designed Dodges were smaller, lighter, faster and less expensive than the cars they were destined to replace. The contrast was particularly evident in the case of the DC8, priced $450 lower than the Senior Six. Carrying a quarter-ton less weight than the big six-cylinder model, the new Dodge eight was a sparkling performer.

As the Depression deepened, sales of the Dodge straight-eight—after a promising start—fell off to almost nothing. Nor was the six setting any records! In 1933 Chrysler made a bold, though not unprecedented, move: Dodge and De Soto swapped places, so that the Dodge—the better-known nameplate of the pair—became the Chrysler Corporation's second-lowest-priced car. Sales scored a spectacular 206 percent increase, and the Dodge leapfrogged over Buick, Pontiac and Hudson's Terraplane to become the industry's fourth-best seller.

But that's getting ahead of our story. In 1930, when our driveReport car was built, Dodge was in seventh place—a big improvement over the number 13 spot it had occupied just two years ear-

Intra-Corporate Comparison Chart

(Note the close resemblance of the Dodge DD6 to the De Soto 6 and the smaller Chryslers of 1930, and of the Dodge DC8 to the De Soto 8. In contrast, observe how totally different in character are the Dodge Six and Senior Six, both of pre-Chrysler origin, as well as the larger Chrysler 70 series.)

	Price*	Net weight	Wheelbase	Cylinders	Bore and stroke	Displacement	Hp/rpm	Comp. ratio	Wgt./c.i.d.	Wgt./bhp	Hp/cu.in.
Dodge DD6	$949	2,668	109″	6	3⅛ x 4⅛	189.8	60/3,400	5.2:1	14.1	44.5	.316
Dodge 6	$994	2,867	112″	6	3⅜ x 4⅞	207.9	63/3,000	5.18:1	13.8	45.5	.303
Dodge DD8	$1,145	3,043	114″	8	2⅞ x 4¼	220.7	75/3,400	5.2:1	13.8	40.6	.340
Dodge Senior	$1,595	3,513	120″	6	3⅜ x 4½	241.4	78/3,000	5.55:1	14.6	45.0	.323
De Soto 6	$885	2,645	109.75″	6	3 x 4⅛	174.9	57/3,400	5.2:1	15.1	46.4	.326
De Soto 8	$995	2,965	114″	8	2⅞ x 4	207.7	70/3,400	5.2:1	14.3	42.4	.337
Chrysler 6	$845	2,745	109″	6	3⅛ x 4¼	195.6	62/3,2000	5.2:1	14.0	44.3	.317
Chrysler 66	$1,095	2,930	112.75″	6	3⅛ x 4¾	218.6	68/3,000	5.0:1	13.4	43.1	.311
Chrysler 70	$1,445	3,650	116.5″	6	3⅜ x 4	268.4	93/3,200	4.9:1	13.6	39.2	.346

*Prices shown are for base four-door sedan, f.o.b. factory.

(There's an oddity here, in that the Chrysler Six, heavier and more powerful than the Dodge DD6 or the De Soto 6, is priced lower than either of them. 1930 was the only year in which this would be true; in 1931 a new Chrysler Six replaced both the Six and the 66 listed above. Powered by a brand-new, 217.8-c.i.d., 70-horsepower engine, it was priced just slightly higher than the Dodge.

Source: *Automobile Trade Journal*, April 1930.

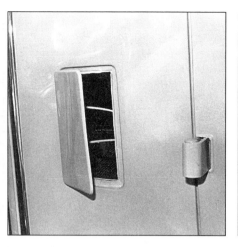

Above left: Additional ventilation was provided by cowl vents. *Above and far left:* Dodge has somewhat of a European flavor when top is in its landau position. *Left:* DD6 uses single tail/stoplamp. Gas tank is neatly concealed under sheet metal panel.

lier, but obviously far short of Dodge's potential, and certainly no match for its record of a decade earlier!

Driving Impressions

We first saw Kent Walker's smart little DD6 convertible at a concours in Lafayette, California. The top, which was arranged in landau position for the show, caught our attention, for a three-position convertible top is an unusual feature for an American car.

Kent found his Dodge through a newspaper advertisement, back in 1976. Mostly complete (though missing a few critical items such as headlight lenses and the radiator cap), it was badly in need of a full restoration. It proved to be a five-year undertaking, with Kent, a Sacramento, California, attorney, tackling a good deal of the work himself. The engine, however, was farmed out to a machine shop, and some of the more difficult body work was done by a genius named Ray Dalke. One fender, for instance, was so badly mangled that Ray was forced to fabricate most of a new one out of sheet metal. And parts of two radiator shells—one rusted through at the bottom, the other hopelessly damaged at the top—had to be welded together to form one usable unit.

Originally equipped with the standard, wooden artillery-type wheels, the little Dodge is now fitted with a set of smart, nipple-spoke wires, an authentic option on the early 1930 cars. (The arched pattern of the hood louvers

reveals the car to have been produced early in the model year, according to Dave Hochhalter, a Vancouver, Washington, aficionado who has made an extensive study of this model and is presently compiling a registry of the remaining DD6 and DD8 cars.)

There is no provision for adjusting the seat and, although the driving position is very good, we found the leg room rather restricted. Dashboard instrumentation includes an electric fuel gauge as well as ampere and oil pressure indicators, but no temperature gauge is furnished, either on the dashboard or the radiator cap. We would find that a bothersome omission, although these cars were not given to overheating.

The Dodge moves out briskly, easily able to keep up with the stream of Sacramento traffic. Steering is rather

quick and easy enough when the car is under way—though parking takes a little muscle. Synchronized gears had not yet come to the Chrysler Corporation in 1930. There's a knack to shifting gears without clashing, and it took a few tries before we mastered the technique. Double-clutching is part of the routine, of course, and we found that a smooth shift is most readily accomplished when the speed is moderate.

The ride is firm and a little bouncy—a predictable characteristic for a relatively light car of this vintage. The engine makes itself heard, especially at highway speeds, but the noise isn't particularly bothersome. Cornering is a real strong point; the car rides through the curves with minimal lean and under good control. Brakes, too, are better than we expected—superior, Kent says,

Price And Production Table, Dodge Brothers DD6

Body style	Price	Weight	Production
Business coupe	$835	2,534	3,877
Coupe with rumble seat	$855	2,603	3,363
Roadster with rumble seat	$855 ($939)	2,462 (2,650)	772
Phaeton*	$875	2,521	542
Convertible*	$935	2,605	620
Sedan	865	2,688 (2,668)	33,432
Chassis	n/a	n/a	899

Sources: McPherson, Thomas, *The Dodge Story; Automobile Trade Journal*, April 1930

DODGE PRODUCTION 1930-33 (MODEL YEARS)

Year	6-cylinder	8-cylinder
1930	43,505	25,250
1931	40,826	11,864
1932	21,042	6,187
1933	104,455	1,652

This table, covering the four years in which Dodge Division manufactured a straight-eight, is interesting in a couple of respects:

First, note that following a moderately successful introductory year, 1930, production of the eight-cylinder car fell off rapidly and steadily until it was discontinued early in 1933.

And second, observe how sales of the Dodge Six took off when it traded places with the De Soto to become the Chrysler Corporation's second-lowest-priced car, in 1933. Remarkably, although Dodge sales were multiplied five times over, very little of this gain appears to have been at the expense of the De Soto, whose 1933 production fell by only 7.2 percent from 1932.

Source: Heasley, Jerry, *The Production Figure Book For U.S. Cars.*

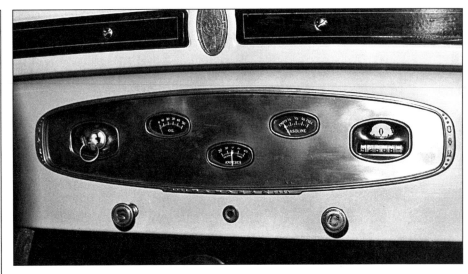

to those of his 1940 Ford. And the body is amazingly tight, particularly for a convertible. No squeaks, no rattles; a nice, solid-feeling automobile.

Kent Walker is a veteran old-car hobbyist. President of the Sacramento Jaguar Club, he owns an XJS, and his next restoration project will be a Mark IV drophead. In addition, along with the Dodge and the '40 Ford convertible, he has a '57 'Bird and a couple of prewar Ford pickups.

"This hobby may borrow your money for awhile," Kent observes, "but if you're careful about your selection, restoring only cars with a relatively high potential

"K.T."

The telephone rang on Kaufman Thuma Keller's desk at Chrysler headquarters. On the other end of the wire was his old friend and colleague, William S. Knudsen, until recently President of General Motors and now—at the urgent request of President Franklin D. Roosevelt—in charge of the Office of Production Management.

It was early June 1940, just a few days following the evacuation of Dunkirk. The Nazi war machine had romped across Norway and Denmark—Knudsen's birthplace—a few weeks earlier, and the plight of the allies was becoming increasingly desperate.

"K.T., will you make tanks?" asked Bill Knudsen of the President of Chrysler.

"Sure. Where can I see one?" promptly responded Keller. That pungent reply epitomized the man. If it was something mechanical, K.T. could master it. If it was needed, Chrysler would build it, although at that moment Keller didn't know where—or how.

Less than a year later, Chrysler turned out its first 25-ton M-3 tank. By the time the war was over, the company had built 23,000 of them—along with military trucks, bombers and rockets.

Keller liked to refer to himself, in a whimsical understatement, as "a machinist by trade." That he was, of course, and a trained stenographer besides. In his youth he had spent two years in England as secretary to an itinerant evangelist. It was an odd hiatus in an otherwise single-minded career, although he remained a church member all his life.

Returning to the United States, Keller "paid his dues" as an apprentice in the machine shops at Westinghouse. His future, he had concluded, lay in mechanics, not paperwork. By 1909, at the age of 24, he was assistant to one of the Westinghouse superintendents.

Moving on, Keller worked successively for the Metzger Motor Car Company, then Hudson, then Maxwell, and in 1911 he joined General Motors. Assigned to Buick, in due time he became that division's General Master Mechanic. Buick's president in those days was Walter P. Chrysler, and a warm, lifelong friendship developed between the two men. Chrysler would later write of K.T., "He had the same love for machines that had dominated my life.... [He] had lots of fire and his feet were on the ground.... When he was told to go ahead, a job was as good as done."

By 1921 K. T. Keller was vice president of Chevrolet, then under the dynamic leadership of Bill Knudsen. Walter Chrysler, meanwhile, had left General and, in 1926, he summoned his old friend, appointing him vice president in charge of manufacturing for the then-fledgling Chrysler Corporation.

Two years later, on July 31, 1928, Chrysler acquired Dodge. The following morning, Walter Chrysler met with Clarence Dillon, the banker from whom the purchase had been made. Dillon told him, as Chrysler later recalled, that "We could let that great Dodge organization run itself, oh, for three months if we wanted to.

"Hell, Clarence," I said, "our boys moved in last night!"

Indeed they had, with K. T. Keller in charge. Signs, prepared in anticipation of the successful outcome of negotiations, were posted: *Chrysler Corporation, Dodge Division.* From that moment on, Chrysler people ran the show at Dodge, and by 1929 K. T. Keller held the title of President.

In 1935, Walter P. Chrysler stepped down as president of his company, retaining the title Chairman of the Board until his death five years later. In his place as the active head of the Chrysler Corporation stood K. T. Keller.

Stood, that is, not *sat,* for K.T. spent as little time as possible behind his desk. He much preferred to be out and about the plants, for he was, first and foremost, a production man; and it was said of him that he could identify a problem simply by listening to the sounds of the plant.

Keller was criticized, doubtless correctly, for his concept of styling. As Don Butler has noted, "He was not an advocate of styling as found acceptable by the public. Principally, his objection was to dimensional aspects of package proportions. He believed that sweeping length, low roofs and wide bodies were excessive, extravagant and impractical." And K.T. jolly well insisted that a man should be able to wear his hat while driving his automobile!

Keller was right in principle, no doubt about that, and he'd have loved the company's current crop of "K" cars. But he was out of step with the times, and as Chrysler's cars became increasingly boxy in appearance, the company's market share declined. Nevertheless, he remains as one of the automobile industry's all-time great production men.

K. T. Keller retired from the presidency of Chrysler in 1950, accepting the position of Chairman of the Board—an office which had remained vacant since Walter Chrysler's death a decade earlier. Keller left Chrysler altogether in May 1956, establishing his own office as a consultant.

"All you get from worrying is a bad heart," Keller once observed Evidently he was not much of a worrier, for his heart carried him past his eightieth birthday. He was in London, traveling as part of a study tour with a group of governors and trustees of Detroit's Institute of Arts museum when death came on January 21, 1966.

specifications

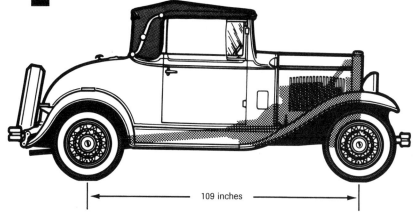

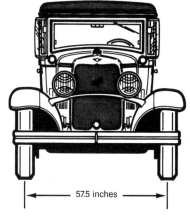

109 inches

57.5 inches

1930 Dodge Brothers Series DD6

Price when new	$935 fob, factory, with standard equipment
Standard equipment	Fuel, amp and oil pressure gauges on dash; rear traffic signal (combination stop/taillight); Delco-Remy shock absorbers;
Optional equipment	Wire wheels; bumpers front and rear

ENGINE

Type	6-cylinder in-line, L-head
Bore and stroke	3.125 inches x 4.125 inches
Displacement	189.8 cubic inches
Max bhp @ rpm	61 @ 3,400
Max torque @ rpm	n/a
Compression ratio	5.2:1
Induction system	Carter updraft carburetor; AC mechanical fuel pump
Lubrication system	Pressure to all bearings
No. of main bearings	4
Cooling system	Pump, thermostatically controlled
Electrical system	Delco-Remy, 6 volt

CLUTCH

Type	Borg & Beck single plate
Diameter	9.875 inches
Actuation	Mechanical, foot pedal

TRANSMISSION

Type	3-speed selective sliding gear
Ratios: 1st	2.15:1
2nd	1.79:1
3rd	1.00:1
Reverse	3.44:1

DIFFERENTIAL

Type	Spiral bevel
Ratio	4.9:1
Drive axles	Semi-floating

STEERING

Type	Gemmer worm and sector
Turns lock-to-lock	3
Ratio	n/a
Turn circle	41.25 feet

BRAKES

Type	Internal 4-wheel hydraulic
Drum diameter	11 inches
Total swept area	125.25 square inches

CHASSIS & BODY

Frame	6-inch channel depth; low-hung, deep section type
Body construction	All steel
Body style	Convertible coupe

SUSPENSION

Front	35.5-inch semi-elliptical leaf springs; solid axle
Rear	53.625-inch semi-elliptical leaf springs
Wheels	19-inch steel wire, drop-center rims
Tires	5.00 x 19

WEIGHTS AND MEASURES

Wheelbase	109 inches
Overall length	155.875 inches
Overall width	69.25 inches
Overall height	69.75 inches
Front tread	57.5 inches
Rear tread	58 inches
Ground clearance	8.25 inches
Shipping weight	2,605 pounds

CAPACITIES

Crankcase	6 quarts
Cooling system	12 quarts
Fuel tank	11 gallons

Facing page: Instrument panel is very straightforward and balanced; typical of Chrysler dash design of the time. **This page, left:** *Reliable, durable six-cylinder flathead engine was highly understressed, with only about 1/3 horsepower per cubic inch developed at 3,400 rpm.*

This page, below: Handy storage pouches in doors were offered in lieu of glove compartment. *Right:* Double bar bumpers in rear helped fend off the park-by-ear crowds. *Facing page:* Rear styling is typical of the times.

Chrysler Corporation's
Moderately Priced Straight Eights, 1930–1933

	Dodge	De Soto	Chrysler
1930	**DC**	**CF**	**No Chrysler eight offered in 1930**
Bore x stroke	2⅞ x 4¼	2⅞ x 4	
Displacement (cu. in.)	220.7	207.7	
Horsepower @ rpm	75/3,400	70/3,400	
Wheelbase	114 inches	114 inches	
Shipping weight (sedan)	3,043 pounds	2,965 pounds	
F.O.B. price (sedan)	$1,145	$995	
1931	**DG**	**CF***	**CD**
Bore x stroke	3 x 4¼	2⅞ x 4¼	3 x 4¼
Displacement (cu. in.)	240.3	220.7	240.3
Horsepower @ rpm	84/3,400	77/3,400	80/3,400
Wheelbase	118 inches	114 inches	124 inches
Shipping weight (sedan)	3,174 pounds	3,025 pounds	3,365 pounds
F.O.B. price (sedan)	$1,135	$995	$1,525
1932	**DK**	**(carried over unchanged)**	**CP**
Bore x stroke	3¼ x 4¼		3¼ x 4½
Displacement (cu. in.)	282.0		298.6
Horsepower @ rpm	90/3,400		100/3,400
Wheelbase	122 inches		125 inches
Shipping weight (sedan)	3,521 pounds		3,860 pounds
F.O.B. price (sedan)	$1,145		$1,475
1933	**DO**	**No De Soto 8 was offered**	**CT**
Bore x stroke	3¼ x 4¼		3¼ x 4⅛
Displacement (cu. in.)	282.0		273.8
Horsepower @ rpm	92/3,400		90/3400
Wheelbase	122 inches		119 1/2 inches
Shipping weight (sedan)	3,580 pounds		3,483 pounds
F.O.B. Price (sedan)	$1,145		$995

Note: the asterisk – * – was Chrysler's symbol for a "second series" car.

1930 DODGE

value, you'll get it back in the end, with a profit!"

As one out of an original production run of 620, this handsome and unusual little Dodge convertible will surely meet Kent Walker's criteria. ⟳

Acknowledgments and Bibliography

Automobile Trade Journal, *January 1930; April 1930; March 1934;* Automotive Industries, *January 4, 1930; February 22, 1930; March 31, 1928;* Stan Greyson, "The Brothers Dodge," Automobile Quarterly, *Volume XVII, No. 1;* New York Times, *January 22, 1966; Time, January 28, 1966;* "Of Arms and Automobiles," Fortune, *December 1940;* Current Biography, *1947;* Don Butler, The Plymouth and De Soto Story; Walter P. Chrysler, Life of an American Workman; Jerry Heasley, The Production Figure Book for US Cars; George Dammann, Seventy Years of Chrysler; B.C. Forbes (ed.), America's Fifty Foremost Business Leaders; Thomas A. McPherson, The Dodge Story; Factory sales literature; Allan Nevins and Frank Ernest Hill, Ford, Expansion and Challenge, 1915-1933.

Our thanks to Dave Brown, Durham, California; Scott Ewing, Sacramento, California; Dave Hochhalter. Vancouver, Washington; Tut Rivoir, San Jose, California. Special thanks to Kent Walker, Sacramento, California.

The Short Saga of the Dodge Straight Eight

As the decade of the thirties opened, straight-eight engines appeared to be the wave of the future. Most of the luxury cars used them: the fabled "Three P's"—Packard, Pierce-Arrow and Peerless—and Stutz, for instance, and, of course, Duesenberg, the car that had started the trend back in 1921.

In the medium-priced field the same movement had begun. Hudson, Nash and Studebaker—not to mention Auburn, Hupmobile and a host of lesser lights—all had straight-eights by 1930, to be followed by Buick a year later (see *SIA* #41). Obviously, the progressive new Chrysler Corporation would have to build them too.

But Walter P. Chrysler played an uncharacteristically cautious game. Taking no chances with the proud reputation of his namesake car, he brought forth the corporation's first two eights—early in 1930—from his Dodge and De Soto divisions. Not until the following year, after the new engines had proved themselves,

would there be straight-eights wearing the Chrysler badge.

From a sales standpoint, as Don Butler has observed (see "The Eights that Nobody Wanted," *SIA* #48) the eight-cylinder Dodges and De Sotos were a terrible disappointment—at least after the first few months. The De Soto version remained in production for only a little over two years, while the Dodge eight soldiered on into early 1933 before being dropped from the line.

Doubtless, the Depression was the key to the problem. Buyers—what few there were to be found—tended to favor the six-cylinder models, both for their lower initial cost and in anticipation of better gas mileage. But the new eights were fine automobiles, and from them were derived the straight eights that for 20 years bore the Chrysler name. The Chrysler Corporation did not permit its various divisions the degree of autonomy found at that time among General Motors' component organizations, and an

examination of the straight-eight sidebar on page 10 will show how closely the Dodge and De Soto eights were related, to one another and to the smaller eight-cylinder Chrysler cars.

At Dodge, the straight-eight started out as a relatively light car, much smaller than the Senior Six whose place it eventually took. But right away it began to grow, in displacement, power, wheelbase, weight—everything but price. One simply didn't raise prices in those Depression days! By 1933, with its demise at hand, the Dodge eight was actually a bigger, heavier, more powerful car than its counterpart from the Chrysler Division.

Given the minuscule production of the Dodge straight-eight (and the even smaller output from De Soto), it is hardly surprising that one seldom sees these cars today.

Had the times been better, perhaps the Dodge straight-eight would have rivaled the enviable sales record of the six, for it was an excellent car and a stellar value.

By Arch Brown
Photos by Jim Tanji

THE year 1933 was a pivotal one for America, and the world: • Franklin D. Roosevelt was sworn in on March 4, inaugurating what was to become the most significant and the most controversial presidency since that of Abraham Lincoln.

• Meanwhile, across the Atlantic, Adolf Hitler came to power as chancellor of the Third Reich.

• Prohibition, the "noble experiment," came to an end with the passage of the 21st Amendment.

• The nation's banks closed for a ten-day "holiday" while steps were taken to restore stability to the Depression-wracked financial system.

• For the first time since the Bolshevik Revolution of 1917, diplomatic recognition was extended by the United States to the Soviet Union.

• And the largest and last of America's great lighter-than-air dirigibles, the *Macon*, was launched. Within a month its sister ship, the *Akron*, would be lost in a storm off the New Jersey coast, carrying 73 members of its crew to a watery death. It was a tragedy that presaged the fate that would eventually befall the *Macon* as well.

Times, of course, were tough. But even so, life had its brighter side.

• The glittering "Century of Progress" Exposition opened in Chicago.

• Broadway fairly dazzled with great new shows. *Tobacco Road* commenced its record-shattering run of 3,182 per-formances, while the brothers Gershwin had another smash hit in *Let 'Em Eat Cake.*

• Radio drama was coming into its own. *The Lone Ranger* started its long series in November of that year, four months after the debut of one of the first and most durable of the "soap operas," *The Romance of Helen Trent.*

• The movies provided a badly needed escape from dreary reality. Fay Wray starred in the thriller *King Kong*, for instance; while a sensational new dance team was featured in *Flying Down to Rio.* Their names: Fred Astaire and Ginger Rogers, of course!

• And Tin Pan Alley had a fabulous season. At least a score of the "pop" tunes of 1933 have long since been recognized as "standards." Tunes like Irving Berlin's "Easter Parade," Duke

1933 DODGE EIGHT

LAST OF THE BREED

Ellington's "Sophisticated Lady," Harold Arlen's "Stormy Weather," Jerome Kern's "Smoke Gets In Your Eyes," Richard Rodgers's "Lover" and Harry Warren's lovely "Shadow Waltz."

A vintage year it was, in more respects than one. And if it was a pivotal year for the United States of America, it was no less critical a time for the Chrysler Corporation's Dodge Division. For 1933 was the year in which Dodge scored the greatest production and sales gains in the entire industry!

It was also the year in which the Dodge straight-eight was dropped. Not for 20 years would Dodge again produce an eight-cylinder car.

The Dodge Eight had been introduced in 1930 as a lower-priced replacement for the heavy, expensive and slow-selling Senior Six. Together with a slightly smaller and less costly eight from De Soto, it represented the Chrysler Corporation's first venture into the eight-cylinder field. Not until the following year would the first Chrysler Eights appear.

Straight-eights were all the rage in

1930. Hudson and Nash introduced theirs that year, joining eights-in-line from such industry stalwarts as Studebaker and Auburn. Buick would follow suit the next year. And the Dodge Eight was modestly successful at first, accounting for nearly 37 percent of Dodge production that first season—despite a stiff, $280 premium over the price of the six-cylinder model. Given the state of the economy in 1930, it was a creditable record.

But as the Depression deepened, sales of the larger Dodge fell off rapidly. From 25,250 cars in 1930, production dropped two years later to 6,187 units, representing only 22.7 percent of Dodge Division's total output.

All of which suggests, of course, that even the less expensive Dodge Six was having a tough struggle. Something dramatic was clearly in order.

And, indeed, something dramatic was done! Walter Chrysler, when he purchased the Dodge Brothers organization in 1928, had positioned the Dodge just below the Chrysler in his corporate price structure, with the newly introduced De Soto occupying the slot between the Dodge and the low-priced Plymouth. To equate the Chrysler Corporation line to

that of General Motors, the Plymouth was positioned opposite Chevrolet; De Soto competed with Pontiac; Dodge occupied Oldsmobile's position; Chrysler banged heads with Buick; and the big Imperial was priced with Cadillac.

But for 1933 the lineup changed. In effect, the De Soto and Dodge sixes traded places. De Soto, whose eight-cylinder series had been dropped at the end of 1931, was upgraded. Instead of sharing most of its components with the Plymouth, as had previously been the case, the 1933 model was more closely related to the smaller Chryslers. A couple of hundred pounds heavier than its 1932 counterpart, the new De Soto was given a massive appearance that suggested an even heavier car than it really was.

The Dodge Six, meanwhile, moved in the opposite direction, with price cuts ranging from $175 to $200. Smaller and lighter than its predecessor, the 1933 model was also a good deal more stylish. Gone was the flat-front radiator; in its place was a sloping, gently curved grille.

The wood-spoked artillery-type wheels were likewise gone, replaced by the buyer's choice of wires or pressed steel spokes. And if the engine was slightly smaller than before, its horsepower was

1933 DODGE

marginally higher than that of the 1932 model.

It was a shrewd move on Walter Chrysler's part. For the Dodge name was far better known than that of the De Soto; and the switch put the Dodge where the market potential was the greatest. Less than a hundred dollars separated it from the Deluxe Plymouth.

Sales took off. Calendar year production trebled over the year before; model year production nearly quadrupled. And, in just one season, Dodge zoomed from eighth place in U.S. auto sales to fourth!

The gain was entirely on the strength of the Dodge Six (see sidebar, page 18). The eight, meanwhile, was fading fast. Its market position had remained unchanged when the Dodge Six was dropped into a lower price field. In fact, remarkably enough, the 1933 Dodge Eight was actually priced $150 higher than the Chrysler Royal Eight! To be

sure, the Dodge was larger, heavier and more powerful than the Chrysler, having grown considerably since its introduction three years earlier. But the Chrysler had by far the more prestigious name as well as a 14 percent price advantage. Not surprisingly, the Royal Eight outsold its counterpart from Dodge by a margin of more than six to one!

So the Dodge straight-eight was doomed; and a pity, too, for it was a particularly nice automobile. Consider some of its salient features:

• A 6.2:1 compression ratio provided the eight-in-line engine with 100 horse-

power—10 more horses than the year before, though the displacement remained the same.

• In terms of power-to-weight ratio, the Dodge was a country mile ahead of its rivals from Chrysler, Buick and Nash. It even edged out the Auburn! Only Hudson and Studebaker's Commander, in Dodge's price class, held the advantage in this respect.

• With 184 square inches of lining surface, the Dodge's brakes were 62 percent larger than those of the Chrysler!

• It also had the fattest tires in its field, and except for Auburn, the longest wheelbase.

• An automatic clutch was furnished as standard equipment. . . .

• And an automatic choke—highly unusual for 1933—was offered as an option.

• Luxury touches, exceptional for 1933, included dual windshield wipers, dual inside sun visors and two dome lights in the sedan—one in the rear compartment, the other over the driver's seat in order to facilitate the reading of maps.

• Chrysler's excellent "Floating Power" engine mountings were retained; and, in company with other Chrysler products,

Facing page, top: Trim lines and an abundance of moldings characterize sides of Dodge's body. ***Below:*** Dodge's famous ram mascot, still in use today as a symbol on Dodge trucks. ***This page, far left, left and below:*** Brand name identification abounds on the Eight, including the use of the old Dodge Brothers initials on the rumble seat step inserts and the sill plates.

the 1933 Dodge featured silent helical transmission gears, advertised by the company as an "industry first."

• There was even a tri-beam lighting system with an intermediate switch position "for country passing," as Dodge put it. The lights were designed with intersecting beams and, when switched to "country passing" position, the left headlamp continued to illuminate the right side of the road well ahead, while the right beam, aimed at the left side of the highway, was depressed.

Five body styles were offered: a four-door sedan (which accounted for 71 percent of the total production), a coupe with rumble seat, a handsome five-passenger coupe—really a victoria, though Dodge didn't use that term—a gorgeous convertible four-door sedan and a smart convertible coupe, exemplified by our driveReport car. Though somewhat more conservative in design than the six-cylinder series, particularly as viewed from the rear, they were all good-looking automobiles—and luxurious ones as well!

And yet, they failed to sell! Only 1,652 Dodge eights were produced for the

1933 season, a miserable 1.6 percent of the division's total output. And of that total only 56 were convertible coupes. So the car you see here is a very rare one indeed!

Driving Impressions

Less than 24 hours after he put the final touches on the restoration of his 1933 Dodge DO convertible, Tut Rivoir found himself guiding the car across the lawn at the Silverado Country Club, to

take its place in the Winner's Circle. In its first show appearance the Dodge had taken First-In-Class at the prestigious Silverado Concours d'Elegance! The award represented the culmination of three years of hard work. When Tut found the car, resting on four flat tires in a Los Angeles garage, it was straight, solid and very, very messy. The paint was shot, the top in shreds, the upholstery torn, and the tires so far gone after 12 years of neglect that when Tut made

1933 Dodge 8 Convertible versus the Competition

	Dodge 8	Auburn Custom 101A	Buick 50	Chrysler Royal 8	Hudson 8	Nash Special 8	Studebaker Commander 8
Price (Conv cpe)	$1,185	$1,045	$1,115	$1,035	$1,145	$1,055	$1,095
Engine	Straight 8	Straight 8	Straight 8	Straight 8	Straight 8	Straight 8	Straight 8
Displ. (cu. in.)	282.1	268.6	230.4	273.5	254.4	247.4	236.0
HP/rpm	100/3,400	100/3,400	86/3,200	90/3,400	101/3,600	85/3,200	100/3,800
Compr. ratio	6.2:1	5.26:1	5.25:1	5.2:1	5.8:1	5.1:1	5.5:1
Valves	L-head	L-head	OHV	L-head	L-head	L-head	L-head
Main bearings	5	5	5	5	5	9	9
Free Wheeling?	Yes	Yes	No	Yes	Yes	Yes	Yes
Brakes	Hydraulic	Mechanical	Mechanical	Hydraulic	Mechanical	Mechanical	Mechanical
Brkg Area (sq. in.)	184.2	236.3	133.2	113.6	175.0	195.0	157.0
Axle ratio	4.3:1	5.1:1*	4.7:1	4.3:1	4.64:1	4.44:1	4.36:1
Tire size	6.50/17	6.00/17	6.00/17	6.00/17	6.00/17	5.50/18	6.00/17
Wheelbase	122 inches	127 inches	119 inches	120 inches	119 inches	121 inches	117 inches
Net weight (lb.)	3,465	3,569	3,525	3,363	3,145	3,270	3,245
HP per c.i.d.	.354	.372	.373	.329	.397	.344	.424
Pounds per hp	34.7	35.7	41.0	37.4	31.1	38.5	32.5
Pounds per c.i.d.	12.3	13.3	15.3	12.3	12.4	13.2	13.8

*Dual ratio

illustrations by Russell von Sauers, The Graphic Automobile Studio
© copyright 1985, Special Interest Autos

specifications

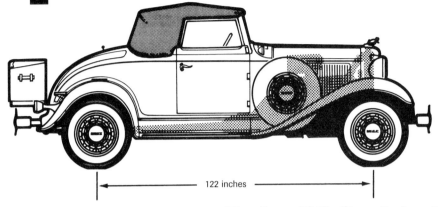

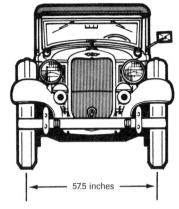

122 inches

57.5 inches

1933 Dodge DO Straight-Eight

Price	$1,220 f.o.b. factory, with standard equipment
Standard equipment	Dual trumpet horns, dual windshield wipers, dual taillamps, automatic clutch, free wheeling
Options on dR car	6 wheels, sidemounted spare tires with metal covers; white sidewall tires; luggage rack with trunk; fog lights; safety glass, all windows; bumpers and bumper guards

ENGINE
Type	Straight-eight
Bore and stroke	3¼ inches x 44 inches
Displacement	282.1 cubic inches
Valve configuration	L-head
Main bearings	5
Max bhp @ rpm	100 @ 3,400
Max torque @ rpm	n/a
Compression ratio	6.2:1
Induction system	1½-inch Carter E8A 2-bbl carburetor, mechanical pump
Electrical system	6-volt

CLUTCH
Type	Single dry plate
Diameter	9⅞ inches
Actuation	Automatic (or mechanical, foot pedal, with automatic clutch and free-wheeling locked out)

TRANSMISSION
Type	3-speed selective, synchronized 2nd and 3rd gears
Ratios: 1st	2.59:1
2nd	1.49:1
3rd	1.00:1
Reverse	3.24:1

DIFFERENTIAL
Type	Spiral bevel
Ratio	4.30:1
Drive axles	Semi-floating

STEERING
Type	Worm and wheel, semi-irreversible
Ratio	17:1
Turns lock to lock	3½
Turn circle	40 feet

BRAKES
Type	Hydraulic, drum type
Drum diameter	13 inches
Brake contact area	184.2 square inches

CHASSIS AND BODY
Frame	Double-drop, bridge type, channel 7 inches deep, X-member
Body construction	All steel

Body manufacturer	Budd
Body style	Convertible coupe, 2-4 passenger

SUSPENSION
Front	35.9375-inch semi-elliptical leaf springs, solid axle
Rear	54⅞-inch semi-elliptical leaf springs, solid axle
Shock absorbers	Delco
Tires	6.50/17
Wheels	Nipple-spoke wire

WEIGHTS AND MEASURES
Wheelbase	122 inches
Overall length	194.46875 inches
Overall height	66 inches
Overall width	68 inches
Front tread	57½ inches
Rear tread	59¼ inches
Ground clearance	9 inches
Shipping weight	3,465 pounds

FUEL CONSUMPTION
Average	14 mpg

Model year production, Series DO (8 cyl): 1,652
Model year production, this body style: 56
Percent of Dodge production in Series DO: 1.56%
Percent of Dodge production in this model/body style: 0.05% (one-twentieth of one percent!)

Dodge exhibits very little body lean even when pushed hard into turns.

Far left: Waterfall-style grille has KA Lincoln-like shape. **Left:** Trunk should be considered a necessity instead of an accessory in a car with so little storage space. **Below left:** Hefty chromed clamps and wing nuts hold sidemounts in place. **Below:** Dual cowl vents add to luxury car feel in Dodge.

The Dodge Straight-Eight and How it Grew: 1930–1933

Year	Series	Bore/stroke	Displacement	Comp. Ratio	Hp/rpm	Wheelbase	Weight*	Price*
1930	DC	2⅞ x 4¼	220.7	5.2:1	76/3,400	114 inches	3,043	$1,145
1931	DG	3 x 4¼	240.3	5.2:1	84/3,400	118 inches	3,174	1,135
1932	DK	3¼ x 4¼	282.1	5.2:1	90/3,400	122 inches	3,527	1,145
1933	DO	3¼ x 4¼	282.1	6.2:1	100/3,400	122 inches	3,580	1,145

* 4-door sedan
Source: *Automobile Trade Journal* (various issues)

1933 DODGE

an effort to pump them up the first one blew sky-high! The convertible had been driven into the garage in 1969 and simply left there. The wheels hadn't been jacked up, nor had the fluids been drained. It was, in short, the epitome of neglect!

Just what the previous owner had in mind when he parked the Dodge is anybody's guess, but by 1981 he had determined to get rid of it. He spoke to someone of his intent to advertise it in *Hemmings.* Word travels swiftly on the car hobbyists' grapevine, and in short order Tut Rivoir, at the other end of the state, heard about the rare Dodge that had suddenly become available. He caught the next flight to Los Angeles, and within an hour of his arrival the convertible had changed hands!

Rivoir hauled the car by trailer to his home in San Jose, and the long job of restoration commenced. The brakes, of course, needed a complete overhaul; leaving the fluid in a set of hydraulics over a span of 12 years is not a procedure to be recommended! This part of the work Tut undertook himself.

There was a lot of surface rust on the engine block, but no serious problems

in that department. Neither the carburetor nor the oil filter were authentic for a 1933 Dodge, however. In time the correct filter turned up at a swap meet, and a new-old-stock carburetor was located at a veteran Dodge dealership. An old-time Chrysler mechanic in East San Jose tore down the engine and found that at some point it had been bored to .0030 oversize. Taper was negligible. New rings were installed, a couple of bearings were poured and with a routine

valve job the old flathead was as good as new.

A number of small parts were missing: door handles, windshield hardware and the like; and a few of the bolts lacked the authentic "DB" embossment. So, for a couple of seasons, Rivoir—determined that the car should be as authentic as possible—haunted the swap meets. Meanwhile, a specialty shop in nearby Santa Cruz reupholstered the convertible, using three flawless English hides

1933 DODGE PRICES, WEIGHTS AND PRODUCTION

Series DO, Eight-Cylinder:

Body style:	Price:	Weight:	Production:
Coupe, 2-4 pass.	$1,115	3,451	212
Coupe, 5-pass.	$1,145	3,540	159
Sedan, 4-door	$1,l45	3,580	1,173
Convertible Coupe, 2-4 pass.	$1,220	3,465	56
Convertible Sedan, 4-door	$1,395	3,961	39
Chassis	n/a	n/a	13
Total:			1,652

Series OP, Six-Cylinder:

Body style:	Price:	Weight:	Production:
Coupe, 2-pass.	$595	2,475	11,236
Coupe, 2-4 pass.	$640	2,520	8,879
Sedan, 2-door	$630	2,591	8,523
Sedan, 4-door	$670	2,650	69,074
Salon Brougham	$660	2,678	4,200
Convertible Coupe	$665	2,523	1,563
Chassis	n/a	n/a	980
Total:			104,455
Grand total, both series (model year):			106,107

Percent of total production, Series DO (8 cyl.):1.56%

Dodge's Sensational Six

Visitors to the Century of Progress Exhibition—the 1933 Chicago World's Fair—were treated to what must have been the most spectacular display of stunt driving that most of them had ever seen. Held at a demonstration track adjoining the Chrysler Corporation pavilion, the show was staged under the direction of the legendary Barney Oldfield.

Billed as "Hell's Drivers," the stunts were a superb demonstration of the performance and durability of the cars, as well as of the skill of the drivers. And the automobiles involved were 1933 Dodge Series DP sixes.

On the face of it, that must have seemed unusual, for it was the Chrysler automobile that had always been thought of as the corporation's hotshot performer. Dodge's image, on the other hand, had been that of a solid, dependable family car—but not, in the parlance of the time, a "speed-burner."

But the Chrysler Corporation had chosen well. For, when equipped with the optional high-compression cylinder head (6.5:1—not much by today's standards), the Dodge developed 81 horsepower. Fitted to a car that weighed, in sedan form, only 16 pounds more than the 70-horsepower Plymouth, it provided a better power-to-weight ratio than anything else in the Chrysler stable—even the straight-eight Imperial. Better, in fact, than Ford's fast-moving V-8!

There was a second reason for selecting the Dodge. Recognizing the economic realities of the times, Chrysler had repositioned the Dodge in a price bracket just above that of the Plymouth. Clipping three inches off the wheelbase of the 1932 model and the better part of 200 pounds off its weight, they had come up with a car that was just an easy step above the "big three" of the low-priced field. It should be, company officials figured, a hot seller; and they pushed it hard.

They were right, of course. In one season Dodge shot from eighth place in the automotive sales race to fourth, elbowing aside Hudson-Essex, Pontiac, Studebaker-Rockne and Buick in the process. And Dodge retained that number four position for five straight years!

It's no criticism to say that the 1933 Dodge looked like a slightly overgrown Plymouth. Cars from the Chrysler Corporation always bore a strong resemblance to one another, just as cars from General Motors do today. But when the Deluxe Plymouth was introduced in April 1933, its wheelbase had been stretched to 111.25 inches, exactly the same as the six-cylinder Dodge. And so, with no fanfare—without even changing the OP Series designation, in fact—Dodge followed suit, maintaining its distinction from the Plymouth by extending its wheelbase to 115 inches. It was a felicitous change; proportions were better, and less than 30 pounds had been added to the weight of the car.

An attractive automobile, a sparkling performer, and—with prices as low as $595—a tremendous value, Dodge's new "six" was sensationally popular.

As indeed it should have been!

1933 DODGE

for the purpose. Finally a gorgeous green and gray finish was applied, smartly accented by orange wire wheels and a new set of wide-whitewall tires.

The Series DO Dodge was optionally available with a 5.2:1 compression ratio, but apparently nearly all the cars—including this one—left the factory with the standard 6.2:1 cylinder head. The horsepower was thus raised from a

Facing page, top: Frontal appearance is big and balanced. **Below:** *Sidelamps are mini-versions of headlamps.* **This page, left and below:** *For a relatively large car, Dodge's rumble seat space is skimpy.* **Below left:** *With top up, driver's compartment is cozy, yet has plenty of head room.* **Bottom:** *Straight eight was a thoroughly understressed engine, developing an even 100 bhp from 282 cubic inches of displacement.*

respectable 91 to a lusty (for 1933) 100. On the gas tank cap is engraved the caution, "Use High-Compression Gas."

For a car of its type and its era this one is a performer! Acceleration is fairly brisk, and the torque is impressive. The Dodge will idle smoothly along in top gear with the driver's foot removed from the throttle; then it will accelerate without complaint—and without the need for downshifting. Hills are flattened in exemplary fashion. The clutch is smooth and shifts are easy, with the short throws to second and high that were typical of Chrysler products in the thirties. The synchronizers are only partially effective, however, and we soon fell into the habit of double-clutching.

Steering is fairly quick and moderately heavy, but there's no "wheel-fight" when the car is driven over rough terrain. It rides comfortably, with only a trace of choppiness, and there's not a lot of lean on the turns. The driver has the reassuring feeling of being "in charge" at

Right: With a price nearly double its six-cylinder counterpart, the Dodge Eight was guaranteed slow sales in the depths of the Depression. Only 56 convertibles found buyers in 1933. *Below:* Plain-Jane steering wheel is out of character for relatively pricey car. *Below right.* Nicely detailed doors include convenient chromed grab handle. *Bottom:* Centrally located instrument panel is easy to read.

Acknowledgments and Bibliography
Automobile Trade Journal, *various issues*; Automotive Industries, *various issues*; Dodge factory literature; Thomas A. MacPherson, The Dodge Story; Motor, January 1933.

Our thanks to Ray Borges and Linda Huntsman, Harrah Automobile Foundation, Reno, Nevada; Dave Brown. Durham, California. Special thanks to Tut Rivoir, San Jose, California.

The Pros And Cons of The Dodge DO

Tut Rivoir hasn't had much opportunity to become intimately acquainted with his Dodge Straight-Eight and, of course, neither have we. But we've had enough experience with it to be able to pass along a few observations:

• In a sense, the DO represents the best of two worlds. It's very rare, yet because it shares a number of components with other Chrysler products, parts are not as scarce as one might expect.

• In every respect but one, it's a superb tour car: powerful, comfortable and easy to drive. The one drawback is its rather lusty appetite!

• Those oversize hydraulic brakes are as good as a lot of modern binders, an unusual feature for a 1933 car—and a comforting one!

• On the other hand, with that low seat coupled with a windshield that doesn't have a lot of height, visibility must be pretty limited for the short driver. For the person of average or greater height, however, it's no problem.

• And, unless you're on terrible terms with your mother-in-law, don't park her in that rumble seat. It's even more uncomfortable than most of the breed!

In balance we'd have to give the Dodge high marks, in terms of its desirability for today's hobbyist, and as a good car and a fine value for the new car buyer of 1933.

---

all times. And the brakes, not unexpectedly, are really superior.

Facing the driver is a full array of instruments. The speedometer, which registers a plausible 96,000 miles, is surrounded by the ampere, oil-pressure, temperature and fuel gauges. Protruding from the dashboard is an interesting little lever. Pulled all the way out, it locks the car in conventional drive. Pushed halfway in, it engages freewheeling. And shoved all the way to the dash, it activates the automatic clutch.

Doors are wide, making for ease of entry and exit. Leg room is ample. The seats are unusually low for a car of this era, which helps account for the generous head room, but the seating position is nevertheless quite comfortable. Back in the rumble seat, however, photographer Jim Tanji found the knee room a little cramped.

With an original production total of 56 units, more than half a century ago, there can't be many cars like this one remaining. You'll be able to see it for a season or two on the West Coast concours circuit, but Tut Rivoir looks forward to the day when he can forget about winning trophies and simply enjoy driving this fine old Dodge.

Certainly it's hard to imagine a more satisfactory tour car! ☞

"I bought my first Dodge nearly twenty years ago

. . . and this new '8' is the finest car Dodge ever built!"

No MATTER what kind of car you've been driving . . . no matter what price you're used to paying, the new Dodge "8" will be a revelation to you.

122-inch wheelbase . . . 100-horsepower—it's big, powerful, fast! And it is ultra-modern in appearance, in comfort, in driving ease.

Floating Power engine mountings give you unbelievable smoothness . . . freedom from vibration. A new feature—"inertia ride control"—automatically adjusts the shock-absorber to all types of road conditions. Oilite springs with metal covers are squeak-proof.

Driving is easy . . . effortless. Shifting is quiet in all speeds, including reverse. Starting is simple . . . turn on the ignition, step on the accelerator and presto! the engine is running.

This new Dodge "8" is speedy . . . and safe! Mono-piece steel body. Hydraulic brakes, with centrifuse drums. Double-drop X bridge-type frame. Low center of gravity. Duplate Safety Plate glass in windshield.

Go to a Dodge dealer and take a look at this new Dodge "8". You'll see why most Dodge owners, when buying a new car, unhesitatingly buy another Dodge!

NEW DODGE "8"
WITH FLOATING POWER
An Aristocrat from bumper to bumper

Dodge "8": Coupe with Rumble Seat $1115 ... Sedan $1145 ... Five-Passenger Coupe $1145 ... Convertible Coupe $1185
Convertible Sedan $1395 ... Dodge "6": $595 to $695 (All Prices F. O. B. Factory, Detroit)

SO RARE

1937 DODGE SERIES D-5 CONVERTIBLE SEDAN

LIKE most of its competitors, Dodge had enjoyed a profitable year during 1936. The depression-ravaged economy had picked up considerably by then, spurred by a substantial bonus granted to veterans of the World War. (Obviously, nobody in those days called it World War I.) The Chrysler Corporation zoomed past Ford that year to become, by a rather substantial margin, the nation's second-largest automaker. Its volume leader was Plymouth, whose production totalled well over half a million cars for the season. But Dodge, since 1933 the industry's fourth-best seller, was also doing well. Production increased that year by 66 percent over 1935, and '35 in turn had

by Arch Brown
photos by Bud Juneau

been 67 percent ahead of 1934's dismal figure.

So there appeared to be every reason to be optimistic about the Dodge Division's prospects for 1937. That upbeat outlook proved to be fully justified, for model year production reached 295,047, a 12 percent increase over the 1936 figure.

The familiar 87-horsepower L-head six was carried forward virtually unchanged, and chassis modifications

were comparatively minor. The Dodge's wheelbase was shortened by one inch, to 115 inches. Similarly, an inch was clipped from the length of the front springs. The frame was stiffened by additional crossmembers and by heavier boxing at the X-member center section. Perhaps the most significant mechanical differences between the 1937 model and its predecessors were, first, its insulated rubber body mountings, an industry "first"; and second, its use of hypoid gears, leading to a reduction in the driveshaft height. The Gemmer worm-and-roller steering mechanism remained unchanged, but surprisingly, braking area was reduced slightly.

If chassis modifications were minor,

Originally published in Special Interest Autos #127, Jan.-Feb. 1992

Driving Impressions

We first saw this particular automobile more than ten years ago. It was sitting in a restoration shop at the time, awaiting its turn. Its paint, light metallic blue in those days, was faded and the top was tatty, but the car was straight and complete. Inquiring, we learned that it belonged to the shop owner, so we secured his agreement that when the restoration was complete the Dodge would become the subject of a driveReport for *Special Interest Autos.*

Some months later we returned, only to find the shop padlocked. We asked around, seeking information on the whereabouts of the owner — and the Dodge. Somebody told us that the shop had gone bankrupt, and the convertible sedan had been sold to a collector in the Middle West, in the St. Louis area, our informant thought.

We put the matter out of mind. St. Louis is too far away, and in any case we didn't even have the supposed buyer's name.

Move the calendar forward now to June 2, 1991. We're attending the Silverado Concours d'Elegance, and here we see a 1937 Dodge convertible sedan. It's finished in an unusual color, something between Bittersweet Chocolate and Eggplant. It didn't occur to us that this might be the same car that we had admired a decade earlier. But when we contacted the owner, we learned that it is indeed that very Dodge. The report that it had been shipped to the Midwest was erroneous; the car had been in California's San Joaquin Valley all the time.

By the time we caught up to it, the convertible sedan had been largely restored. Its owner had gone through the engine, clutch and brakes, though oddly enough he had left the original wiring harness in place. The interior had been reupholstered in dark brown leather, similar to the original. (Even the door panels are done in genuine leather.) And it had been painted in its present, very attractive color.

The Dodge's current owner, Rhonda Madden, of San Rafael, found the car at an auction in January 1990. A long-time MoPar fan, she "simply had to have it." Rhonda has carried the restoration work several additional steps, tightening every nut and bolt ("Everything was loose!" she explains), overhauling the front suspension and the rear end, replacing the shock absorbers, and of course installing a new wiring harness. A new top was fitted by Armand Annereau, of Walnut Creek. Also replaced were the headlamp lenses, which proved to be very difficult to find.

After purchasing the Dodge, Rhonda went over it carefully with a magnet. There is no Bondo to be found in it anywhere, and it is apparent that this car has never been in a major accident. Neither is it a high-mileage unit. Clutch and brake pads, which appear to be original, show remarkably little wear. We even found a factory instruction tag, tied to the cord for the optional electric clock.

That clock, by the way, is an interesting little timepiece, and a very attractive one. But it is very small, and its location, in the glove box door, is so far removed from the driver that it would be impossible for him to read it while the car is under way.

A few more items need attention before the restoration can be considered complete. The striker plates are poorly adjusted, resulting in an abundance of door rattles, and there is more whine in the second gear than there ought to be. Evidently a buffer was applied to the car with more enthusiasm than skill, so the paint needs to be touched up in two or three places; and the trunk lid is slightly out of alignment. But these are minor matters that will probably have been attended to by the time this driveReport is in print.

This is a comfortable car. Front and rear seats were moved three inches forward in the 1937 model, contributing to a smooth ride — despite the rigid front axle — and the Dodge corners without leaning excessively. Seats are fairly supportive and leg room is ample, both front and rear. So

is head room, even for the six-foot-plus driver. (K.T. Keller would have loved this car.)

We found the Dodge to be a pleasant car to drive. Steering, while heavy by modern standards, is lighter than that of many cars of this vintage. The clutch is smooth, brakes are very effective, and neither pedal requires heavy pressure. Shifts require little effort, though it's easy to override the synchronizers if the floor-mounted lever is moved too fast. Throws are longer than those of some earlier Chrysler products — a "plus," in our view.

Putting the convertible sedan's top down (or back up again) is a two-person proposition, and not an easy one at that. It's worth the effort, however. We went topless for our test drive, and found it a delightful experience. On the other hand, with the top in place, rearward visibility would obviously be somewhat impeded.

Acceleration from rest isn't bad, but when the Dodge takes to the hills one becomes aware that, especially with the heavy convertible sedan body, it is really somewhat underpowered. And it's not about to chug smoothly along in top gear with the engine at idle, as at least one competing make will do. But that's what downshifting is all about. On the open road the Dodge will cruise at 55, but at that speed the 217.8-c.i.d. flathead is thrashing about rather noisily. Owner Rhonda Madden comments, "It really could use an overdrive!" Indeed it could, but oddly enough, that feature — offered by both Desoto and Chrysler in 1937 — was unavailable in the Dodge.

Of all the makes in this car's price range, only Dodge and Pontiac offered the four-door convertible body style during 1937. Neither found much of a market for it, and by 1939 both had abandoned the effort. It's simply too heavy, too clumsy and too expensive to be really practical for most buyers. But for our part, we consider the Dodge convertible sedan to be among the most desirable of all the thirties MoPars.

1937 DODGE

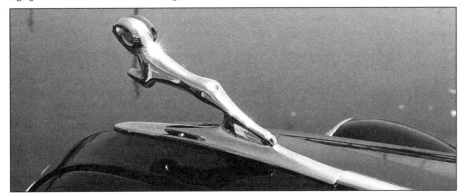

Wheel covers and hood ornament designs were carried over from 1936 cars, but the majority of sheet metal on the '37 Dodge bodies was all-new.

differences in styling were substantial — and attractive. The Chrysler Corporation's chief stylist in those days was Ray Dietrich, formerly of the coachbuilding firm bearing his name. Dietrich obviously drew some of his inspiration from the curvaceous lines of the Chrysler Airflow, then in its final year of production. But his designs, while softly rounded and entirely contemporary were not at all controversial, as the Airflow's had been.

The corporation's stamping plant had been enlarged and upgraded, permitting the use of a seamless, one-piece steel roof in lieu of the metal insert previously employed for the closed body types. Bodies were engineered by the Chrysler staff this time, rather than by Briggs though most of them were still Briggs-built.

Interiors were designed with safety in mind, an almost totally unknown concept in 1937. Knobs and switches were recessed; gauges were set flush with the surfaces. Door handles curved inward in order to reduce the chance of snagging. Gone were the usual protruding knobs and handles, that could be so hazardous in the event of a sudden stop.

Only one trim level was offered, and there were eight body styles on the standard, 115-inch wheelbase. Included were two coupes, one with a cavernous

trunk, the other with a rumble seat. Two- and four-door sedans came with or without a built-in trunk, and convertibles were offered in either two- or four-door style. In addition there were two larger cars, a seven-passenger sedan and a limousine, each built on a stretched, 132-inch chassis. Both were presumably intended primarily for the commercial trade, for the family that could afford to hire a chauffeur would surely have been able to choose a Chrysler Crown Imperial instead of a Dodge.

Prices, initially, were shaved by about five dollars, just enough to permit the company to advertise that reductions had been made. But along with virtually the entire industry, at mid-year the division posted substantial increases. In Dodge's case the boost amounted, in most instances, to $75, a difference of about ten percent. In the case of the convertible sedan, however, the price was boosted by a whopping $235.

It was 1935 when Dodge had first introduced its two- and four-door "touring sedans" — that is, sedans with bustle-backs that provided for built-in trunks. They had been an immediate success; from the very start they outsold the flat-back type by a margin of better than two to one. By 1936 fully 96 percent of all Dodge sedans were of the "touring" style. The price differential was only $10, little enough to pay for the convenience of a luggage compartment. Similarly, in 1937 the four-door touring sedan ranked first in sales, followed by its two-door counterpart.

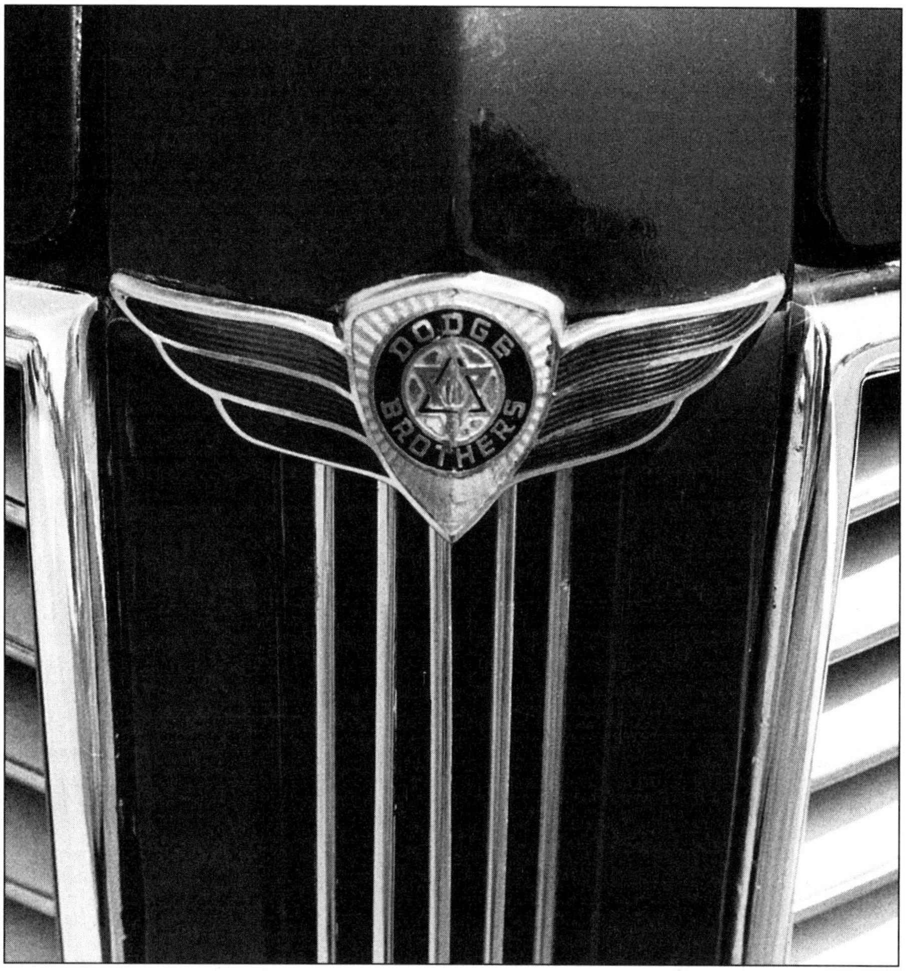

Traditional Dodge Brothers badge with wings and six-pointed star leads the way down the road.

1937 Comparison Table: Five Lower-Medium-Priced Cars

Dodge's principal competitor in its particular price bracket was the Pontiac, but there were some other fine cars in the field as well. The following table covers, in addition to Dodge, the Nash LaFayette 400, Pontiac Deluxe Six, Studebaker Dictator and Terraplane Super 6-72. Because only Pontiac and Dodge offered four-door convertibles, four-door touring sedans (meaning, sedans with built-in trunks) are used here for purposes of comparison. Note that all five makes posted steep price increases at mid-year.

	Dodge	**Nash**	**Pontiac**	**Stude**	**Terraplane**
Price, November 1936	$755	$700	$770	$795	$745
Price, July 1937	$830	$810	$861	$900	$885
Wheelbase	115 inches	117 inches	117 inches	116 inches	117 inches
Overall length	196⅛ inches	196 7/16 inches	193 1/16 inches	192 7/16 inches	193 3/16 inches
Front track	56 inches	58 inches	58⅜ inches	57⅜ inches	56 inches
Rear track	60⅛ inches	60¼ inches	59 inches	60⅜ inches	57½ inches
Shipping weight	2,995 pounds	3,240 pounds	3,235 pounds	3,130 pounds	2,905 pounds
Engine displacement	217.8	234.8	222.7	217.8	212.0
Bore x stroke	3¼ in. x 4⅜ in.	3⅜ in. x 4⅜ in.	3 7/16 in. x 4 in.	3¼ in. x 4⅜ in.	3 in. x 5 in.
Stroke/bore ratio	1.346:1	1.296:1	1.164:1	1.346:1	1.667:1
Compression ratio	6.50:1	5.67:1	6.20:1	6.00:1	6.25:1
Horsepower @ rpm	87/3,600	90/3,400	85/3,250	90/3,400	101/4,000
Torque @ rpm	155/1,200	171/1,200	161/1,600	198/1,800	170/1,200
Engine revolutions per mile	3,071	3,078	3,273	3,408	3,078
Number main bearings	4	7	4	4	3
Lubrication system	Pressure	Pressure	Pressure	Pressure	Splash
Clutch diameter	10 inches	9¼ inches	10 inches	10 inches	8⅝ inches
Transmission ratios, 1st/2nd	2.57/1.55	2.72/1.63	2.94/1.66	2.57/1.55	2.42/1.61
Final drive ratio	4.10:1	4.11:1	4.37:1	4.55:1	4.11:1
Overdrive available?	No	Yes	No	Yes	No
Braking area (square inches)	148.4	177.0	161.0	138.0	154.8
Drum diameter	10 inches	10 1/16 inches	12 inches	11 inches	10.06 inches
Tire size	6.00/16	6.00/16	6.00/16	6.00/16	6.00/16
Horsepower/c.i.d.	.399	.383	.382	.413	.476
Weight (pounds) /horsepower	34.4	36.0	38.1	34.8	28.8

specifications

illustrations by Russell von Sauers, The Graphic Automobile Studio

© copyright 1992, Special Interest Autos

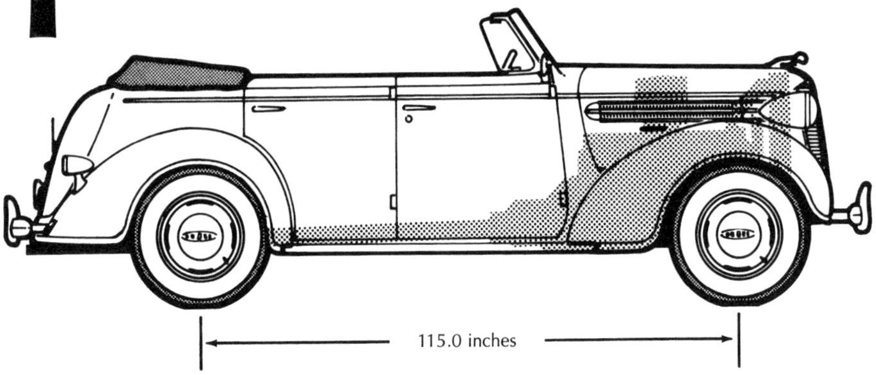

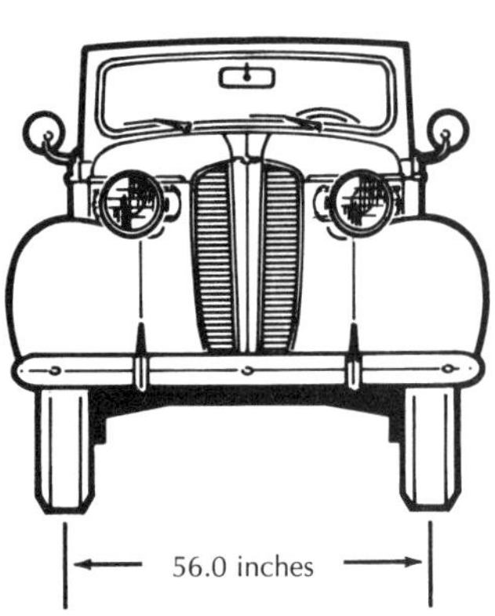

1937 Dodge D-5 Convertible Sedan

Price	$1,230 f.o.b. factory w/standard equipment
Options on dR car	Wheel trim rings, white sidewall tires, electric clock, wind wings, front and rear bumpers, passenger-side wiper, oil filter
Aftermarket accessories on dR car	Locking gas cap, dual outside mirrors, exhaust extension

ENGINE

Type	6-cylinder in-line, L-head
Bore x stroke	3¼ inches x 4⅜ inches
Displacement	217.8 cubic inches
Compression ratio	6.50:1
Horsepower @ rpm	87 @ 3,600
Torque @ rpm	155 @ 1,200
Engine revs per mile	3,071
Taxable horsepower	25.35
Valve lifters	Mechanical
Main bearings	4
Fuel system	Stromberg 1¼-inch single downdraft carburetor, camshaft pump
Cooling system	Centrifugal pump, thermostatic control
Lubrication system	Pressure to main, connecting rod and camshaft bearings
Exhaust system	Single
Electrical system	Auto-Lite 6-volt

CLUTCH

Type	Single dry plate
Diameter	10 inches
Actuation	Mechanical, foot pedal

TRANSMISSION

Type	3-speed selective, synchronized 2nd and 3rd gears; floor-mounted lever
Ratios: 1st	2.57:1
2nd	1.55:1
3rd	1.00:1
Reverse	3.48:1

REAR AXLE

Type	Hypoid
Ratio	4.10:1
Drive axles	Semi-floating

STEERING

Type	Gemmer worm-and-roller
Ratio	16.4:1
Turns, lock to lock	4
Turning diameter	33 feet 6 inches

BRAKES

Type	4-wheel internal hydraulic, drum type
Drum diameter	10 inches
Total swept area	148.4 square inches

CONSTRUCTION

Type	Body on frame
Frame	Double-drop, channel section steel with x-member
Body	All steel
Body style	4-door convertible sedan
Body builder	Murray

SUSPENSION

Type	"Synchronized springing"
Front	Tubular axle, 37 in. x 1¾ in. semi-elliptic springs; sway eliminator
Rear	Rigid axle, 53⅝ in. x 1¾ in. semi-elliptic springs
Wheels	Budd steel disc
Tires	6.00/16 4-ply, tube type

WEIGHTS AND MEASURES

Wheelbase	115 inches
Overall length	196⅛ inches
Overall width	68 inches
Overall height	67¼ inches
Front track	56 inches
Rear track	60⅛ inches
Road clearance	8 1/16 inches (minimum)
Shipping weight	3,262 pounds

CAPACITIES

Crankcase	5 quarts
Fuel tank	16 gallons
Cooling system	16 quarts
Transmission	2¼ pints
Differential	3¼ pints

CALCULATED DATA

Horsepower per c.i.d.	.400
Weight per hp	37.5 pounds
Weight per c.i.d.	15.0 pounds
Weight per sq. in.	22.0 pounds (brakes)

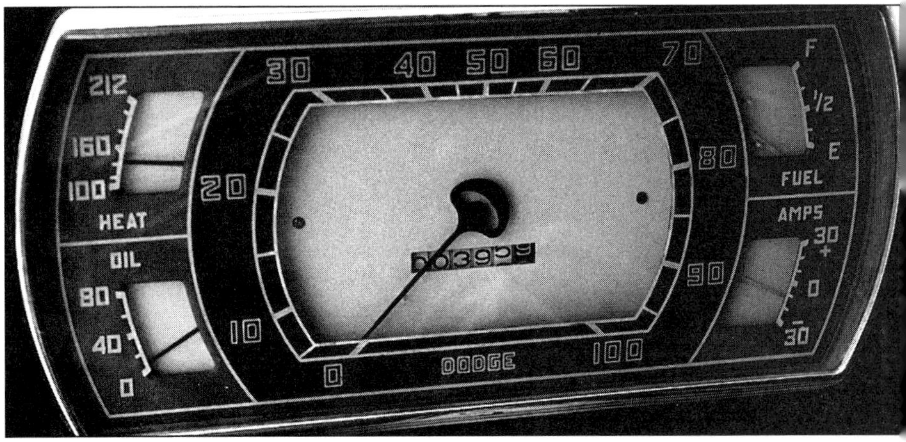

This page: *There's a full complement of gauges for the driver.* ***Facing page, top:*** *Windwings add a practical and sporty touch.* ***Center:*** *Taillamps are typical of Chrysler Corp. cars of the period.* ***Bottom:*** *Front end styling is straightforward.*

1937 DODGE

An equally conspicuous shift in the public's preference was to be found in the coupes. As recently as 1933, nearly 45 percent of all Dodge coupes were fitted with rumble seats. But by 1937 motorists had evidently grown tired of the wind, the dust and the sunburn that went along with the fresh-air ride. That year, the dickey appeared in fewer than eight percent of all Dodge coupes. By 1938 that figure would drop to less than six percent, and at season's end the rumble would become history, at least as far as Dodge was concerned.

The convertible coupe had for years enjoyed a small but steady market. Dealers liked to keep a ragtop on hand, for as the style leader of the line it helped to attract visitors to the Dodge showrooms. But during 1936 Dodge had added another attraction: the convertible four-door sedan. It was an expensive car, selling at a 31 percent premium over the touring sedan; so its market was a very limited one. Only 750 examples were built for the 1936 season. But the company probably considered it to have substantial prestige value, and again, the four-door ragtop was an effective showroom "draw." So the style was continued for 1937 and on into 1938. The numbers kept dwin-

Upside, Downside

1937 DODGE

As is so often the case, we found much to like about our driveReport Dodge — along with few characteristics that do not appeal to us. It's the classic Good News/ Bad News standoff. Let's take the positive side first.

Door rattles notwithstanding, this is a solidly built automobile, especially for a convertible. And yet, in body styles other than the convertibles, the '37 Dodge — though at least equally sturdy — is lighter than most of the competition.

For a car with a 115-inch wheelbase, it's a roomy vehicle. Seating is comfortable, access is good, and the ride is better than we anticipated, especially considering that it lacks independent front suspension.

We like the relatively flat floor, achieved by means of the hypoid axle. In 1937 most of the competition, including Pontiac, Dodge's principal rival, still used the older spiral bevel design.

It's an easy car to drive. The steering wheel is positioned so as to minimize fatigue, the clutch is smooth, brakes are excellent and steering effort is not excessive.

The 217.8-c.i.d. L-head engine, whose lifespan extended from 1933 (in the DeSoto) through 1954 (in the Plymouth), isn't flashy, but it's a dependable, absolutely unbreakable piece of machinery.

And Dodges of this era were relatively economical to operate. The company used to claim 18 to 24 miles to the gallon of gasoline. The latter figure was almost certainly an exaggeration, but 18 to 20 on the highway would have been readily obtainable.

The downside has to do principally with the Dodge's power, or lack thereof, and to some extent that problem is a reflection of the convertible sedan's excessive weight. The two-passenger coupe carried 33.35 pounds per horsepower, while the four-door touring sedan carried 34.45 pounds. For the convertible sedan featured here, on the other hand, that figure comes to 37.49 pounds, and the little flathead has to work somewhat harder than it should. A high-compression cylinder head was available at that time for the six-cylinder Chrysler Royal, providing it with an additional seven horsepower. We regard it as unfortunate that the company failed to offer a similar option to Dodge buyers.

Then, Chrysler had yet to perfect its transmission synchronizers in 1937. Several competing automobiles, notably but not exclusively the General Motors makes, did a much better job when it came to clash-free gearshifts.

And why, for heaven's sake, did Dodge abandon independent front suspension, after offering it as standard equipment on its 1934 models? Not until 1939 did this important feature return to the specification table.

One more criticism, a relatively minor matter: There's a good deal of wasted space in the trunk, space that could be put to good use if the spare tire were relocated and mounted vertically. But built-in trunks were a relatively new idea in 1937, and evidently automakers had yet to learn how to get the most out of them — or into them.

dling, though, to 473 in '37, then to 132 for 1938, the Dodge convertible sedan's final season.

Which, of course, means that our feature car represents a body style that is seldom seen. Hence the title of this driveReport, taken from one of 1937's popular songs, "So Rare."

In this day and age of lavishly equipped (though costly) automobiles, it's interesting to note that in 1937 Dodge supplied only one windshield wiper as standard issue. The passenger-side wiper seen on our driveReport car was an extra-cost option, though it appears to have been fitted to most new

Above: *Rear seat passengers have the luxury of dual ashtrays.* **Below:** *Sturdy, ultra-reliable flathead six pumps an understressed 87 bhp.*

1937 DODGE

Dodges that year. Even more surprising is the fact that even the bumpers were optional. Few new cars left the factory without them, but in fact they cost extra. So did the oil filter, an important item that nowadays is considered to be *de rigueur*. But in 1937 it was considered critical to keep the advertised cost as low as possible.

At that, the $1,230 list price of our driveReport car was a stiff one in 1937. For that price the buyer could have had a new LaSalle sedan, with $85 left over. But the four-door ragtop is a special body, built — in limited numbers, obviously — by Murray rather than by Briggs. All four-doors are front-hinged, in contrast to the sedans, whose rear doors were hinged at the back. The structure is heavy; this model outweighs the best-selling four-door touring sedan by 265 pounds, a difference of nearly nine percent. And a great deal of skilled hand work must have gone into its construction. ❑

Above: Centerposts must be removed by hand. *Above left:* Restricted rear visibility with top up. *Left:* Dash design is pleasant and uncluttered. *Below left:* Scads of rear seat room. *Below:* Top goes up and down easier with four hands.

Acknowledgments and Bibliography
Automobile Trade Journal, July 1937; Automotive Industries, *October 17, 1936, November 21, 1936, February 27, 1937;* Heasley, Jerry, The Production Figure Book for US Cars; *Kimes, Beverly Rae and Henry Austin Clark, Jr. (eds.),* Standard Catalog of American Cars, 1805-1942; *Langworth, Richard M. and Jan P. Norbye,* Complete History of Chrysler, 1924-1985; *McPherson, Thomas A.,* The Dodge Story.
Our thanks to Dave Brown, Durham, California; National Automobile Museum, Reno, Nevada, Charles C. Hilton, Executive Director; Bobbie'dine Rodda, Glendale, California. Special thanks to Rhonda Madden, San Rafael, California.

1937 Dodge Table of Prices, Weights and Production

	Price 11/36	Price 7/37	Weight	Production
115-inch Wheelbase				
Coupe, 2-passenger	$640	$715	2,902	41,702
Coupe, 2-4 passenger	$695	$770	2,967	3,500
Sedan, 2-door	$705	$780	2,992	5,302
Touring Sedan, 2-door	$715	$790	2,997	44,750
Sedan, 4-door	$745	$820	2,982	7,555
Touring Sedan, 4-door	$755	$830	2,997	185,483
Convertible Coupe	*	$910	3,057	1,345
Convertible Sedan	*	$1,230	3,262	473
Chassis only	N/A	N/A	N/A	2,514
132-inch Wheelbase				
Sedan, 7-passenger	*	$1,075	3,367	2,207
Limousine, 7-passenger	*	$1,175	N/A	216
*Not Yet announced				

Sources: *Automotive Industries,* November 21, 1936; *Automobile Trade Journal,* July 1937

Dodge Coronet, 1949-1976

By Robert Gross

1949 Station Wagon

Dodge's first postwar restyling came in 1949, and with it came new names: The base model Wayfarer, intermediate Meadowbrook and the top-line Coronet. With minor trim and interior variations, the Coronet and Meadowbook models differed only slightly. In the Coronet line, buyers had no less than 6 body styles to chose from including this 3,830-lb., six-passenger station wagon—Chrysler's first all-steel wagon. Standard power for all Dodge models this year was a 230-cu.in. straight-six. The 103hp engine had a 7.1:1 compression ratio, solid valve lifters, and a Stromberg 1-barrel carburetor. A three-speed transmission with Fluid-Drive came standard. When new, this simulated wooden wagon cost more than $2,900, but today one of these classy wagons in good condition can be yours for around $6,700.

1952 Sedan

Because Dodge was supporting the Korean War effort building military vehicles, changes from 1951 to 1952 were minimal. Although they used the same basic body styling first seen in 1949, a sloping hood, revised grille, and more pronounced bumpers gave the cars a fresh new look. Coronets continued to be the upscale version, with six models to select. Priced at $2,300, the 1952 4-door sedan was only $200 more than the mid-level Meadowbrook, though the only additional features were chrome wheel rings and special badging. Powering all Dodges through 1952 was the prewar, 230-cu.in. straight-six, and Fluid Drive was still the standard transmission, The Gyromatic semi-automatic with Sprint-Away passing gear was optional. For a mere $3,600, a Coronet sedan in decent condition is economically priced for today's market.

1953 Coupe

Inside and out, the 1953 Dodge lineup was completely revised. With all new sheet metal, a one-piece curved windshield and wraparound rear window, its exterior had a lean, smooth look. Under the hood was a new, 140hp, 341-cu.in. V-8—the first of Chrysler's renowned Hemi-head designs, and it was exclusive to the Coronet in Dodge's model line. On the majority of cars such as the staid 4-door sedan, the old straight-six came standard, with the new V-8 offered as an option; the convertible and hardtop Diplomat had the hot Hemi as standard equipment. It could be specified with a new optional transmission, the Gyro-Torque automatic, or the semi-auto Gyro-Drive, but the 3-speed manual was still standard. Prices for these early Hemi-powered Dodges ranged from $2,100 to $2,500; today they can be obtained for between $3,000 and $7,000.

1949   1952   1953   1954   1957   1959

1954 Coupe

Although the 1954 Dodge lineup was advertised as "Elegance in Action," very little changed from the 1953 models. A tastefully restrained grille, higher side moldings, and revised taillight panel were among the more notable features. The new Royal series bumped the Coronet as the top offering this year, and by 1955 this once premium Dodge would be the company's base-level model. A Carter two-barrel carburetor and a slight increase in compression to a 7.5:1 ratio boosted the power from the aging straight-six to 110hp. In the Coronet and Royal series, the 241-cu.in. Hemi engine gained 10 horsepower. Automatic and manual transmission choices were the same as the previous year. When new, this 3,200-lb., 2-door club coupe sold for $2,100, an additional $100 was required if the Hemi engine was specified. Today a nice club coupe will cost about $7,000.

1957 Sedan

The 1957 model featured Dodge's new "Forward Look." Its styling was lower and wider than ever before. Quad headlights, finned rear fenders, and a compound-curved windshield were some of its features, but under its skin were a larger Hemi engine and an all-new torsion-bar suspension. Torsion-Aire replaced the front coils and shocks. In the midst of the horsepower race, Dodge offered five engines. The 230-cu.in. six that developed 138hp came standard in the Coronet lineup, while four versions of the 325-cu.in. Hemi were available—all were optional in the Coronet including the powerful 310hp Super D-500 with two Carter 4-barrels. Six-cylinder Coronet sedans sold for $2,400, while the V-8s began at $2,500. Today, one of these handsome four-doors will cost $5,000, while the Super D-500 Hemi commands $30,000 or more.

1959 Convertible

Little was changed at Dodge in 1958, but for 1959, the cars received even longer, lower, and wider styling than before. Fins were higher, and the headlights had more pronounced chrome "brows." Swivel front seats and Co-Pilot speed control were popular options. The 383-cu.in. and 361-cu.in. "wedge" V-8s displaced the smaller Hemi as the top performance offerings. The Bendix electronic fuel-injection system that was first used in 1958, though unpopular, was still offered on the 361 engines. Standard power for the Coronet was the prewar six, and it was the only Dodge to use this engine. The lavish 1959 convertible was the most expensive Coronet and cost just over $3,000. Today, one of these drop-top dreamboats fetches upwards of $15,000. Though 97,000 cars were sold this year, the name Coronet wouldn't be used again until 1965.

Dodge

1965 440 Convertible

Riding on a 117-inch wheelbase, the Coronet was back. Dodge needed a name for its new intermediate line that was to compete with the Chevelle and Fairlane, so it revived one from the past. The base model was simply known as the Coronet, mid level was the 440 (not to be confused by the large engine that powered these cars in later years) and the 500 was the top trim level. In 1960 the 230-cu.in. six was replaced by a 145hp 225-cu.in. "Slant Six," and it was still used in 1965 as the base engine in the Coronet and 440. Engine options included the 365hp, 426-cu.in. street wedge, and a handful came with a high-compression 426 race Hemi. Manual 3-speed was the standard transmission, but a TorqueFlite automatic or manual 4-speed were optional. This 440 convertible cost $2,600 when new, and one in similar condition today can be taken home for under $10,000.

1967 440 Sedan

The Coronet lineup in 1967 was broadened with the addition of the sporty R/T. The body styling was similar to the 1966 design, but incorporated a grille similar to the one used for the Charger and a slightly revised rear end. The venerable Slant Six was standard in the Coronet, but its output was increased to 180hp. Five V-8s were available with power levels ranging from 180hp to 425hp. Of the 92,000 440 Coronets built, nearly 90 percent were ordered with a V-8. This 4-door 440 sedan has a 230hp, 318-cu.in. V-8 and is further optioned with power steering and brakes. When new, the standard 440 sedan cost $2,500. It was the lowest-priced offering in its range. The 318-cu.in. V-8, power steering and brakes brought the price up another $113. Today, this affordable four-door would only set you back $3,500. Not much more than it sold for when new.

1968 440 Coupe

With a smoother and more streamlined profile than the previous year, this Coronet is revered by some critics as the most attractive of them all. A full-width grille, housing quad headlights, coke-bottle rear-quarter-panel styling, and recessed rear taillights marked just some of the upgrades. Six-cylinder engines were available in the Deluxe, 440 and 500 models, but the high-performance R/T version had a 440-cu.in. Magnum V-8 as its base level engine. Typical examples such as this mid-level 440 coupe were more than likely optioned with a 318-cu.in. V-8 and a TorqueFlite automatic, but could also have been equipped with a 383 or 426 Hemi. The average 1968 Coronet cost about $2,500 when new. A coupe like the one shown can be bought for $7,000, while a rare and powerful Hemi-powered R/T is valued close to $60,000 in today's market.

1965 **1967** **1968** **1970** **1971** **1976**

1970 Super Bee

First available in 1968, the Super Bee was considered to be Dodge's high-performance "stripper" model. Like all 1970 Coronets, the Super Bee was basically a face-lifted 1969 version. Its front end was restyled with a split front grille with chrome surrounds. Based on the entry level Deluxe coupe, the Bee package came with a 335hp, 383-cu.in. V-8, 3-speed manual transmission, dual exhaust, Rallye suspension, special decals, and a dual-scooped hood. A 440-cu.in. V-8 with three two-barrel carburetors and the dual-quad 426 Hemi were optional, and so was a four-speed manual or TorqueFlite automatic. Just under 15,000 Super Bees were ordered in 1970. Their $3,100 price tag was some $400 more than the standard coupe when new. Today a Bee can average between $20,000 and $50,000 depending on its engine option; a standard coupe costs about $3,500.

1971 Brougham Sedan

With the Charger as Dodge's decidedly high-performance offering, the Coronet shed its sporty image for a more family oriented demeanor. Looking more like the full-sized Monaco for 1971, it was only available as a four-door sedan or station wagon. The car's styling resembled the rest of the Dodge line, with a wraparound front bumper and lower side trim. Series designations changed once again: Coronet was the base offering, Custom the midway package, and the Brougham and Crestwood were the premium packages. Standard power was a Slant Six, but a 300hp, 383-cu.in. V-8 could be specified. This 4-door Brougham, which included the deluxe wheel covers and extra chrome trim, cost $3,400 new. A driver in nice shape today can be had for a mere $3,000.

1976 Custom Sedan

A split grille and single headlights first appeared in 1975 and were retained through 1976. The coupe again made a brief appearance in '75 but was unceremoniously deleted from the option list for its final year. In the sedan, power was sadly limited to the 225-cu.in. Slant Six, and the station wagons came with a 360-cu.in. V-8 as standard. Optional engines included the 318-cu.in. V-8 and a large, 175hp 400-cu.in. V-8 with a four barrel carburetor, respectively. The Custom 4-door sedan, such as the one shown here, was a part of the standard model line and cost nearly $4,000 when new. Today, you can find one in excellent shape for about the same price. As the Coronet was bowing out for good, Dodge was proudly displaying the then-all-new Diplomat as the intermediate successor to the long-standing Coronet.

Photos by Douglas Mellor and Chrysler Corp.

1950 Wayfarer Sportabout

By Ken Gross, *Managing Editor*

Dodge's roadster tried bravely to recapture the spirit of a bygone era.

The Wayfarer roadster was another of Mr. K. T. Keller's brainstorms," recalls former Dodge chief engineer Harry Chesebrough. "He wanted to market the least expensive full-sized convertible in the country."

K.T. Keller was Chrysler Corp.'s powerful and implacable president, and what Mr. Keller wanted, Mr. Keller got.

Adds James W. Shank, who's now an executive engineer with Chrysler but who worked on the postwar roadster, "In 1949, convertibles were usually the most expensive body styles in any manufacturer's line. Mr. Keller felt that here was an opportunity for a really low-cost open car. So we developed the roadster and had a true 3-seater convertible without the expense of a power top, roll-up windows, and other frills."

The idea, then, was to create a car with youth appeal, sports appeal, and yet one not costing a fortune—a personal, uncomplicated, jaunty roadster in the 1930s tradition, but with up-to-date styling. Dodge, with its bank-clerk/*hausfrau* image, needed something to perk up the line, and the Wayfarer Sportabout seemed just the ticket.

K.T. Keller's conservative styling posture had ensured that Chrysler Corp.'s $90 million restyling budget for 1949 hadn't resulted in anything too radical. Chrysler's proud heritage from its founder was an *engineering*, not a styling, reputation. The '49 Dodges were billed as handsome, smart, distinguished automobiles that would be in style for years to come.

Enlarging an oft-repeated quote of Mr. Keller's, Dodge admen proudly claimed their practical new '49s were, "lower outside, higher inside,

Square gauges are easy to read, but driver has a stretch to reach ashtray under clock.

Narrow rear bench seats two in a pinch, makes plenty of room for sample cases.

Roll-up windows became an option in 1950 after buyers balked at plastic sidecurtains

Manual one-woman top can be raised or lowered from driver's seat with little fuss.

Short cockpit makes the deck and hood look longer, gives Wayfarer its sporty aura.

narrower outside, wider inside, shorter outside, longer inside." After you digested that equation, you had to conclude that the '49 Dodges weren't going to walk off with any styling awards but were probably pretty functional.

Tom McCahill agreed. Writing about Chrysler Corp.'s 1949 efforts in *Mechanix Illustrated*, the father of American roadtesting noted, "While there isn't a champion in the line, at the same time there isn't a stinker, either. Chrysler products rate high in the dependability class. They are a product of excellent industrial planning, are reliable, hold their value and have excellent sales appeal."

Dodge's sober interpretation of Keller's marketing philosophy had assured them a solid sixth in 1948 sales—behind Chevrolet, Ford, Plymouth, Buick, and Pontiac. The 1949 model year at Dodge didn't start until February 1949 (traditionally, it had begun in January). "There was confusion over some styling decisions," Harry Chesebrough recalls. Mr. Keller had made his choices, but they were opposed by some top executives. There was a stalemate, as Mr. Keller refused to compromise. Finally, at the last minute, the four operating heads of Chrysler, De Soto, Dodge, and Plymouth had an unprecedented showdown with Mr. Keller.

When he saw their unanimous stance, he agreed to a few concessions. Changes in the taillights on some models required last-minute tooling. Mr. Keller saw that the market was holding and agreed to stick with the '48s until the new tooling was ready. Thus some '48s were titled "first series" 1949s.

For their "second series"—the real '49 models—Dodge adopted a wider marketing stance than their previous efforts. They offered two distinct car sizes and three different models, all designed to appeal to a broader range of buyers. The Coronet was Dodge's top of the line, on a 123.5-inch wheelbase, and its models ranged from a 6-passenger coupe to an 8-passenger sedan (on a 137.5-inch wheelbase).

If you wanted a stripped-down Coronet, Dodge marketed its austerity model, the less expensive Meadowbrook. Meadowbrooks and Coronets had identical specifications, except for trim and interiors.

Today, when we hear the name Wayfarer, we think of the roadster only, but Wayfarers made up a third separate and complete series of 1949–52 Dodges. There were three body styles on the new-for-1949 115-inch wheelbase: a 3-window, 3-passenger business coupe ($1,611), a 2-door fastback sedan ($1,738), and the Sportabout roadster ($1,727). The Wayfarers remained in production from February 1949 through February 15, 1952—just three years. (Plymouth, too, had a shorter-wheelbase car that also lasted three years.)

In price, Wayfarers were just above Plymouths, and they shared a good number of Plymouth components. Wayfarer engines and running gear, though, were primarily Dodge. Chrysler Corp., as you know, pioneered component and sheet metal interchangeability.

"We called it commonization," states Harry Chesebrough. "Chrysler was really unique among the Big Three. Certain components were the same in most of our cars—had been since the '30s. Commonization was limited primarily to mechanical items that were functional and didn't contribute to individual line uniqueness.

"These components included such items as door locks, window regulators, some engines, almost all components of certain powertrains, brakes, clutches, gears, axles, steering, and some suspension pieces—except springs, which were tailored to an individual model's length and weight.

"Also included in the commonization program were selected central parts of the body structure—dashes, floorpans, windshield openings, inner door panels, hinges, and seat frames. We commonized most items which performed a function but did not contribute to distinct appearance."

The Get-Away 6 was a good example of the commonization program's adaptability. This engine started life in late 1932 as the 189.9-c.i.d. Plymouth PC. Subsequent boring and stroking brought it up to Plymouth's 1949 217.8-c.i.d. Another 1/4-inch stroke along with 1/8-inch shorter rods raised it up to Dodge's specifications. The same game went on between De Soto and Chrysler—their 6-cylinder engines were very similar except for 1/4-inch stroke differences. And these engines stayed in production for boats and industry through the late 1960s.

Adds Jim Shank: "Chrysler's divisions all grew out of one another—sharing parts and manufacturing facilities. Chrysler's Central Engineering did all design work for all four car divisions. We designed many of the cars with a close eye on our interchangeability charts.

"Basically, almost all sheet metal was unique to each car line. Most fenders and outer panels were different, but some decklids were common, as were some roof panels. It all depended on a car's external dimensions. Of course, soft and hard trim and bumpers were unique."

The little Wayfarer, on its abbreviated wheelbase, contended nicely in the low-price range. Mr. Keller's admen were quick to call it "America's lowest priced full-sized convertible." Although the Willys Jeepster undersold the Wayfarer, Dodge's ad agency must not have felt that the Jeepster's 104-inch wheelbase qualified it as full-sized.

Certainly the most unusual feature about the new Wayfarer roadster was its plastic "take-out" (Dodge called them demountable) side windows. The demountable windows followed the traditional fresh-air roadster practice. "More important to Mr. Keller," notes Harry Chesebrough, "they eliminated the window crank mechanism, were cheaper to manufacture than conventional roll-up windows, and lightened the simplified door structure."

Early Wayfarer roadsters had no ventipanes and came with plastic inserts instead. The ventipane inserts dropped into each door belt line and were secured at either end with two extensions formed as a part of the aluminum window framing. Plastic ventilating wings, for use only after you popped out the sidecurtains, were available optionally for $22.50.

The demountable windows caused a number of problems. You couldn't remove or install them with the car in motion. This prohibited hand signals (turn indicators were another extra-cost option), and you couldn't simply "roll them down" when the sun came out. Customers and dealers complained.

The first solution—a hasty one—proved halfway. Ventipanes were built into the existing plastic windows. This solved the fresh-air problem but still prevented signaling for all but contortionists.

Dodge's reliable L-head 6 shared much with Chrysler/De Soto/Plymouth engines.

Large trunk stretches far forward, has low loading sill and very little top intrusion.

Harry Chesebrough told *SIA* that the Wayfarer roadsters' thin doors wouldn't accept conventional Dodge window mechanisms. It took time to design new regulators and, in the interim, sales probably suffered. Finally, on September 22, 1949, normal glass door windows with internal regulators became a $35 option on Wayfarer roadsters, rendering them convertibles, for better or worse. Plastic demountable windows were still available, reduced to $12.50—perhaps to unload excess stocks. At the same time, almost by way of compensation to true roadster lovers, a new color, Atomic Yellow, became available only on Wayfarers.

Wayfarer roadsters (the model designation was officially changed to Sportabout in 1950 and 1951) came with Fluid Drive, a single sunvisor, an oilbath aircleaner, and an automatic choke as standard equipment. Optionally, buyers could choose from a long list that included rear fender stone shields, stainless hubcaps or wheel discs, a second sunvisor, a horn ring, heavy-duty seat cushions, and whitewalls.

The Sportabout offered comfortable seating for three on the 58-inch-wide front seat, and a Dodge brochure suggested, "With the top down, the package shelf can be utilized as a seating ledge for three more people." It should also have suggested only the shortest of rides on that hard bench.

Dodge had made a number of improvements for 1949. One of the Wayfarer's strong selling points was that the little car shared all of the new features with its bigger brothers. Suspensions were bolstered with tubular hydraulic shock absorbers. Dodge called them "Sea Leg shock absorbers similar to those used on the giant airliners," and boasted that "for added protection against flying stones and dirt, they have been raised five inches."

Dodge's "Safe-Guard" hydraulic brakes featured dual front wheel cylinders and "Cycle-Bonded" (rivetless) brake linings. A fuel tank filter, safety wheel rims, and a reinforced front bumper rounded out the chassis improvements.

All Wayfarers shared the same "Get-Away" 103-bhp, 230-c.i.d. flathead 6 as the larger Meadowbrooks and Coronets. The roadster weighed 415 pounds less than the 6-passenger Coronet convertible. Thomas McPherson's *The Dodge Story* shows Irish Horan and his Lucky Hell Drivers using a Wayfarer in a spectacular cannon jump. The car's light weight and low cost made it a natural for stunt driving.

For 1949, the venerable Dodge 6's compression ratio was upped to 7:1 (vs. 6.7:1 in 1948) and fed by a new high-capacity fuel pump and Stromberg carburetor. Dodge claimed its "Speed-Proofed" cylinder walls "eliminated tedious engine break-ins." Dodge director of service, B.B. Settle, explained this feature in *Automotive News*, saying, "Cylinder walls in Dodge engines are machined to precise tolerances and then given a chemical coating that serves two purposes. First, the chemical reduces the possibility of scuffing contact between pistons or rings and cylinder walls during the first few hundred miles of operation. Second, the chemical creates microscopically fine pockets in the cylinder walls... which serve as minute lubrication reservoirs and provide an extra source of lubrication—a factor in extending the life of cylinder walls and rings."

New oil control rings, full pressure lubrication, Oilite alloy bearings, an improved clutch, and redesigned accelerator linkage rounded out the mechanical improvements. Electrically, the new '49s now had the industry's only combined ignition and starter switch, a 40-amp generator, 105-amp-hour battery, and an improved voltage regulator. A "splash pocket" on the fender apron protected the low-mounted distributor from drowning. Armored ignition cable discouraged thieves. A 10,000-ohm suppressor eliminated car radio and home TV set interference.

The 1949 Wayfarers had a unique rear quarter and trunk treatment. The license plate was recessed, but the expensive chrome framing of the larger Dodges was eliminated to save money. Similarly, Wayfarers lacked the bigger cars' plastic Dodge hood crest. Side identification was a chromium nameplate which read simply: *Wayfarer, Fluid Drive*. First year sales of only 5,420 roadsters made the open car the least popular of the new Wayfarer line.

Although 1949 Wayfarer sales had been disappointing, Dodge retained sixth place with a total of 298,399 units. It was the division's best year since 1937.

When the 1950 models arrived on January 4 of that year, the division had a brave new sales strategy. Bob Gordon, writing in *Automotive News*, interviewed E.C. Quinn, Dodge's general sales manager. "Dodge plans to ship more cars in the first two months of 1950 than it did in the first five months of 1949," predicted Quinn. Dodge was after fourth place in the sales standings. Quinn told a Detroit meeting of 1,250 cheering dealers that Dodge had the capacity for fourth place and the ability to handle a sustained output of 1,800 cars daily.

According to *Automotive News*, "Mentions of fourth place in sales were frequent at the meeting." Quinn told his dealers that the new models, "... are going to get a 4th place national announcement... and the company will support dealers all year long with a 4th place advertising job." Quick to get in the spirit, dealers wore hats and badges proclaiming, "Go 4th With Dodge in '50."

But Dodge wasn't the only manufacturer eyeing fourth. Buick, fourth at the time, wanted to oust Plymouth from third. Pontiac and Oldsmobile also had fourth in sight. When the smoke cleared at the end of the year, Quinn's men had sold 332,782 Dodges. While that figure represented an improvement over 1949, in 1950 it was enough only for eighth place. Despite valiant catch-up efforts following a 100-day strike, Dodge had been passed by Oldsmobile and Mercury. Plymouth, Buick, and Pontiac kept their holds on third, fourth, and fifth, respectively.

Dodge had continued the Wayfarer Sportabout in 1950, along with the business coupe and fastback—probably to give the division the widest possible sales appeal for its drive toward fourth place. The price stayed the same, but even fewer buyers were attracted to the "trim beauty packed with surprises." Just 2,903 Sportabouts found buyers. The marketing strategy of positioning the Wayfarers "just a few dollars more than the low-priced cars" flopped.

The Korean police action caused production cutbacks and saw the cost of critical ingredients begin to rise. On October 18, whitewalls were discontinued as an option on Wayfarers. By 1951, the Sportabout's pricetag had climbed to $1,942, canceling the car's low pricing feature. Harry Chesebrough reminisces, "By that time, the car had an unpopular image. Although we'd solved the window problem, the Sportabout still had a non-automatic top and people didn't want it." The last ads billed the Sportabout as, "Gay as a circus poster and nimble as a polo pony." Sadly, only 1,002 found homes.

Only the Wayfarer coupes were continued in Dodge's 1952 lineup, which was relatively unchanged due to the corporation's heavy war

specifications

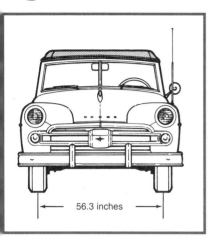

56.3 inches

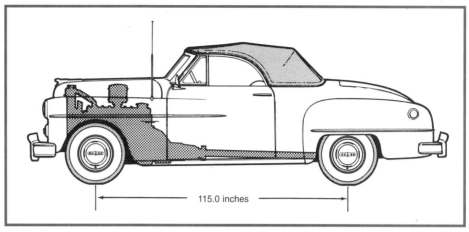

115.0 inches

1950 Dodge Wayfarer Sportabout roadster

Price when new . . . . $1,745 fob. Detroit (1950)
Options . . . . Radio, heater, clock

ENGINE
Type . . . . In-line, L-head 6, water-cooled, cast-iron block, 4 mains, full pressure lubrication
Bore & stroke . . . . . . 3.250 x 4.625 inches
Displacement . . . . 230.2 c.i.d.
Max. bhp @ rpm . . . . . 103 @ 3,600
Max. torque @ rpm . . . . 190 @ 1,200
Compression ratio 7.0:1
Induction system . . . . . 1-bbl. Stromberg downdraft carburetor, mechanical fuel pump
Exhaust system . . . . . . Cast-iron manifold, single muffler
Electrical system . . . . . 6-volt battery/coil

CLUTCH
Type . . . . Single dry plate, woven asbestos lining
Diameter . . . . 9.0 inches
Actuation . . . . Mechanical, foot pedal

TRANSMISSION
Type . . . . Fluid-Drive 4-speed semi-automatic with fluid coupling, column lever
Ratios: 1st 3.57:1
2nd 2.04:1
3rd 1.75:1
4th 1.001
Reverse 3.99:1

DIFFERENTIAL
Type . . . . Hypoid
Ratio 3.73:1
Drive axles . . . . Semi-floating

STEERING
Type . . . . Worm & roller
Turns lock to lock 4.0
Ratio 18.2:1
Turn circle . . . . 38.0 feet

BRAKES
Type . . . . 4-wheel hydraulic internal expanding drums, dual wheel cylinders, rivetless shoes
Drum diameter . . . . . . 10.0 inches
Total lining area . . . . . 157.8 square inches

CHASSIS & BODY
Frame . . . . Channel-section steel, boxed siderails, crossmembers, central X-member
Body construction . . . . All steel
Body style . . . . 2-door, 3-pass. convertible roadster

SUSPENSION
Front . . . . Independent, unequal A-arms, coil springs, tubular hydraulic shocks
Rear . . . . Solid rear axle, longitudinal semi-elliptic leaf springs, tubular hydraulic shock absorbers

Tires . . . . 6.70 x 15 4-ply
Wheels . . . . Pressed steel discs, drop-center rims, lug-bolted to brake drums.

WEIGHTS & MEASURES
Wheelbase . . . . 115.0 inches
Overall length . . . . 194.4 inches
Overall height . . . . 64.6 inches
Overall width . . . . 74.4 inches
Front tread . . . . 56.3 inches
Rear tread . . . . 59.0 inches
Ground clearance . . . . . 8.5 inches
Curb weight . . . . 3,155 pounds

CAPACITIES
Crankcase . . . . 5 quarts
Cooling system . . . . . . 15 quarts
Fuel tank . . . . 17 gallons

FUEL CONSUMPTION
Best . . . . 17–20 mpg
Average . . . . 15–18 mpg

PERFORMANCE (from *Motor Trend*, 1951 Coronet with 3.90 axle & Gyromatic):
0–30 mph . . . . 7.5 sec.
0–60 mph . . . . 24.8 sec.
Standing 1/4 mile . . . . 23.68 sec. and 58 mph
Top speed (av.) . . . . . . 86.37 mph

commitment. Production of all Wayfarers ceased on February 15, 1952. No '52 Sportabouts were built at all. The few examples sold and titled as '52s were really 1951 leftovers.

Jack Wishnick, owner of Roaring 20 Autos, in Wall, New Jersey, lent us his 1950 black Sportabout. Although its fast, 1.5-turn roll-up windows cure the roadster's original problem, the hand-operated top is difficult to raise and lower. Fluid Drive shifts languidly and won't be hurried. (Harry Chesebrough told me that K.T. Keller liked Fluid Drive and its various companions. "GM's patents were not a factor," said Chesebrough. "Less cost and simplicity were the reasons behind Fluid Drive. This revolved around Mr. Keller's obsession with keeping things simple. He thought a completely automatic transmission was too complicated and costly. We could have built one, but he didn't want it.")

Brakes are above average. Ride feels a bit choppy, and fast cornering reminds the driver that Sportabout is not synonymous with sports car. Visibility, with blind quarter panels, presents a challenge. Performance of the "Get-Away" 6 isn't necksnapping, but at today's highway speeds, which approximate those of the 1950s, the Sportabout cruises comfortably.

What killed the Wayfarer? Probably a combination of factors. The demountable windows were the first strike against it. And, although Mr. Keller couldn't have anticipated it, lowered prices on competitive convertibles made the single-seat, manual-topped Wayfarer no real bargain.

The most valuable Wayfarers today are those first few cars equipped with the infamous plastic windows. Ironically, the very factors that doomed the little roadster make it a sought-after special-interest car today. ☙

Our thanks to James J. Bradley, National Automotive History Collection, Detroit Public Library, Detroit, Michigan; Don Butler, Detroit, Michigan; Harry Chesebrough, Bloomfield Hills, Michigan; Jeff Godshall, Tom Jakobowski, Chuck Tomlinson, Peter Sawchuk, John Schwarz, James W. Shank, Bill Stempien, and Ed Vosburgh, Chrysler Corp., Detroit, Michigan.; Henry T. King, Fort Lauderdale, Florida; and Rhys Miller, Walnut Creek; California. Our special thanks to Jack Wishnick of Roaring 20 Autos, Wall, New Jersey.

DODGE RULED the salt that year. And took 1-2-3-4-6-9 in the fifth Pan American Road Races. And a stick Red Ram V-8 became class champ in the 1954 Mobilgas Economy Run. It turned out to be a big year for Dodge in every way but sales.

The season started in September 1953 at Bonneville. Danny Eames and a factory team set 196 new AAA-certified stock car speed records with four 1954 Dodge V-8s—twin sedans and convertibles. The sedans' best speed came for the flying 10 miles—108.36 mph. The year before, driving a 1953 Dodge V-8 at El Mirage dry lake in California, Eames broke the then-record at 102.62 mph.

Eames, now Autolite-Ford performance program manager, recalls, "The objective for 1954 was to better as many AAA stock car records as possible. These records were comprised of standing and flying starts on the straightaway, from one kilometer to 10 miles, and standing and flying starts on a 10-mile circle from one kilometer to 31,000 miles. Our...4-door and convertible were run simultaneously and driven by a staff of four drivers alternating in 4-hour shifts."

Dodge sent nearly 50 men to Utah that year, including two pit crews of eight men each, working 12-hour shifts. Eames was project manager and chief driver. Other drivers were Bill Taylor, Jimmy Jackson, and Hal Cole. Goodyear, Mobil, Autolite, the AAA and, of course, Chrysler all had engineers or representatives on hand. It marked the largest factory assault on the salt up to that time.

After Dodge had seared the salt and then had done so well in Mexico and in the Mobil run, it seemed only fitting to make a Dodge Royal V-8 convertible that year's official Indianapolis 500 pace car. In commemoration, Dodge brought out a mid-year option package (not actually a series) called the Royal 500, the 500 designating the car's status in the Indy 500 that year. The option package transformed regular Dodge Royal V-8 convertibles into Royal 500 pace car replicas by the addition of chromed Kelsey-Hayes wire wheels, a continental kit, plus special insignias and trim. Under the hood, buyers could order a dealer-installed 4-barrel Offenhauser manifold with a Stromberg carb. Output with the 4-barrel was never given. The stock V-8 used a 2-barrel carburetor and delivered 150 bhp on regular gas.

In all, Dodge sold a total of 701 factory-built pace car replica Royal 500

1954 Dodge Royal 500

*By Michael Lamm, **Editor***

Originally published in Special Interest Autos #8, Nov.-Dec. 1971

The factory built 701 pace car replicas, and dealers outfitted untold number more. Test car uses 4-barrel Offy manifold from dealer kit.

Wilbur Shaw (right) and Dodge president W.C. Newberg smile in 1954 Indy pace car. The "500" is what gave this model its designation.

Bonneville Dodges did 108.36 mph (see page 40), but we didn't get Bill Geyer's up to quite that. It's a spirited car nevertheless, especially above 40.

Cantilevered continental kit swings to the right for access to trunk. Squared-off decklid lets tall suitcases stand upright, side by side.

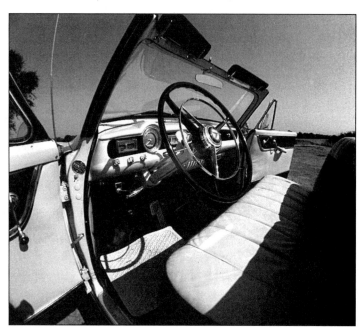

No jukebox dash here. It's complete, simple, and easy to read, with Leathertex non-reflecting top. Seats use black and yellow vinyl.

convertibles, plus another 1,299 standard Royal convertibles. But the 500 equipment could also be dealer-installed, so no telling how many replicas were put together in toto. There were actually two different types of continental kits that dealers could install—one for wire wheels and one for disc wheels with fake wires.

The 1954 Dodge hardtop, convertible, and some wagons were built on the Plymouth's 114-inch chassis, making these the shortest-wheelbase Dodges since 1933. 1954 Dodge sedans and 4-door wagons shared a wheelbase of 119 inches. Thus Dodge had a "B" body that year, just as most intermediates have today.

Before leaving Dodge's racing conquests for 1954, we should squeeze in a mention of Tommy Drisdale's class win in the Pan American Road Race. Lincoln captured the Large Stock class and most of the glory, but Dodge dominated the Medium Stock class that year. Out of 46 cars entered, Dodge took the first four spots, plus sixth and ninth. Drisdale's fellow Texan, C.D. Evans, took second, and Ray Elliott from Portland, Oregon, captured third. Drisdale's average speed had been just under 90 mph for the 1,908 grueling miles.

In 1953–54, with the dawning of the Red Ram V-8, Dodge was just beginning to emerge from the Dependable era, heading into a time of 3-tone paint jobs, spiraling horsepower, spinner wheel covers, and an entirely new image. "Dependable" no longer sparked the public interest, or, at least, so thought Dodge Div. management. The faithful old flathead 6 couldn't run with the younger set (the Olds 88 had become the car to look up to), so Dodge management made the right decision in going to the Red Ram hemi V-8 (although the Dodge 6 would continue in production through 1959, after which the ohv Slant 6 replaced it).

Chrysler Corp. had just instituted a program of corporate decentralization, and Dodge was much more on its own after 1953 than it had ever been before. Dodge's managers decided that the venerable ram needed more than dependability to talk about, and that's how the AAA records came to be. Overnight, Dodge turned from a rather staid bank teller's automobile into a muscular medium-sized car that could move out with the best.

As in any change of life, this one took its share of adjustments. Generations of Dodge faithful who'd never bought anything but Dodges suddenly weren't so sure this soupier, jazzed-up version was what they really wanted. Sales took a drastic tumble in 1954, the worst year Dodge had had since 1939 (if we exclude 1946, which wasn't a capacity production year anyway). Unpredictably, in 1955, when Dodge brought out still wilder models—3-tone paint, the potent D-500, baloney-slicer spinners—sales boomed again, up 130,000 units (154,789 in 1954 vs. 284,323 in 1955). But then, 1955 was a record year for the entire industry.

Bill Geyer, who's a legislative consultant in Sacramento, California, and an ardent S-I car collector (he likes convertibles, owns a ragtop Chrysler 300-C, this Dodge 500, a 1949 Chrysler T & C convertible, a 1949 Lincoln Cosmopolitan convert, plus a 1948 Packard station sedan), bought our driveReport car in April 1970. It had been in the same family since new, now has 72,000 miles on it, and the only mechanical repair needed in Bill's possession has been a new set of mufflers.

Bill Geyer's bright yellow-and-black convertible is one of a handful of cars we've tested with automatic transmission and power steering. This is Chrysler's full-time power steering. Full-time means there's no resistance to steering-wheel inertia. You get no feedback through the wheel. Steering is light to a fault—too light, and it makes the front end feel unrealistically light.

Earlier Chrysler Corp. power steering (actually supplied by both Monroe and Ross) had an indefinite centerpoint. But by 1954, they'd given it good return power, so Bill's car proved very comfortable to drive once we made up our minds that we weren't going to get any road feel. The lack of it is especially disconcerting on high-crown roads, where we would simply see ourselves starting to drift to the right, although we couldn't feel the slope in the wheel.

1954 marked the first year Dodge offered a fully automatic transmission—PowerFlite. PowerFlite was the same unit Chrysler Corp. used in all its 1954 offerings except Plymouth. Before PowerFlite, Dodge offered two semi-automatics, one called Gyro-Matic and one called Gyro-Torque. Gyro-Matic used a clutch pedal, and even with Gyro-Torque, which had no clutch pedal, you had to lift your foot off the gas pedal to shift gears. Both Gyros were offered in 1953, but for 1954 Gyro-Torque gave way to

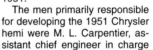

A Bit of Hemi History

Dodge's Red Ram ohv V-8, introduced in 1953, was a scaled-down version of the potent and legendary Chrysler hemi. Dodge used the same hemispherical combustion chamber and all the same essentials as laid down by Chrysler for 1951.

The men primarily responsible for developing the 1951 Chrysler hemi were M. L. Carpentier, assistant chief engineer in charge of engine design, and W.E. Drinkard, supervisor of Chrysler's engine development lab at Central Engineering. Carpentier was one of Chrysler's old guard, having come into the company after leaving Studebaker in 1920, along with Breer, Skelton, and Zeder. Drinkard had held his title since 1943.

Chrysler Corp. began experimenting with V-8s during WW-II for military use. They started testing passenger-car V-8s in 1946. Trying numerous combustion-chamber configurations in one-cylinder test engines, they finally settled on the hemi. Advantages of the hemispherical combustion chamber had long been known and used, both here and abroad, especially in racing cars. Duesenberg, Offy, and Jaguar's dohc engines were perhaps the most famous hemis before Chrysler's.

The hemi head's advantages are briefly these. 1) much smoother porting and manifolding are possible; 2) less crowding of the valves, thus they can be bigger and farther apart; 3) more central sparkplug location; 4) good thermal efficiency via low surface/volume ratio; 5) plenty of room for water passages, thus good cooling; 6) low heat rejection to the coolant, thus smaller, lighter, less expensive radiators needed.

Chrysler's initial FirePower hemi V-8 of 1951 displaced 331.1 c.i.d. and delivered 180 bhp. Next came the 1952 De Soto's 276.1-inch hemi at 160 bhp. In 1953, Dodge got its version—241.3 c.i.d. and 140 bhp. That same engine was used in the 1955 Plymouth, rated at 157 bhp.

The Chrysler hemi became an instant hit with hot rodders, sports-car builders, and luxury car manufacturers. With a little judicious tinkering, a good peppertree mechanic could double the hemi's output. And the engine seemed to stay together no matter what—it was marvelously overbuilt. Briggs Cunningham used hemis in his Le Mans cars; they powered Facel Vegas, Dual Ghias, plus a variety of rails, lakesters, and specials.

Chrysler Corp. continued the production hemi through 1957, when they finally decided to replace it with the wedge. Reason: the hemi cost too much to manufacture. But in 1964, they re-introduced the hemi on a very limited basis for racing only. In 1966, they brought out a new street version—the 426 hemi. This last was dropped again after 1971, and that looks like the last of the hemis for awhile—perhaps forever.

Dodge 500 shows relatively little lean in corners, and tires remain upright. 1953–54 convertibles and coupes used Plymouth's wheelbase; sedans were 119.

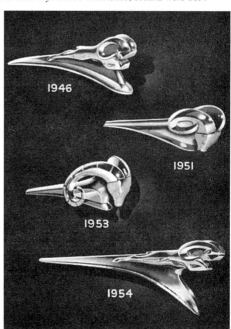

Chrome finlet crests fender kickup, and gas filler cap is balanced by backup lamp on right side.

Convertible's C-pillars sport sewn Dodge patches in red, white, and gold against black.

Dodge ram has undergone many changes over the years, but 1954 was similar to 1946 version.

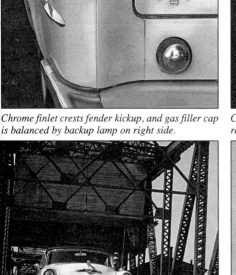

With automatic and power steering, this 18-year-old feels, handles, looks better than many '72s.

Crossed flags, like crossed fingers, symbolize Indy 500; also victory in '54 Mexican road race.

Test car was probably dealer assembled because it has false wires instead of the Kelsey-Hayes.

Danny Eames spearheaded Salt assault with 1954 Dodges. He and 3 co-drivers set 196 AAA records that season. There were 2 sedans and...

Danny Eames

...2 convertibles, all with 4-barrel carburetors and standard 3-speed...

PowerFlite (you could still have Gyro-Matic in 1954 Meadowbrooks).

Having tested both the 1953 and 1954 Dodge V-8s, *Motor Trend* found that the 1953 with Gyro-Torque would beat the 1954 PowerFlite below 40 mph but that the 1954 model had it on the top end. That's where PowerFlite and the 10 extra horses came into their own. Over the quarter mile, the 1954 Dodge beat the 1953 by precisely one second.

Our 1954 Dodge Royal 500 convertible handled well, with minimal lean on hard turns and a solid, stable feel on all road surfaces. The front weight bias causes some tendency to plow, and with the very light power steering this plow comes suddenly and unexpectedly. The car will also fling its rear end around on gravel, but that's par.

Workmanship on the '54 looks good, although *Motor Trend* noted that their 1953 test car was put together rather haphazardly. By 1954, these assembly mistakes were apparently corrected.

One touch we especially appreciated was the crinkle-finished dashboard top. Dodge called this "Leathertex," although it was merely paint over metal. It completely eliminates glare and windshield reflection.

Since PowerFlite has no PARK position and no parking pawl, we soon developed a habit of setting the emergency brake whenever we stopped. The brake itself is a separate 7-inch drum on the driveshaft, just behind the transmission. All Chrysler Corp. cars used this system for years, and it's very effective. The parking brake handle is a T-pull at the left of the dashboard—very easy to operate.

Motor Life rated the 1954 Dodge's service brakes tops, saying "Dodge's brakes are excellent; gave us, in fact, some of the shortest stopping distances ever recorded for an American passenger car. These were...panic stops and one reason the distances are so short is that our car never threatened to swerve during the most violent braking."

Overall, we'd judge this 1954 Indy pace car replica very satisfying in all important aspects. One thing we especially like is its size. Even with the continental kit, Bill Geyer's 500 convertible is roughly the same overall length as the 1972 Dodge Dart. Too, this car has that extra touch of verve that makes it stand out in any crowd of collectibles, both old and new. ᓂ

Our thanks to Bill Geyer, Sacramento, California; John Bunnell, Ed Vosburgh, H.D. Schaerer, Bill Stempien, Bob Cahill, and Frank Wylie of Chrysler Corp.; Jack McFarland of Dodge Div.; Danny Eames, Autolite-Ford Div., Livonia, Michigan; and members of the W.P.C. Club, 17916 Trenton Dr., Castro Valley, California 94546.

transmissions. They drove in a 10-mile circle at Bonneville, 24 hours a day, cracking records in Class C (183–305-c.i.d.) from one kilometer to 31,000 miles. Eames later beat his own records in a '56 Dodge, then the next year broke those in a fleet of blown 1957 Fords.

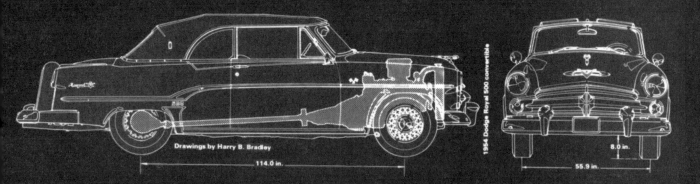

114.0 in.   8.0 in.   55.9 in.

Drawings by Harry B. Bradley

1954 Dodge Royal 500 convertible

SPECIFICATIONS
1954 Dodge Royal 500 conv., Model D-53-3

Price when new . . . . $2,632 f.o.b. Detroit (1954)
Current valuation* . . . . Xlnt $1,865; good $450
Options . . . . Radio, heater, wire wheel covers, continental kit, whitewalls, power steering, PowerFlite, 4-bbl carb

ENGINE
Type . . . . Ohv V-8, cast-iron block, water-cooled, 5 mains, full pressure lubrication
Bore & stroke . . . . 3.4375 x 3.250 inches
Displacement . . . . 241.3 c.i.d.
Max. bhp @ rpm . . . . 150 @ 4,400
Max. torque @ rpm . . . . 222 @ 2,400
Compression ratio 7.5:1
Induction system . . . . One 4-bbl. Stromberg carb, Offen-hauser manifold, mechanical fuel pump
Exhaust system . . . . Cast-iron manifolds, twin mufflers
Electrical system . . . . 6-volt battery/coil (Autolite)

CLUTCH
Type . . . . None

TRANSMISSION
Type . . . . PowerFlite 2-speed automatic with torque converter, planetary gears
Ratios: 1st . . . . 1.72:1 x 2.60 conv. ratio
       2nd . . . . 1.00:1 x 2.60 conv. ratio
       Reverse 2.39:1

DIFFERENTIAL
Type . . . . Hypoid, open driveshaft
Ratio 3.54:1
Drive axles . . . . Semi-floating

STEERING
Type . . . . Monroe hydraulic power steering, link-type, worm and roller gears
Turns lock to lock 4.5
Ratio 20.4:1
Turn circle . . . . 39.5 feet

BRAKES
Type . . . . 4-wheel hydraulic drums, internal expanding, duo-servo
Drum diameter . . . . 11.0 inches
Total lining area . . . . 173.5 square inches
Emergency brake . . . . Independent, on driveshaft

CHASSIS & BODY
Frame . . . . Double-dropped, channel-&-box-section steel, 4 crossmembers
Body construction . . . . All steel
Body style . . . . 6-pass. conv. cpe, hydraulic top

SUSPENSION
Front . . . . Independent, unequal A-arms, coil springs, tubular hydraulic shocks, linkless stabilizer bar
Rear . . . . Solid rear axle, longitudinal semi-elliptic leaf springs, tubular shocks, stabilizer bar
Tires . . . . Tube type, 7.10 x 15 whitewalls
Wheels . . . . Drop-center rims, pressed steel discs, lug-bolted to brake drums

WEIGHTS & MEASURES
Wheelbase . . . . 114.0 inches
Overall length . . . . 199.5 inches
Overall height . . . . 60.25 inches
Overall width . . . . 73.875 inches
Front tread . . . . 55.938 inches
Rear tread . . . . 58.750 inches
Ground clearance . . . . 8.0 inches
Curb weight . . . . 3,575 pounds

CAPACITIES
Crankcase . . . . 5 quarts
Cooling system . . . . 19 quarts
Fuel tank . . . . 17 gallons

FUEL CONSUMPTION
Best . . . . 19.9 mpg
Average . . . . 16.8 mpg

PERFORMANCE (from *Motor Trend*, Aug. 1954, for Royal V-8 sedan with PowerFlite)
0-30 mph . . . . 5.2 sec.
0-40 mph . . . . 7.9 sec.
0-60 mph . . . . 16.2 sec.
0-70 mph . . . . 21.8 sec.
Standing 1/4 mile . . . . 20.3 sec. and 68 mph
Top speed . . . . 108.36 mph (AAA record sedan)

* Courtesy Antique Automobile Appraisal.

1955 Dodge, Mercury and Oldsmobile

by Arch Brown
photos by Vince Manocchi

LOOKING back on It, 1955 was really the best of times. The Korean War was behind us and the world was at peace. Well, most of the world, anyway.

The paterfamilias was in the White House, and there was the feeling that all was well. A chill ran through us on September 24 when it was announced that President Eisenhower had suffered a heart attack, but it soon became apparent that the tough old general was on the road to recovery, and our fears were allayed.

Dr. Jonas Salk perfected his vaccine against polio, and another of our fears was put to rest

With Mary Martin in the title role, NBC telecast *Peter Pan* in compatible color—a landmark event in the development of color television.

Marian Anderson sang at the Metropolitan Opera, the first black person to be engaged as a regular member of the company. One more barrier down!

Hollywood gave us such notable films as *Mister Roberts* (Henry Fonda), *The Seven Year Itch* (Marilyn Monroe) and *East of Eden* (James Dean).

And on Broadway, audiences were captivated by the likes of *Bus Stop, Cat on a Hot Tin Roof, The Diary of Anne Frank* and the Cole Porter musical smash, *Silk Stockings*.

It was a record-breaking year for the American automobile industry. Business had literally never been so good—at least for General Motors, Ford, and Chrysler. It was a prosperity in which the independent firms did not share, however. Most of them were sinking fast.

Nineteen-fifty-five was a particularly felicitous time for cars of the medium-priced field. Their customary share of the market had faltered a bit in recent years, but in '55 they scored a resounding comeback. (Seeing this as a portent of what was to come, the folks at Ford began to plan a new entry for this already crowded field. But that's another story.)

If the somber hues in which so many of today's cars are finished can be said to reflect the tenor of the times, the same was no less true of the bright colors that characterized the equipage of the Eisenhower era. The economy was booming; it was a happy time, and America enjoyed its expression in brightly painted automobiles. Even pink was popular, for heaven's sake, prompting the speculation that somebody in Detroit may have been inspired by his wife's false teeth! Dodge, among others, actually offered three-tone color schemes, combining yellow or pink with black and white. It was all a bit much, and mercifully the fad died a rapid death.

Important changes had been made by the major manufacturers in nearly all of their product lines: new developments in engineering, and especially in styling. The most obvious differences in the latter respect were to be found in the cars from the Chrysler Corporation.

Take, for instance, the Dodge. The division's 1953–54 models had been stubby and stodgy, not to say downright ugly. Corporation President K.T. Keller, a practical-minded man, had decreed that they should be "smaller on the outside, larger on the inside." And so they were, but at what a cost!

Dodge's 1955 line, however, was a totally different story. Wearing a completely redesigned body shell, based on but attractively differentiated from that of the Plymouth, the new Dodge in sedan form was nearly seven inches longer than its predecessor. And in convertible, hardtop, and station wagon configurations the stretch came to no less than sixteen inches! Less curvaceous than the General Motors products, the new Dodge presented a lean, trim appearance that stood in marked contrast to its dumpy predecessor. And its windshield, wide enough to provide maximum visibility, managed to avoid the knee-rapping, distortion-producing "dogleg" so common at the time.

Three trim lines were offered by Dodge, all on the same chassis. The Coronet name, which only a couple of years earlier had designated the top trimline, was now applied to the base car. Gussied up a little, it was known as the Royal, while the top series was called the Custom Royal.

Dodge's familiar hemi V-8, bored for an additional 29 cubic inches of displacement, was retained for the Custom Royal models, while the same block, fitted with conventional heads, was used in the less expensive Royal and Coronet series. The latter could also be ordered with Chrysler Corporation's hoary L-head six, but fewer than one out of every eight 1955 Dodges was so equipped.

The public's reaction to the new car was almost overwhelming. A former Dodge dealer told *SIA* that the reception accorded the 1955 model was "by far the most enthusiastic I ever saw, in more than 20 years in the business!"

Dodge sales shot up by an astonishing 106 percent!

At Mercury the changes were less dramatic. The new, overhead-valve V-8, introduced just the year before, was bored and stroked, raising its horsepower rating from 162 to 188. The horsepower race, most visible among cars of the luxury class, was making itself felt even among the more modest automobiles of the day.

Like the Dodge, the Mercury came in three series, all sharing the same 119-inch wheelbase. The base car was called the Custom. With upscale trim, the same automobile became the Monterey. And at the top of the heap rode the Montclair, a slinky number standing two-and-a-half inches lower than the less expensive cars.

Sheet metal, derived from that of the Ford, was brand new for 1955, though there was enough resemblance to the 1954 model to make the new Mercury readily identifiable. A wraparound windshield similar to that of the GM cars was featured. Dimensions, apart from the Montclair's lowered roof line, were nearly the same as those of the previous year's Merc, yet the new car's lines somehow contrived to make it appear longer and lower than before.

Buyers responded on cue; Mercury scored an impressive 69 percent sales increase.

Meanwhile, over at GM the price dis-

All three cars were styled with trim which encouraged two-tone paint schemes. Mercury had most conservative trim, Dodge the wildest.

tinctions between the various divisions had become blurred. For years it had been the Pontiac that had slugged it out with Dodge (and later with Mercury as well) for leadership in the lower-medium-priced field. But with the 1939 introduction of the "60" series, Oldsmobile had invaded Pontiac's territory, and by 1954 Olds sales had surpassed those of Pontiac. (Buick, its somewhat higher price structure notwithstanding, was still ahead of both of its sister divisions.)

Olds, along with Buick, had been rebodied for 1954; for 1955 there was only a minor facelift to distinguish the new car from its predecessor. There were

some mechanical refinements such as recalibrated front springs and a new front stabilizer, but essentially the people at Lansing had refrained from messing with what was obviously a very good thing.

The policy paid off. Olds set a sales record that year that would stand for a decade.

Three distinct Oldsmobiles were offered for 1955. Flagship of the line was the 98, a sumptuously trimmed automobile built on an extended wheelbase. The division's bread and butter came, however, from the more modest 88 and Super 88 lines. Sharing the mechanical

Comparison Chart: 1955 Dodge, Mercury, Oldsmobile—And Pontiac

Series tested	Dodge Custom Royal	Mercury Montclair	Oldsmobile Super 88	Pontiac* Star Chief
Body style	Convertible	Convertible	Convertible	Convertible
Price, model tested**	$2,723	$2,712	$2,894	$2,681
Price, base V-8 sedan**	$2,171	$2,277	$2,362	$2,164
Engine	ohv V-8	ohv V-8	ohv V-8	ohv V-8
Bore/stroke (inches)	3.63/3.25	3.75/3.30	3.875/3.4375	3.75/3.25
Displacement (cubic inches)	270.0	292.0	324.3	287.2
Compression ratio (model tested)	7.6:1	8.5:1	8.5:1	8.0:1
Compression ratio (base engine)	same	7.6:1	same	7.4:1
Bhp @ rpm (model tested)	183 @ 4,400	198 @ 4,400	202 @ 4,000	180 @ 4,600
Bhp @ rpm (base engine)	175 @ 4,400	188 @ 4,400	185 @ 4,000	173 @ 4,400
Bhp per c.i.d. (model tested)	.678	.702	.623	.627
Bhp per c.i.d. (base engine)	.648	.644	.570	.602
Torque @ rpm (model tested)	245 @ 2,400	286 @ 2,500	332 @ 2,400	264 @ 2,400
Torque @ rpm (base engine)	240 @ 2,400	274 @ 2,500	320 @ 2,000	256 @ 2,400
Carburetor	Dual downdraft	4-barrel	4-barrel	Dual downdraft
Electrical system	6-volt	6-volt	12-volt	12-volt
Automatic transmission	PowerFlite	Merc-o-Matic	Hydra-Matic	Hydra-Matic
Torque converter?	Yes	Yes	No	No
Number of speeds	2	3	4	4
Ratios (:1)	1.72/1.00	2.40/1.47/1.00	3.82/2.63/1.45/1.00	4.10/2.63/1.55/1.00
Differential	Hypoid	Hypoid	Hypoid	Hypoid
Drive axles	Semi-floating	Semi-floating	Semi-floating	Semi-floating
Ratio	3.54:1	3.15:1	3.23:1	3.08:1
Front suspension	Ind. coil spring	Ind. coil spring	Ind. coil spring	Ind. coil spring
Steering (power, type)	Recirc. ball nut***	Worm and roller	Ball nut	Recirc. ball brg.
Ratio (:1, gear)	16.2	20.1	19.1	21.3
Turn circle (curb/curb)	42' 3"	42' 4"	42' 0"	42' 11"
Brakes (type)	Hydraulic, drum	Hydraulic, drum	Hydraulic, drum	Hydraulic, drum
Drum diameter	11"	11"	11"	12"
Effective area (sq. in.)	173.5	190.9	191.7	178.0
Tread, front	58.9"	58"	59"	58.7"
Tread, rear	59.1"	59"	59"	59.1"
Capacities:				
Cooling system (qts, w/heater)	20	20	21.5	26
Fuel tank (gallons)	17	18	20	20
Shipping wgt, car tested (lbs)	3,610	3,490	3,989	3791
Shipping wgt, base sedan	3,395	3,450	3,707	3511
Measurements:				
Wheelbase	120"	119"	122"	124"
Overall length	212.1"	206.3"****	203.4"	210.2"
Overall width	74.5"	76.4"	77.8"	75.4"
Overall height (sedan)	62.6"	60.5"	62.2"	62.5"
Minimum road clearance	5.0"	6.6"	6.3"	6.7"
Tire size	7.10 x15	7.10 x 15	7.60 x 15	7.10 x 15
Front leg room	44.5"	43.8"	42.9"	42.7"
Rear leg room (sedan)	35.5"	35.4"	35.6"	35.6"
Front head room (sedan)	35.5"	33.5"	35.6"	35.6"
Rear head room (sedan)	34.9"	32.2"	34.6"	35.9"
Front hip room	62.5"	60.6"	62.3"	61.8"
Rear hip room (sedan)	62.8"	60.3"	62.4"	63.1"
Front shoulder room	58.0"	57.0"	58.2"	56.6"
Rear shoulder room (sedan)	57.8"	56.8"	56.7"	56.4"
Front seat adjustment	5.0"	4.9"	4.4"	4.4"
Front seat height	13.4"	12.0"	13.2"	13.7"
Rear seat height (sedan)	12.8"	13.1"	12.4"	12.0"
Registrations (calendar year)	284,323	371,837	589,515	530,007
Production (calendar year)	313,088	434,911	643,459	581,860
Production (model year)	276,936	329,808	583,179	553,808
Production, this body style	3,302	10,668	9,007	19,762
Performance factors				
Lbs per bhp (car tested)	19.73	17.63	19.75	21.06
Lbs per bhp (base sedan)	19.40	18.35	20.00	20.20
Lbs per c.i.d. (car tested)	13.37	11.95	12.30	13.20
Lbs per c.i.d. (base sedan)	12.57	11.82	11.40	12.22

*The Pontiac was not tested. Figures are shown here for comparative purposes.

**Price f.o.b. factory, including federal excise tax.

***Test car was equipped with worm-and-roller manual steering, ratio 18.2:1.

****Length shown does not include optional continental kit.

Primary source: *Automotive Industries*, March 15, 1955.

Below: Dodge taillamp treatment was very space-age, while Olds, **far left**, stayed with its traditional bullet treatment. Merc, **left**, opted for busy vertical effect. **Below center and bottom:** All three cars present a pleasant rear appearance, with Olds having the cleanest styling of the lot.

components of the larger car, they were priced within the reach of the Pontiac (or Dodge or Mercury) buyer. (See comparison chart, page 44.)

Statistically, the Dodge-Mercury-Oldsmobile trio of 1955 have much in common, though the Olds is a little heavier and more powerful than the other two—as well as marginally more expensive.

The Dodge, though a bit narrower overall than its competition, furnished a little extra shoulder and hip room, and for the tall driver it had a substantial advantage in leg room.

But perhaps the most obvious difference among the three cars, appearance aside, lay in their optional automatic transmissions. Oldsmobile used, as it had since 1940, the venerable four-speed Hydra-Matic. Mercury employed, for the fifth straight year, the Merc-o-Matic, a three-speed unit tied to a torque converter. Dodge, whose first fully automatic transmission had been introduced only two years earlier, stayed with the PowerFlite, a two-speed planetary arrangement coupled to a torque converter. All three transmissions had excellent records in terms of durability.

Options abounded. Dodge, Mercury and Oldsmobile all came with three-speed manual transmissions as stan-

dard equipment, to which the Dodge would append an overdrive for an extra hundred or so. But the automatic transmission had captured the public's fancy, and most of the cars left the factories equipped to suit the "shiftless" driver. Power steering and power brakes were becoming increasingly popular as well. Radios and heaters, technically extras, were so widespread as to be virtually standard, and white sidewall tires were also highly popular. Power windows and power seats, though seldom seen at that time in cars of this class, were available to buyers who wanted them; and Dodge was beginning to push its Chrysler Air-Temp air-conditioner, at

$567 the most costly of all options. At that price there were few takers.

Thanks to some vigorous legwork on the part of photographer Vince Manocchi, *SIA* was able to bring together three particularly choice convertibles for this comparisonReport—one from each of the major US manufacturers.

• Representing the Chrysler Corporation was Nick Dezmura's Dodge Custom Royal Lancer.

• Carrying the flag for the Ford Motor Company was Cindy Keetch's Mercury Montclair.

• And upholding the honor of General Motors was an Oldsmobile Super 88 belonging to Norb Kopchinsky.

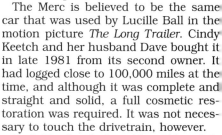

Above: Dodge rolls on factory-option Kelsey-Hayes wires, while Merc and Olds hubcaps are quite restrained in design: **Right and below:** Model ID appears on Merc's continental kit. Olds need only say "88" for instant recognition, but Dodge spells it out. **Bottom, left to right:** '55 was first year for Mercury's full wraparound windshield. Dodge opted for semi-wraparound and Olds continued its raked wraparound, introduced in 1954.

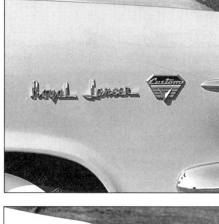

We drove them all—and we loved them!

Our Dodge's early history is shrouded in mystery, since Nick bought it in 1979 off a consignment lot. But there is every indication that the 77,000-mile odometer reading is probably correct. The car even has its original Goodyear wide-whitewall spare tire.

The Merc is believed to be the same car that was used by Lucille Ball in the motion picture *The Long Trailer*. Cindy Keetch and her husband Dave bought it in late 1981 from its second owner. It had logged close to 100,000 miles at the time, and although it was complete and straight and solid, a full cosmetic restoration was required. It was not necessary to touch the drivetrain, however.

Norb Kopchinski found his Oldsmobile in 1982, in a Pennsylvania barn where it had been stored for many years, forgotten and neglected. A 36,000-mile original car in generally sound mechanical condition, it was suffering from rusted-out front fenders and quarter panels. Without laying a wrench on it, Norb was able to drive the Olds home to California at speeds that he would be reluctant to discuss with the Highway Patrol. The original leather interior is still in good condition, but of course the car's exterior needed extensive attention.

We have owned Chrysler Corporation

cars of 1953 and 1958 vintage in years gone by, and we were not impressed with the body structure of either of them. So it came as something of a surprise when we found the Dodge to be—seemingly, at least—the most solidly constructed of the three ragtops used for this report. Leg room is ample, front and rear—the best of the lot in that respect. Seating is comfortable, too, though the edge in that department would have to go to the Olds.

We appreciate the absence of a dogleg in the Dodge's panoramic windshield. Not only is this design kinder to the knees of a long-legged occupant, but it produces almost no distortion.

A full set of dashboard instruments characterizes all three of these cars. We like that. The people who invented and promoted idiot lights have a lot of penance to do.

The Mercury's front seat is wide and comfortable, if a bit low for our taste. Leg room is ample in the driver's compartment. Seated in the rear, however, we found our knees tucked up under our chin. The back seat is wide enough for two, but for three people it would be an impossibly tight squeeze. And the head room, thanks to the Montclair's low profile, is limited.

Boarding the Oldsmobile, we found the best seating accommodations of the lot—in front. Rear knee room is nonexistent for a six-footer, however. The seat cushions seem more supportive than those of the other two cars, an important comfort factor. But that miserable dogleg seems even more obtrusive than that of the Mercury.

Head room is good, about on a par with the Dodge, and although the Olds has the smallest trunk of the three, it's still reasonably spacious.

The best part of an assignment such as this one is, of course, getting to drive the cars. We took the Dodge out first.

We were surprised to find that the Royal Lancer convertible, though a top-of-the-line car, is not equipped with power steering. That may have been a wise move on the part of the original owner, for Chrysler's power steering in the fifties was too sensitive for many drivers. In any case, we found the manual steering to be light, easy and precise—

Top left, top right and above: Olds carried rocket theme over to its hood ornament. Mercury ornament doesn't have any particular theme; Dodge used very abstract knight's helmet. **Left:** *Olds headlight rim treatment gave a slightly hooded effect.* **Below left:** *Mercury used a very heavy hood on their lights.* **Below:** *Dodge treatment looks like a highly stylized eyebrow.*

though a little slow. The car, as Nick says. goes exactly where you point it.

Acceleration is handicapped by the Dodge's two-speed PowerFlite transmission. Which isn't to say that the car is sluggish; it's not. But off-the-line it would do much better if the transmission had an extra gear. The shift from low to high is a smooth one; the driver is hardly aware of it.

The ride is good, very comfortable indeed. There's quite a bit of lean in the turns, but control is easy to maintain at all times.

Like its steering, the Dodge's brakes are non-powered. They take a bit of getting used to, for a lot of pedal pressure

is required. But they do their job smoothly and well.

We had forgotten that the early Merc-o-Matic transmissions start the car in second gear. We were reminded of this characteristic quickly enough, for the Mercury's acceleration from rest is less brisk than that of the Dodge. By starting off in Low, then shifting manually to Drive, performance is substantially improved.

This Merc is equipped with just about every option the company offered in 1955. The power steering preserves a fair amount of road feel, and the power brakes are—like the laxative ad says—smooth and effective. In addition, Cindy's

Right: Oldsmobile front carries typical GM combination bumper/grille styling. Below: Dodge uses split grille effect. Below right: Mercury also goes the bumper/grille route, but in a more angular manner than Olds.

car boasts power windows, power seats, a rare deluxe steering wheel, and even a factory continental kit.

If one were to stage a drag race among these three cars, the Oldsmobile would win it going away. The enormous torque of the 88 engine—largest of the three powerplants by a substantial margin—combines with the four-speed Hydra-Matic transmission to give this car a strong advantage in that department. Shifts are smooth, and so are the

The Traditional Rival: Pontiac

It had been General Motors President Alfred P. Sloan, Jr., who—back in the early twenties—had come up with the idea of arranging the corporation's various marques in the form of a "ladder." Thus, as Sloan conceived the notion, as the motorist's social, professional and financial status improved, he could progress step-by-step to ever finer and more expensive automobiles. All within the GM family, of course.

Initially there had been a couple of gaps in that ladder, and Alfred Sloan made it his business to close them. The most important of these was the considerable stretch between the price of the Chevrolet and that of the Oldsmobile. Strategically placed at the bottom of the medium-priced market, it was a segment that for years had been dominated by the Dodge Brothers four-cylinder cars.

Sloan's response to Dodge's implicit challenge was, of course, the Pontiac. (See *SIA* #44.) Introduced in 1926, it was an attractive L-head six. And it was an immediate success.

As time went along, the steps of Sloan's ladder became less well-defined. By 1939 the top-of-the-line Pontiac was actually priced substantially higher than the cheapest Olds, for instance. And by the mid-fifties, even Buick was marketing automobiles that directly competed with the upscale Pontiac models.

But still, in the public's mind—and doubtless in the thinking of the corporate planners as well—it was the Pontiac that was the traditional and natural rival of the Dodge—and of the upstart Mercury as well.

The Intra-corporate rivalry among Buick,

Olds, and Pontiac is a story in itself. For years the Buick, despite the disadvantage of carrying the highest average price tag of the trio, had been General Motors' best-selling medium-priced car, followed by Pontiac and Oldsmobile, in that order. But the fifties saw some drastic shifts in the automobile market. Olds eased past Pontiac in 1954 and passed Buick in numbers of cars produced four years later. And then in 1959, with the introduction of the dramatic new "wide track" models, Pontiac leapfrogged over both of its sister divisions to take over fourth place in the industry, behind Chevrolet, Ford and Plymouth. By 1961 the Ponty was the industry's number three nameplate, a distinction it was to hold for several years to follow.

As it happened, 1955 was a banner year for Pontiac, despite the fact that the division was out-produced by both Buick and Oldsmobile. Scoring a 57 percent sales increase over the previous year, Pontiac was a country mile ahead of both Mercury and Dodge. And perhaps not surprisingly, for the car they offered was almost completely new. Fitted with GM's freshly styled A body, which it shared with Chevrolet, it featured the then-popular dogleg wraparound windshield, and was distinguished by twin "silver streaks" (a Pontiac trademark in those days) running the length of the hood. Those streaks, taken together with the comparatively massive appearance of the new model, led one critic to refer to the '55 Pontiac as "a fat man wearing suspenders." No matter; the public loved it

But significant as the new styling was, the

real change in the Pontiac was to be found under the hood. From the time of its introduction, Pontiac had used side-valve engines exclusively. There had been a short-lived and none-too-popular V-8 back in 1932, but the bulk of Pontiac's production had been of sixes and—especially—straight eights.

Pontiac's 1955 powerplant set a new direction for the marque with a modern, short-stroke, overhead-valve V-8. Not for more than a decade would Pontiac again offer a six. With a modest increase in displacement over the old L-head eight (287.2 versus 268.4 cubic inches), the new engine boasted a healthy 42 percent boost in horsepower, from 127 to 180 (as fitted to Hydra-Matic-equipped units). So, despite an extra hundred and fifty pounds of heft compared to its predecessor, the 1955 model was by far the fastest, liveliest car produced by the Pontiac Motor Division up to that time.

Three series were offered: The Chieftain 860 (Special), Chieftain 870 (Deluxe), and the Star Chief. The latter, a beautifully appointed car with two extra inches of wheelbase, measured more than seven inches longer overall than the Chieftains, the extra length taking the form of an extended rear deck. The convertible body style was offered only in the Star Chief series.

The automotive world didn't know it yet, but Pontiac was about to enter its halcyon days—the period of the marque's greatest sales success.

Continued on page 57

Color Gallery

Photograph from Hemmings Motor News archives

1918 Open Tourer
Now in its fifth year as a manufacturer, Dodge's 1918 cars were essentially unchanged from the first Dodge that bowed in 1914. Available in 6 different body configurations, total series production reached 62,000 units. A 35hp, 212.3-cu.in. inline-four was its only engine.

Photograph from Hemmings Motor News archives

1925 Two-Door Coupe
With their balloon-type tires on large, 20-inch diameter wheels, the 1925 models were the first Dodges to have one-piece windshields, automatic windshield wipers, lift-open rear windows, cowl vents, and rubber motor mounts to reduce vibrations.

Photograph from Hemmings Motor News archives

1926 Sport Roadster

Stylistically unchanged for several years, the 1926 Dodges now featured a conventional "H" shift pattern on their three-speed manual gearboxes and three hinges per door. Power was provided by the same 35hp, L-head 212.3-cu.in inline-four engine used since 1914.

Photograph from Hemmings Motor News archives

1929 Victory Six

Now in its second year, the Victory Six, as well as all Dodges, featured more rounded, high-crown fenders that provided it with a more contemporary look. There were some 124,000 cars built this year; all were powered by a 63hp, 208-cu.in. straight-six engine.

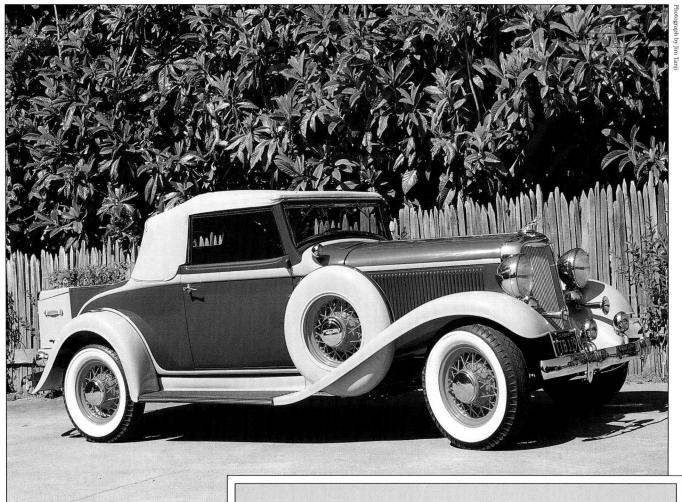

Photograph by Jim Tanji

1933 Model DO Straight 8

With its waterfall grille, dual cowl vents and abundance of chrome moldings, the Dodge 8 has many of the same details that the far more expensive full Classics are appreciated for. Under the hood lies a 282.1-cu.in. straight-eight engine that makes an even 100hp.

Photograph by Bud Juneau

1937 D-5 Convertible Sedan

Looking quite modern for its day with its elegant split grille and horizontal hood louvers, the spacious D-5 convertible sedan comfortably seated 5 passengers; yet only 473 were produced. Priced at $1,230, it was the most expensive Dodge model produced that year.

Photograph from Hemmings Motor News archives

1949 Wayfarer
Featuring Dodge's first all-new body style since before the war, the Wayfarer was a huge hit, with nearly 64,000 produced. Available only in two-door trim, just 5,420 convertibles were built, and all were powered by the 103hp, 230-cu.in. straight-six.

Photograph from Hemmings Motor News archives

1951 Meadowbrook
As had been the case since its introduction in 1949, the Meadowbrook was only offered as a four-door model, and only in base-level trim. Like all Dodge models this year, it used the 103hp, 230-cu.in. L-head straight-six.

Photograph by Don Spiro

1955 LaFemme

Designed for the fashionable woman on the go, the La Femme was outfitted with loads of accessories, including an umbrella, purse, rain hat, lipstick, lighter, pocketbook and a gold-trimmed compact case to help the "American Woman" always look her best.

Photograph from Hemmings Motor News archives

1957 Custom Royal Lancer

Well appointed throughout, the Custom Royal was the top trim level model, and the most expensive. Reflecting its upscale image, its Dodge lettering had a gold finish, and the front bumper featured six vertical bars. The base Red Ram 325-cu.in. V-8 made 260hp.

Photograph from Hemmings Motor News archives

1959 Coronet
As one would expect of a '59 model car, the Coronet had trendy fins that were quite tall and visually striking with their twin protruding taillamps. Engine choices were many on Dodge's base model, and included a straight-six or four different V-8s.

Photograph by John Matras

1959 Custom Royal Convertible
Powered by a dual-quad 383-cu.in. V-8 producing a mighty 345hp, this Custom Royal is an aggressively styled convertible that packs a powerful punch. Its Super D-500 engine featured a high-lift cam, heavy-duty valve springs and a dual-point distributor.

Photograph by Bud Juneau

1961 Dart Phoenix

With the sleekly designed profile of its hardtop-styled roof and oddly shaped protruding rear fins, the Dart Phoenix is a real standout of early Sixties American automotive fashion. Power is supplied by a 360-cu.in. V-8 that develops 305hp.

Photograph by Don Spiro

1962 Lancer

Ghia-inspired body lines, quad headlamps and heavily sculptured rear fenders are just a few of the hallmark styling cues that made the Lancer so distinctive. Chrysler's ever-reliable 145hp, 225-cu.in. slant-six resides under the hood.

Photograph by Bud Juneau

1964 Dart Convertible
Well appointed and stylish, the mid-size Dart convertible had lots of welcome features including an electronically controlled convertible top, push-button TorqueFlite automatic transmission and a 180hp, 273-cu.in. V-8 that provided plenty of go.

Photograph by Josiah Work

1972 Dart Demon
Powered by Chrysler's rugged 340-cu.in. small-block V-8 that produced a user-friendly 240hp, the Demon 340 was created as an entry-level muscle-type car for those on a budget. It featured twin hood scoops, bucket seats and a devilish cartoon-like emblem.

Left, below left, and below: *All three cars will break into noticeable understeer when pushed in corners.* **Below center, left to right:** *Thanks to continental kit, Merc wins largest trunk contest.* **Below, top to bottom:** *Olds's big, round speedo is highly readable. Merc's speedo sweeps across the dial in an arc. Dodge's gauges are each carried in separate pod. All three cars boast full instrumentation as standard equipment.*

brakes, and the power steering is at least the equal of the Merc's in preserving the feel of the road.

It seems to us that the Olds doesn't lean as much as either of the other cars in hard cornering. And yet it's no easier to control on winding roads. Maybe not quite as easy, in fact, as the Dodge. Hard to say; the difference between power and non-power steering could be a factor here. And in terms of ride we'd rank the Olds about equal with the Dodge—and just a bit ahead of the Mercury.

All right: so which to choose?

As usual there were characteristics in each car that had the edge over the other two, and what we would really prefer is a composite.

• We like the Oldsmobile's transmission best, though the Merc might get the edge here if only it would start off in first gear.

• It's entirely a matter of personal preference, but the sleek styling of the Dodge appeals to us. Again, the Merc is a close second—a potential winner except for that misbegotten dogleg. The curvaceous lines of the Olds are the sexiest of the lot, but they've always seemed to us to be a trifle bulbous.

• The torque output of that Oldsmobile engine is impressive, and evidently there's little penalty attached in terms of fuel mileage.

• Seating comfort up front is best in the Olds, though the margin is narrow. In the rear seat, the advantage goes to the Dodge.

• The lady at our house tends to pack everything in sight every time we go anywhere, so of course we can appreciate the Mercury's enormous trunk.

Taken all-in-all, had we been keeping a point score, perhaps the nod would have gone to the Olds—by a nose. But that's as it should be, for it was the costliest of the three, back in 1955. All three cars offer a comfortable ride, more than adequate performance, and durability that has proven itself over the years.

And when you contemplate the progress in automotive design that these cars represent, compared to their precursors of a quarter-century—or even nine years—earlier, you know it's really true: 1955 was indeed a very good year! ☙

Acknowledgments and Bibliography
Automotive Industries, March 15, 1955, and March 15, 1954; Thomas Bonsall, Mercury Identification Guide, 1939-1969; *Dennis Casteele,* The Cars of Oldsmobile; *Jerry Heasley,* The Production Figure Book for US Cars; *James H. Mahoney and George H. Dammann,* American Cars, 1946-1959; *Thomas A. McPherson,* The Dodge Story.
Our thanks to Al Allande, Van Nuys,

Right, below and below right: All three engines have good accessibility to the basics, though in their day these were considered fiendishly busy engine compartments. Bottom: Dodge's tail is beginning to hint at fins; Olds looks nearly identical to '54 cars; Merc gains added inches because of wind-catching continental kit.

The Fickle Fortunes of the Lower-Medium-Priced Four

Dodge had been, from 1933 until the close of the decade of the thirties, the number-one seller in the lower-medium-price sales race—with Pontiac hard on its heels and Oldsmobile a strong third. In 1940 Pontiac took the lead, and the following year Dodge fell to third place behind Oldsmobile. Ford's new Mercury, meanwhile, was making its opening bid.

In the years just after World War II, Dodge forged ahead once again, with Pontiac, Olds, and Mercury following in that order. But fate is capricious and the public is fickle. By 1948 Pontiac had regained the lead, only to lose it to Oldsmobile six years later. Mercury, meanwhile, had slipped ahead of Dodge, leaving the one-time leader of the field in fourth place.

Calendar Year Production, 1946-1955

Year	Dodge	Mercury	Oldsmobile	Pontiac
1946	156,080	70,955	114,674	131,538
1947	232,216	124,612	191,454	222,991
1948	232,390	154,702	194,755	253,472
1949	298,399	203,339	282,885	336,466
1950	332,782	334,081	396,757	469,813
1951	325,694	238,854	285,634	345,617
1952	259,519	195,261	228,452	278,140
1953	293,714	320,369	319,414	415,335
1954	151,766	256,730	433,810	370,887
1955	313,038	434,911	643,459	581,860

Source: Jerry Heasley, *The Production Figure Book for US Cars.*

California; W.H. Braley, Santa Cruz, California; Gary Goers, Santa Fe Springs, California: Tom and Nancy Howard, Riverside, California; Franca and Vince Manocchi, Azusa, California; Jerry Olmstead, Hilltop Classics, Escondido, California; Telford and Ada Work, Pacific Palisades, California. Special thanks to Nick Dezmura, Northridge, California; Dave and Cindy Keetch, Spring Valley, California; Norb Kopchinski, Downey, California.

New Dodge Custom Royal Lancer . . . most glamorous car on the road.

What's all this talk about "Price Class"?

It gets to be a little confusing—this talk about "price class."

Take that dashing Custom Royal Lancer up above. People who are used to paying a *thousand dollars more* for a car are asking themselves, "What more could I get—*what more is there?*"

Money can't buy more flashing style, more dashing beauty, more exciting features.

Then take the Dodge Coronet 4-door sedan shown below. A really *big* car in every way—up to a foot-and-a-half longer than the so-called "lowest priced" cars. Big in V-8 power. Big in luxury. Big in solid comfort.

But the shocker is this: *You can own this Dodge sedan for less than you'd pay for many models in the small car field! You can step up to "The Big One"—and actually step down your costs!*

Price class? Forget it! The new Dodge is stealing hearts in every "bracket." Don't let *anything* keep you from yours! See your Dodge dealer.

DODGE
FLASHES AHEAD IN '55

New Dodge Coronet V-8 Four-Door Sedan . . . value buy of the year.

Sweet Dreams

Dodge Firearrow vs. Dual-Ghia

By John Katz
Photos by Roy Query

It's funny how different two siblings can be. One may be brilliant and mannerly, a straight-A achiever, with a straight-arrow style; the other a rebellious cut-up with a bad attitude and an aversion to effort. ("Why can't you be more like your brother/sister?") Then, just when you think you've got them both neatly labeled, the cut-up starts climbing the corporate ladder, while the "brilliant" one can't seem to hold a job.

These two automobiles—each a unique prototype, as well as a relative of the glamorous Dual-Ghia— are a little like those rival siblings Comparing them illustrates just how rapidly automotive technology marched through the fifties: Only four years separate one from the other, yet in those 48 months Chrysler engineering advanced from decidedly vintage to surprisingly modern. Which means that this comparison is no contest: The '58 Dual-Ghia 400 is superior to the '54 Dodge Firearrow by any measure you can mention. Still, the Firearrow led to an actual series-produced automobile, while the 400 merely pointed down a deceptively intriguing dead end.

Examined side-by-side, they neatly bracket the actual production run of the Dual-Ghia convertible.

    Originally published in Special Interest Autos #154, Jul.-Aug. 1996

Above: Front profiles of both cars are softly rounded in appearance. Below: Taillamp treatment on Firearrow shows its Italian roots. It could as easily be a Ferrari. Dual-Ghia taillamp treatment is much more in the Exner/Forward Look mode.

The Dodge Firearrow

Virtually all printed sources render the name "Firearrow," although the script on all four examples looks more like "fire arrow"—two words and all lower-case. Widely attributed to Virgil M. Exner, Sr., who then headed Chrysler's Advanced Design section, the Firearrow in fact originated at the Ghia coachworks in Turin where, according to Dual-Ghia engineering chief Paul Farago, it was based on a model submitted by the 16-year-old son of a Ghia woodworker. "Ex" offered some guidance on its development but never claimed credit for it.

According to Virgil M. Exner, Jr., however, the Firearrow was designed "to Farago's taste." And it was Farago, who at that time represented Ghia in the United States, who pushed each successive Firearrow ever closer to producible reality.

The first Firearrow, a brilliant red barchetta, appeared at the Turin auto show in 1953. A metallic gray molding bisected its oval grille, rounded its front fenders, and ran all the way down both sides; while maroon piping highlighted its yellow-buff leather interior. Its shifter sprouted promisingly from the floor, and its quad headlights, peering from under the bumper-like molding, were unusual then, even for a show car. Alas, Firearrow I was just a non-running mockup.

But Firearrow II, which followed in 1954, was a runner, built on a stock 119-inch Dodge chassis and packing a Red Ram Hemi under the hood—ostensibly hotted up to 250 bhp. A column-mounted shifter communicated with Dodge's "Gyro-Torque" four-speed semi-automatic transmission. Firearrow II featured pale yellow paintwork and black leather inside, set off by a black wraparound molding. Its single headlights were set at a more realistic height.

But with no windshield wipers, wind-

shield frame, side windows, top, or exterior door handles, it still made a poor candidate for production. Reportedly sold in 1955 to a private party in Hawaii, it happily survives to this day.

By mid 1954, however, the series moved much closer to a viable production car with Firearrow III. A dark blue coupe with a silver belt molding and a blue-and-white interior, the third Firearrow offered real door handles, roll-up windows, and even a modicum of bumper protection. It was also the first Firearrow to feature bucket seats. Racer Betty Skelton used it to set a new ladies' closed-course speed record of 143.44 mph at Chrysler's Chelsea Proving Grounds. It too survives.

Our comparisonReport Firearrow is number IV, and is extremely similar to

Firearrow III, but with a folding fabric top. Its exterior color reverted to red, but it sports the same silver molding as the coupe. By this time Dodge offered the fully automatic PowerFlite transmission on most models, but the basic Meadowbrook Six retained the old Gyro-Matic (like Gyro-Torque, but with a simple fluid coupling instead of a torque converter), and oddly, that is the transmission Dodge chose for this Hemi V-8 sportster.

The late Maury Baldwin, who worked closely with Exner on all of Chrysler's Ghia-built "idea cars," once told Richard Langworth that Dodge *could* have produced Firearrow IV. Dodge didn't, of course, but Gene Casaroll did. A devout car enthusiast, Casaroll owned a Detroit-based new-car transport company

Above: Firearrow front-end treatment also has that pure Italian sports car appearance, while the Dual-Ghia is like a dream car from a fifties auto show. *Below:* Quad headlamps for the Dual-Ghia, a pair of Marchals and Heil fog lamps for the Firearrow.

SIA comparisonReport

called Automobile Shippers, Inc., as well as Dual-Motors, which had assembled twin-engine trucks for the Army Air Corps during World War II. Farago introduced him to *Carrozzeria Ghia* owner Luigi Segre, after which Casaroll bought the rights to the Firearrow design from Dodge and arranged for Ghia to re-engineer the show car for production. Ghia updated the Firearrow around 1955-56 Dodge mechanical components and switched to unit-body construction to gain interior space without increasing overall height. The first result of this effort, which Casaroll dubbed the Fire-bomb, proved disappointing for several reasons, but then Farago took direct control of the engineering work at Ghia and developed an extensively revised and improved version of the car. This was the Dual-Ghia, of which Dual-Motors and Ghia produced some 100 examples in 1956-58.

The Dual-Ghia never sold quite as well as Casaroll initially predicted, but it was a simple supply problem that finally stopped production: Dual-Motors used up the last available '56 Dodge running gear in the summer of 1958. And Chrysler Corporation's '57-59 torsion-bar suspension wouldn't fit the existing Dual-Ghia body without major modification.

Furthermore, the Firearrow-based Dual-Ghia was starting to look stale next to Exner's latest creations. Ex had significantly lowered Chrysler's 1957 production cars relative to the '55-56 models. "They were almost as low as the original Dual-Ghia," remarked Farago, who naturally wanted to keep his limited-production sports car one step ahead of Detroit's styling studios. So he decided to design an all-new car, a coupe this time.

Dual-Ghia 400

At this point, the Dual-Ghia story grows murky, with little documentation and few survivors willing to share their memories. Logically enough, Dual-Motors seems to have experimented with the '57 Chrysler 300 as a basis for a new Dual-Ghia. Ghia built at least two 300-based prototypes for Dual-Motors, the first a surprisingly upright and formal two-tone coupe, with only high ridges atop its front fenders and a square-oval grille to suggest a Dual-Ghia identity. Nonetheless, historic photos clearly show the Dual-Ghia crossed-flag badge on its nose. Its modest tailfins sport the numerals "375" (the actual gross horsepower of a '57 300-C with standard heads), surrounded by a chrome circle and pierced by a chrome dart. At least one source erroneously attributes this car to the Shah of Iran, probably confusing it with a vaguely similar but sleeker Chrysler 300 coupe that Ghia built (without any involvement from Dual-Motors) for the Shah around the same time. The Dual-Ghia "375" now resides in the United States. According to Dr. Paul Sable, who heads the Dual-Ghia registry (and who loaned his own Dual-Ghia and Facel Vega FVS for a comparisonReport in *SIA* #131), it bears Dual-Motors serial plate #201.

The number is significant. The production Dual-Ghias of 1956-58 were numbered from 101 onward, and despite what has been written before (by your humble author and others), Dr. Sable is now convinced that Dual-Motors assembled fewer than 100 of them. The highest known serial number is 197. So 201 suggests the start of a new generation. It is also significant

Evolution to Production I

1954 Dodge Firearrow IV vs. 1956-58 Dual-Ghia

	1954 Dodge Firearrow IV	1956-58 Dual-Ghia
Engine	V-8	V-8
Bore x stroke	3.44 X 3.25 in.	3.63 X 3.80 in.
Displacement	241.3 cu. in.	315 cu. in.
Compression ratio.	7.5.1	8.5.1 (9.25:1)*
Rated bhp @ rpm	150 @ 4,400	240 @ 4,400 (260 @ 4,800)*
Rated torque @ rpm	222 lb.ft. @ 2,400	316 @ 2,400 (330 @ 3,600)*
Combustion chamber	Hemi	Polyspheric (hemi)*
Valve lifters	Hydraulic	Hydraulic (mechanical)*
Carburetor	1 x 2-v	1 x 4-v
Exhaust system	Single with crossover	Dual
Electrical system	6 volts	12 volts
Transmission	4-speed semi-auto.	2-speed automatic
Axle ratio	N.A.	3.54:1
Steering	Manual worm & roller	Power recirc. ball**
Brakes	4-wheel hydraulic drums, unassisted	4-wheel hydraulic drums with vacuum servo**
Construction	Box-section frame with separate body	Unitized
Front suspension	Independent, unequal-length A-arms, coil springs anti-roll bar	Independent, unequal-length A-arms, coil springs anti-roll bar
Rear suspension	Live axle, semi-elliptic leaf springs, anti-roll bar	Live axle, semi-elliptic leaf springs
Wheels	Wire, 15 x 5K	Steel disc, 15 x 5K
Tires	7.00 x 15	6.70 x 15
Wheelbase	119.0 in.	115.0 in.
Stroke/bore ratio	.945:1	1.047:1
Bhp/c.i.d.	.622	.762 (.825)*

*Specifications with D-500 option are in parentheses)
**Power steering and brakes were optional on early production Dual-Ghias.

Left: *Stock Dodge badge is used on Firearrow.* **Above:** *Both front ends are distinct and flashy.* **Below:** *Crossed flags presaged Dual-Ghia logo. Kelsey-Hayes wire wheels carry the Firearrow along.*

because our comparisonReport car—although totally different in appearance—is Dual-Ghia number 202.

With number 202, Ghia seems to have abandoned any design continuity with the Firebomb and first-generation Dual-Ghia and turned instead for inspiration to another Chrysler show car—the 1957 Dart. Compared to the sleek Dart, however, 202 is bulked up considerably to provide adequate interior space on an unmodified, 126-inch Chrysler 300-C chassis. In fact, about the only thing 202 shares even with 201 is a stock 300 chassis and its dart-and-circle fender badges—although on 202 the number in the circle has been raised to an arbitrary "400" (390 gross bhp with the optional 10:1 heads, generously rounded up?). Its designer remains anonymous, and Ex Jr. recalled that "it didn't make any waves with my father or Farago."

Its first private owner was Alex Freeman, of New Jersey, who bought it at the New York Auto Show in 1958. The sale didn't come easily. Freeman repeatedly asked the price, while a Dual-Motors official patiently explained that the show car wasn't for sale. To which Freeman replied, "Everything's for sale. What's the price?" The harried employee finally fetched Casaroll himself, who agreed to sell the "400" after it had completed its show tour. Freeman wrote a check on the spot for $15,000, and took delivery of his prize almost a year later.

Almost immediately, the 400 proved troublesome as real-world transportation. Freeman must have found the front-mounted air conditioner inadequate, because a second air conditioning unit was added in the trunk, with outlets in the rear package shelf. In a letter to Freeman dated October 14, 1959, Casaroll acknowledged that "Chrysler New York" had performed "repairs and painting necessary to bring your Dual-Ghia 400 up to your expectations." For the painting, he enclosed a check for $500; for the rest, well, Casaroll was "indeed sorry you were put to this expense, and I do hope that the

car is now in top condition." Freeman tried to sell the car in 1970 but found no buyers.

It is currently owned by Dan and Fred Kanter, who supply restoration parts for Packards and other collector cars at Kanter Auto Products in Boonton, New Jersey. Fred told us how he had admired the 400 since it first appeared

in the enthusiast magazines some 37 years ago. "Then, in '77," he said, "a friend of mine who has a transmission shop said to me, 'I worked on a Dual-Ghia yesterday, did a transmission on it.' And I asked 'What color is it?' And he said, 'yellow and black.' And I said, 'Alex Freeman's car?' And he said, 'Yes, and it's for sale.'" Fred had the 400 parked

Evolution to Production II

	1958 Duall-Ghia 400 vs.	1960-63 Ghia L6.4
Engine	V-8	V-8
Bore x stroke	4.00 x 3.90 in.	4.25 X 3.38 in.
Displacement	392 cu. in.	383 cu. in.
Compression ratio.	10.0.1	10.1:1
Rated bhp @ rpm	390 @ 5,400	335 @ 4,600
Rated torque @ rpm	430 lb.ft. @4,200	410 @ 2,400
Combustion chamber	Hemi	Wedge
Valve lifters	Mechanical	Hydraulic
Carburetor	2 x 4-v	1 x 4-v
Exhaust system	Dual	Dual
Electrical system	12 volts	12 volts
Transmission	3-speed semi-auto.	3-speed automatic
Axle ratio	3.36:1	3.23:1
Steering	Power recirculating ball	Power recirculating ball
Brakes	4-wheel hydraulic drums with vacuum servo	4-wheel hydraulic drums with vacuum servo
Construction	Box-section frame with separate body	Unitized
Front suspension	Independent, unequal-length control arms, torsion bars, anti-roll bar	Independent, unequal-length control arms, torsion bars, anti-roll bar
Rear suspension	Live axle, semi-elliptic leaf springs	Live axle, semi-elliptic leaf springs
Wheelbase	126.0 in.	115.0 in.
Stroke/bore ratio	.975:1	.95:1
Bhp/c.i.d.	.995	.875

Above: Firearrow looks opulent without overstatement on the outside. Below: Dual-Ghia looks like a cross between a Mopar dream car and a 1957 production car. Above right: Coachbuilder's signature on Firearrow. Bottom: Difference in size of the cars is obvious. Facing page: Flashy framework for Firearrow's license plate.

SIA comparisonReport

in his garage that night.

Dual-Ghia historian Bruce Wennerstrom believes that the 400 "was considered as a potential production car—I don't know why it didn't go further." Yet, when I spoke to Farago about the car in January 1993, he dismissed it with a single sentence: "I didn't like it anyway," he said, in his musical Italian accent. "It was too damned wide." Certainly, the 400 was not significantly lower than a production Chrysler 300—or much sportier, for that matter.

So as far as anyone knows, the 400 was not only the second, but the last Dual-Ghia to carry a 200-series serial number. The definitive successor to the original convertible was instead the L6.4, which debuted at the Paris auto salon in 1960 wearing Dual-Ghia badges and serial number 301. (The 26 subsequent L6.4s were badged as Ghias, not Dual-Ghias, as an ailing Casaroll distanced himself from the venture.) Interestingly, the circle-and-dart logo appears on Ghia renderings made for this car before Ex Sr. assumed responsibility for its styling in 1959.

Driving Impressions

Noted collector Noel Thompson owned the Firearrow when I drove it for this comparisonReport, but the car has been sold at least twice since then, so that by the time that Roy Query took these photos it belonged to Sam and Emily Mann. Ex Jr. told me that he prefers the simpler, cleaner Dual-Ghia to any of the Firearrows; it seems presumptuous to disagree, but personally I love the roundness of the Firearrows—particularly III and IV—as well as their exquisitely fashioned jewelry. Inside, as well as out, the Firearrow is all curves—curves that sneak up from behind you, sweep across the dash in front and then vanish again behind the passenger seat. A bold pattern of black and white leather

diamonds fairly leaps off the upholstery, accented by red-painted metal, engine-turned aluminum, and flowing rivers of chrome. It's either deliciously bold—or it looks like the inside of a diner—depending on your point of view.

Compared to the production Dual-Ghia, which benefited from Farago's clever unit-body design, the Firearrow does seem rather shallow inside—though hardly cramped. It would be reasonably comfortable, in fact, if it weren't for the flabby and unsupportive seats. The instruments look great, but even with the top up, we couldn't pick out the indicators against all the dazzling reflections. Accessory controls are simple enough, once you decipher the cryptic abbreviations that label them, but they require an awkward reach to the center of the cockpit. And, although this fourth and final Firearrow was billed as a four-seater, the rear compartment lacks even child-size leg room. Fortunately, the rear seat cushions lift out to reveal a beautifully crafted wooded luggage rack.

The Hemi lights off with a loud, wild, cammy, hot-rod rumble. With all that audible fuss, however, actual acceleration was a little disappointing. Noel admitted he had just gotten the car and hadn't had a chance to properly tune the engine. The semi-automatic transmission may have needed some attention as well, as the upshifts from 1-2 and 3-4 came painfully slowly. The clutch is stiff; fortunately, you don't use it much with the Gyro-Matic. The brakes also require a bit of effort, and return about average performance for a mid-fifties automobile.

Standing next to it, the Firearrow looks narrow and compact, yet from behind the wheel it seems intimidatingly long and wide enough to be cumbersome. Fortunately, the sharp blades at the tops of its fenders mark its forward extremes. There's no rear-view mirror (and no evidence there ever was one), which further complicates driving in even light traffic. The twin outside mirrors help, but not enough. The wood-rimmed Nardi steering wheel is beautiful to see and sensuous to hold, but it connects to a vintage Detroit steering gear that's typically vague on center. The Firearrow wanders in a straight line and understeers in the turns. Yet, even though it doesn't handle like a sports car, it still rides like one, i.e. stiff and busy. The cockpit got hot, too, even in October.

Remember, however, that this is a *show* car; we should be surprised that it works as well as it does and pleased that it works at all. Farago and Ghia deserve a great deal of credit for re-engineering the Firearrow into the swift, comfortable, refined, and thoroughly practical Dual-Ghia. Meanwhile, the best way to appreciate this show car is to *show* it: cruising slowly with the top down, soaking up the sunshine along with the looks of astonishment and admiration on every face you pass.

Then there's the Dual-Ghia 400: Outside it's wedgy, attractive, dramatic, and interesting—if not exactly beautiful. The bucket-seat interior retains all the glamour of the Firearrow's, yet is functionally superior in every way. In a complete turnaround from the Dodge show car, the 400 seems *smaller* from behind the wheel, probably because the sloping hood and wraparound windshield provide such excellent forward visibility. You have only to look behind you, however, to remember that you're driving a full-sized U.S. chassis, vintage 1957. Still, the fastback roof and tall fins don't hamper visibility as much as you might think.

There's plenty of room in front—more front leg room, in fact, than you'll find in most US production cars from that era—and the firm bucket seats approach perfection. The rear compartment is just as comfy, although foot space is a little tight back there.

As with most Chrysler products of the era, pushing the transmission's "neu-

Specifications: '54 Dodge Firearrow IV vs. '58 Dual-Ghia 400

	1954 Dodge Firearrow IV	1948 Dual-Ghia 400
Engine	V-8	V-8
Bore x stroke	3.44 x 3.25 inches	4.00 x 3.90 inches
Displacement	241.3 cubic inches	392 cubic inches
Compression ratio	7.5:1	10.0:1
Bhp @ rpm	150 @ 4,400	390 @ 5,400
Torque @ rpm	222 lb.ft. @ 2,400	430 lb.ft. @ 4,200
Taxable horsepower	37.8	51.2
Valve configuration	Ohv (hemi head)	Ohv (hemi head)
Valve lifters	Hydraulic	Mechanical
Main bearings	5	5
Carburetor	1 Stromberg WW-3-108 2-v	2 Carter WCFB 4-v
Fuel system	Mechanical pump	Mechanical pump
Lubrication system	Pressure/spray	Pressure/spray
Cooling system	Pressure/vent	Pressure/vent
Exhaust system	Single with crossover	Dual
Electrical system	6 volts	12 volts
Transmission	GyroMatic: 4-speed semi-auto countershaft gearbox w/fluid coupling	TorqueFlite: 3-speed auto., planetary gearbox with torque converter
Ratios: 1st	3.57.1 .	2.45:1
2nd	2.04:1	1.45:1
3rd.	1.75:1	1.00.1
4th	1.00.1	
Reverse	3.99.1	2.20:1
Max. torque converter	N.A.	2.30:1 @ 1,950 rpm
Rear axle	Hypoid; semi-floating	Hypoid, semi-floating
Ratio	N.A.	3.36:1
Steering	Kingpin	Ball joint
Steering gear	Ross worm & roller	Mopar recirculating ball with hydraulic servo
Gear ratio	18.7:1	16.3.1
Overall ratio.	20.4:1	19.8.1
Turns, lock-to-lock	4.0	3.3
Turning circle	N.A.	43.9 ft.
Brakes	4-wheel hydraulic drums	4-wheel hydraulic drums with vacuum servo
Effective area	173.5 square inches	251 square inches
Parking brake	On transmission	On transmission
Construction	Box-section frame with separate body	Box-section frame with separate body
Front suspension	Independent, unequal-length A–arms, coil springs, anti-roll bar	Independent, unequal-length control arms, torsion bars, anti-roll bar
Rear suspension	Live axle, semi-elliptic leaf springs, anti-roll bar	Live axle, semi-elliptic leaf springs
Shock absorbers	Mopar direct-acting	Mopar direct-acting
Wheels	Wire, 15 x 5K	Steel disc, 14 x 6.5K
Tires	7.00 x 15	9.00 x 14
Wheelbase	119.0 inches	126.0 inches
Overall length	189.6 inches	N/A
Overall width	75.8 inches	N/A
Overall height	54.9 inches	N/A
Front track	55.9 inches	61.2 in..
Rear track	58.8 inches	60.0 in.
Crankcase capacity	5 quarts (less filter)	5 quarts (less filter)
Cooling capacity	20 quarts (w/heater)	25 quarts (w/heater)
Fuel tank	17 gallons	23 gallons
Transmission oil cap.	N.A.	21 pints
Rear axle oil cap.	3.2 pints	3.5 pints
Bore/stroke ratio	.945.1	.975.1
Bhp/c.i.d.	.622	.995

Below and right: Two distinct approaches to auto design are represented by these exotics. Center left: Firearrow went totally flamboyant on the interior. Right: Firearrow's custom-fitted luggage straps down behind seats to allow extra trunk space. Bottom: Rear fender exhausts are purely decorative.

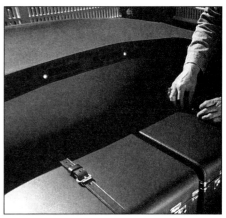

Darting Into The Future

The Dual-Ghia 400 clearly evolved from the Chrysler Dart show car, which in turn grew out of the Gilda, a non-running aerodynamic study by Ghia design chief Giovanni Savonuzzi that debuted at the Turin auto show in 1955. Virgil Exner, Jr., emphasized that the Gilda was purely a Ghia effort that appeared without Chrysler's sponsorship. As early as June 1955, however, Chrysler engineers were developing a running derivative of the Gilda, beginning with wind-tunnel tests of a 500-pound, 3/8-scale model that featured an operating engine fan, rotating wheels, and a detailed undercarriage based on the torsion-bar chassis proposed for 1957. Ex Jr. recalled that Cliff Voss, his father's close friend as well as colleague, was "primarily involved" with the prototype's styling at this stage.

The full-scale, running Dart appeared in 1957, riding the 129-inch wheelbase of the '57 Imperial but boasting unit-body construction and a "streamlined" undercarriage, and powered by a 300-C Hemi with its compression ratio boosted to 12.5:1. The radiator, leaned rearward to allow the radically plunging hood line, and twin ducted fans assured adequate engine cooling. A rubber-mounted bumper wrapped all the way around the sleek, wedge-shaped body—itself hardly more than a taut, oval-section tube stretched between two enormous fins. One of the wildest ideas on the car was its retractable hardtop: The for-ward section of the roof slid back under the fastback rear window, which then folded flat against the deck, remaining exposed but lying nearly horizontal ahead of the trunk lid.

Motor Trend contributor William Carroll tried the Dart out in 1959; by that time the prototype had accumulated some 85,000 miles on the Chelsea proving ground. Carroll only commented that the Dart "rode like a truck" and "wasn't a happy car at slow speeds." He complained also of restricted leg and head room in the rear, the invisibility of the front fenders, and a windshield header "only inches from the brow of a tall person."

Nonetheless, Exner himself told Carroll that, "The Dart theme is part of our basic philosophy. In our opinion, this is what an automobile should look like. It's a contemporary car with a feeling of motion. And we use the same approach to interior design. The instrument panel should have enough mechanical feeling to convey the impression that you are in an object that *has* motion." Ex hedged, however, when Carroll asked if future Chryslers would look like the Dart, but added that "in case you're curious, we'll be using fins until something better comes along."

The Dart survives today, although it has been significantly modified, with its retractable roof discarded in favor of a folding fabric top.

SIA comparisonReport

tral" button starts the engine; the hemi clatters to life but quickly settles into a subdued, distant *thrum-thrum-thrum-thrum*. The 400 doesn't sound much different once under way—until you crack open the throttle, which brings on a wave of intake rush and road-racer rumble accompanied by enough g-force to split your face into an ear-to-ear grin.

The 400's handling will feel familiar to any Mopar maven of the Exner era. The steering is utterly numb (of course), but the big car goes exactly where it's pointed; and it corners securely, despite some lean. The ride is solid, smooth, controlled, and more luxuriously comfortable than it ought to be, given the

Left and below: Dodge Hemi has 150 cubes less than 300-C Hemi in Dual-Ghia. **Center:** Harlequin-design seats in Firearrow contrast with Chrysler-style treatment in Dual-Ghia. **Bottom:** They're both sporty, but in quite different ways.

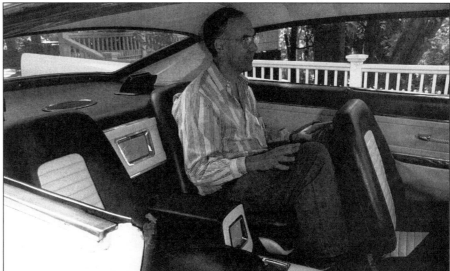

Below and right: Both dashboards have their fill of shiny chrome knobs and controls. Below center and right: Firearrow gauges are virtually unreadable because of reflections. Neat "Dodgematic" clock lives in center of Nardi steering wheel. Center: Dual-Ghia's instruments and steering wheel are from Imperial. Bottom: Take your pick—a sassy barchetta or a Detroit spaceship.

SIA comparisonReport

400's handling capabilities. Only the brakes disappointed me, with some swerving in hard use and a weak performance overall. Fred suggested that they might need some work, and no sooner had he spoken than a wisp of acrid smoke from the right front wheel confirmed his suspicion.

Not only is the Dual-Ghia 400 a better car in every way than the Firearrow, it's also better in most ways than the production Dual-Ghia: quicker, roomier, with more poised and balanced handling. At the same time, however, I understand why Casaroll and Farago didn't pursue this course any further. The 400's space-ship styling would surely have alienated as many buyers as it intrigued. And no matter how well it handles, with 126 inches of wheelbase the 400 is just too big to take seriously as even a boulevard sports car. Had they produced it, Dual-Motors would have had to charge too much for a car that wasn't that different from the (relatively) mass-produced Chrysler 300. Whereas the L6.4 packed all of Chrysler's latest unit-body, torsion-bar, and wedge-head technology into the same 115-inch wheelbase as the '56-58 original.

They did the right thing. ෨

Acknowledgments and Bibliography

Books: David Burgess-Wise, Ghia: Ford's Carrozzeria; *John A. Gunnell (editor),* Standard Catalog of American Cars 1946-1975; *Richard M. Langworth,* Chrysler and Imperial: The Postwar Years; *Valerio Moretti,* Ghia Automobilia.

Periodicals: William Carroll, "I Drove Tomorrow's Cars!" Motor Trend, *September 1958; Richard M. Langworth, "1953-54 Firearrow: Fifties Sports Car from Dodge,"* Collectible Automobile, *February 1992.*

Thanks to Bill Brownlie; Virgil M. Exner, Jr.; Jeffrey I. Godshall; Kim M. Miller of the AACA Library and Research Center; Dr. Paul Sable; Henry Siegle; Bruce Wennerstrom; and, of course, special thanks to owners Fred Kanter, Noel Thompson, and Sam and Emily Mann.

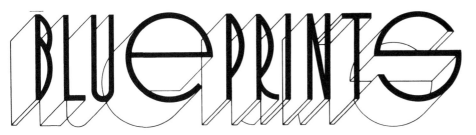

BLUEPRINTS

1956 Dodge D-500

by Bob Hovorka

Back in 1955, Chrysler dropped a 300-horsepower Hemi into a de-chromed New Yorker Deluxe hardtop, tacked on a two-piece Imperial grille, and called it C-300. Magazines called it America's most powerful car!

The following year, De Soto joined the growing ranks of "Super Stocks" with a limited number of gold-trimmed hardtops dubbed "Adventurer." Not to be outdone by its upscale brethren, Plymouth stuffed a number of off-white hardtops with 303-cubic-inch V-8s, speckled their sides with strips of gold anodized aluminum, and labeled them "Fury."

Aside from performance, all of these factory-built hot rods had one thing in common: a special look to set them apart from the go-for-the-groceries hardtops. What the Chrysler 300 accomplished by taking the chrome off, De Soto and Plymouth accomplished by spreading the gold on. Either way, it created a high-performance image that was designed to intimidate most would-be stoplight Grand Prix racers.

But Chrysler had one more division. Over at Dodge, there were no limited pro-duction gold-trimmed hardtops. There was, however, a little known option called D-500. Unlike the specialty models of other divisions, "the D-500 is available in all models." That meant not only in heavy-weight luxury hardtops and convertibles, but the cheapest, lightest, two-door sedan.

Externally, the entire option consisted of a pair of small crossed checker flags, with tiny "500" letters beneath them. Placed in the lower corners of the trunk and hood, they were hardly noticeable. But pity the poor hot shoe who pulled alongside one of these Q ships without noticing them. For nestled beneath the sloping hood was a 315-cubic-inch Hemi that boasted 260 horsepower, and could crack 60 from rest in under ten seconds. Some magazine testers were even claiming mid eights. In fact, a 1956 Dodge held "every AAA American and international performance and endurance record for American closed cars up to 31,224 miles."

More than just a straight line rocket, the D-500 package included a beefed up chas-sis and suspension system, with heavy duty springs and shocks. Up front, a hefty stabi-lizer bar with special snubbers helped its cornering prowess. That, coupled with a sil-houette that was a full inch and a half lower than standard Dodges, made high speed highway driving a dream. To compare a nearly two-ton, six-passenger automobile to a sports car for handling was, of course, ludicrous, but for a typically nose-heavy American car, the D-500 was no slouch.

In keeping with its overall performance potential, Dodge fitted "12-inch center-plane brakes with 15½ pounds of car weight per square inch of lining area—a figure unequaled in American passenger cars—and one that approaches most sports cars and even racing cars." Al-though it sounded like typical fifties adver-tising hype, the massive 12-inch by two and a half-inch drums were highly rated—even by the usually critical "sports car" magazines.

Wrapped with Chrysler's new high-flying "Flight Sweep" styling, the '56 Dodge D-500 looked great! For a price of approximately one hundred and seventy five dollars, the D-500 option might just have been the per-formance bargain of the year! ❧

La Femme

The rare and not-as-provocative-as-hoped-for 1955 Dodge La Femme

By Don Spiro
Photography by the author

"Gee Wally.... all the guys are callin' me a sissy.... a pink and white car and it says La Femme on the side.... I just can't be driven to school in mom's new car anymore...."
"Yeah, Beave.... I know what ya mean.... that's why I ride with Eddie.... and besides, mom's not all that thrilled with the car either!"
[Line from a long-lost episode of "Leave it To Beaver"?!]

Oh those wild, finned and chromed days of the Fifties; it seems that no matter what the auto makers built, the American buying public lined up at their downtown dealer troughs to ogle and buy. Bigger, lower, wider, faster, more streamlined, more powerful; if there was a usable adverb or adjective, you could find it in automobile ads. Success was still, seemingly, a given in the Detroit of the mid-fifties. Though consumer spending and demand for durable goods lingering from the war years had slackened, a strong economy seemed to assure continued sales. Detroit became more marketing "savvy" and began to target various specific segments of the mass market. For the most part, this targeting was successful and laid the foundation for automotive marketing strategies for decades to come.

There were, however, notable and not so notable exceptions to this en masse consumer gorging. Failure in the marketplace during this period did happen. First to mind is Ford's Edsel; even the most auto-illiterate individual will tell you about that "horse-collar" blunder. It is the stuff of legends. Then there were the less obvious ground balls through the infield: the entire Crosley line, the Pinin Farina-designed Nash Ambassador Custom, the Kaiser Darrin, and the Ford hardtop/convertible Sunliners, to name a few. Over at Chrysler there was a slight blip of failure on the sales chart about mid-decade. The specific car was a model variation of the 1955 and '56 Dodge Lancer.

This blip passed by almost unnoticed, as scant few examples were produced over the two-year run. There are so few examples of this car extant today that most enthusiasts have never seen one.

Unless you are a dyed-in-the-wool Mopar enthusiast, chances are you have never heard of this car. Count me as one of the uninformed, until Spud Sperdutti of Tucson's Suburban Motors beckoned me into his back warehouse to show me something that he was sure I had never seen. Spud's warehouse is a veritable shrine, and time line from the weird and wonderful to the most pedestrian of everyday cars, covering all decades from the Thirties on up. Wedged between a gold '47 Cadillac Sedanet and a green

> *"Her Majesty...*
> *The American Woman*
> *was not about to be*
> *re-defined in*
> *Heather Rose with*
> *feminine accessories."*

metallic '42 Buick fastback coupe was what appeared at first glance to be a common, mid-fifties Dodge Lancer sedan. A handsome car, this particular one was finished in a garish pink and white two-tone, never one of the most popular color combos from the two- and three-tone era. "Go have a close look at it while I go get the *real* reason I bought this particular car." I carefully worked my way through the rows of gleaming beauties until I reached the Dodge. I gave the car a quick going over. It was wedged into the back row, so it was impossible to stand back and really appreciate its lines. It looked like a run-of-the-mill Lancer for sure, but a small gold stylized-script trim piece on the front fender caught my eye. "LA FEMME". Interesting name for a model. I'd never heard of it, and the thought that it might be a show car or design study crossed my mind. "Come on back to my office; I found what I was looking for," boomed a voice from the adjacent service room.

"This is only the second one of this model Dodge I've ever found, and I passed on the first one because the stuff in this box was missing," remarked Spud as he settled into his desk chair. An excited look was fixed on Spud's face as he carefully opened the flaps of a tattered cardboard box." A pink floral-patterned collapsible umbrella and matching plastic rain hat emerged from the box. "HUH," I thought.... Now what did this rain gear have to do with the car. I didn't see the connection, unless the car was strictly for the Seattle market. Next, a stylized gray presentation box emerged, with fancy gold script on top. As Spud opened the box, a strange-looking wedge-shaped object lay inside. Because of its unusual shape, I thought at first glance that it might have been a special protective carrying case for Spock's Tri Corder on Transporter beam-downs to some of the more hostile alien planets in *Star Trek.* "Here; look at this," remarked Spud as he unfastened the gold hasp on the lid of the strange object, and began to carefully remove the contents. Onto Spud's desk emerged a gold-edged tortoise-shell comb, a lipstick, an elegant gold make-up compact, a tube-shaped container of powder, a Fifties chic cigarette case and matching lighter and, finally, a pink change purse with a delicate gold chain attached. All were in pristine condition; it was apparent that the strange-shaped object was a purse. I remained clueless as to the connection between this array of seemingly high-end feminine accessories and the Dodge back in the shop, though. Last to emerge from the musty box was a small pamphlet. On the cover was one of those great stylized illustrations of a quintessential Fifties woman. She possessed features and fashion stylings that seemed to be the prototype for the Barbie Doll. Suspended in a sea of flowers, with a relaxed yet confident expression on her face, she fingered in her delicate hand a thin baton, replete with the Dodge hood ornament on the top. Across this vision of feminine postwar loveliness was a pink banner, on which a simple line of text suddenly connected the contents of the box and the pink and white Dodge, "By Appointment to Her Majesty...the AMERICAN WOMAN." La Femme by Dodge.

The auto show circuit of the early Fifties was the springboard for new de-

Originally published in Special Interest Autos #186, Nov.-Dec. 2001

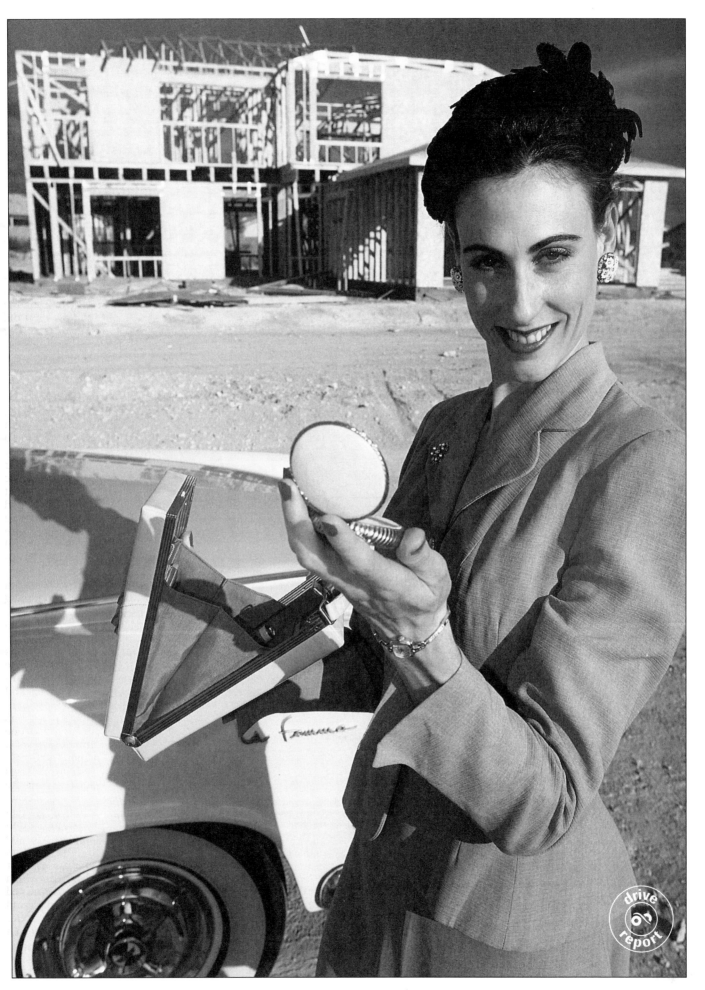

signs and engineering. These shows were also used as a barometer of sorts to see just what new designs and options might inspire a purchase in the buying public. These shows were big too; in 1955 GM used 150 tractor-trailers to haul the Motorama show from town to town. The stars of the shows were the dream cars. These dream cars, while certainly futuristic and glitzy, usually featured highly impractical design and engineering features. Some items appearing on dream cars might find their way onto the eventual production model, but for the most part, the dream cars were strictly for ooohs and aaahs. La Femme can trace its origin to a show car, one designed especially for the feminine buyer. In 1954, Chrysler unveiled two show cars; Le Comte and Le Comtesse. Le Comte was the masculine and brawny of the two and was finished in a no-nonsense bronze and black. La Comtesse was painted pink and pale gray. Both cars were reported to be identical under the paint and both show cars were built on the Chrysler New Yorker platform. The design of those cars was more reflective of the late Forties Chrysler design then what was

about to come in 1955. Apparently, show interest in La Comtesse, particularly in Chicago and New York, was responsible for Chrysler making the

Even the brochure was designed for women.

PROS & CONS

Pros
Eye-catching color scheme
Powerful Chrysler Hemi V-8
Ideal car for Interior Designers

Cons
Production was very limited
Original upholstery not available
Accessories almost always missing

final decision to market a car expressly to women.

Chrysler adopted Virgil Exner's "forward look" in design in 1955. Gone were the tall and slab-sided conservative designs that had been Chrysler's hallmark since the end of the war. Bold, sleek, aircraft-inspired themes appeared across the line. Fins topped the rear fenders, tempered and tasteful for '55. Exner would flex his wings to the fullest over the next few years however. In 1955, Chrysler had some of the boldest and freshest designs in the industry. Dodge for '55 was "flair fashioned," or so touted the ads from the period. Split grille openings with stylized bars over each opening that wrapped into the front fenders gave the Dodge a unique and no-nonsense look coming at you. The chrome headlight trim was highly reminiscent of jet-engine nacelles. The hood featured a chrome band surrounding an implied scoop that continued around the sides of the car as a trim piece. Just forward of the rear wheel wells this trim piece dipped, came back up and ended at the dual-lens aircraft-exhaust-like taillight assembly. A very provocative and harmonious design.

Dodge went one up on an industry enamored with two-tone paint schemes, and offered three-tone schemes. How successful the three tones looked was strictly dependent on the colors; some were stunning, others best rolled out at night. Top of the line were the Custom Royal Lancer hard-tops and convertibles. La Femme would be an option available on this top-line model. Base price of the Custom Royal Lancer was $2,543, and the La Femme option added another $143.30, which got you the two-tone Heather Rose over Sapphire 36White paint. The all-important "La Femme" badging appeared on the front fenders and glove-box door. Inside, you got the special Jacquard Fabrics upholstery; the compartments on the front seat backs were covered in Heather Rose Cordagrain and held all of the "feminine" accessories to not only keep your styling intact, but dry should you be caught in the rain. These rainy-day necessities included a fisherman's-style rain hat, stylish rain cape, rain boots and an umbrella that featured the Jacquard motif. There were slight detail variations between cars built in Los Angeles and those in Detroit, most notably the colors of the wheels. There also seemed to be variations in the color of the taillight area as well. Most appeared painted pink; some were white.

There were two variations of the same engine available for La Femme in '55: the standard Super Red Ram Hemi-head V-8, which made 183hp at 4,400 rpm; and the optional, 193hp Super-Powered Super Red Ram Hemi V-8. "Super-Powered" and its neck snapping increase of ten horsepower came via a Carter 4-barrel carburetor, instead of the standard Stromberg 2-barrel. The one key-spotting feature of a genuine La Femme is the gold La Femme badging. (It appears on Spud's example that the gold plating either peels off or fades to more of a silver/chrome-like color. The badges are original, though, as under scrutiny you can see remnants of gold plating on all of the lettering, especially at the base of the badge closest to the fender.) While La Femme would re-appear as an option on the '56 Dodge Royal Lancer, the colors changed to two-tone lavender, and gone was the purse and all its wonderful feminine accessories.

Was La Femme successful? Far from it, in spite of flowery press releases to the contrary prior to the '56 models

Levittown 1955? Randy and Sistine Casellini look back.

Umbrella, purse, lighter, rain hat, lipstick, etc....

release. While there are no exact figures for how many La Femmes were produced, I have seen estimates ranging from 300 to 500 for each year. A report by an owner of a La Femme I came across on the internet reported contacting Chrysler's PR department and was told that a total of 1,140 La Femmes were produced over the two-year run. Whatever the figure is, these were very rare cars in their time; and if these numbers are accurate, how many are still around today? Until I saw Spud's, I

never had heard about, let alone seen one. It would appear that, in spite of great interest on the show circuit level, when it came time to plunk down the hard-earned cash, women cared little about La Femme; and if women didn't buy it, how many Fifties-era men would? The car had too narrow an audience. But let's not dwell on failure; happily, there are a few around, and Spud was most gracious in allowing us behind the wheel.

"She runs fine," assured Spud, "no need to baby her." Pink and white; what a combination, I thought, sliding behind the wheel. This was definitely an acquired taste in color. Now I have fond memories of so many of the two-tone color schemes applied to cars from the Fifties. I think back to those summer drives as a kid down New Jersey's Garden State Parkway to Point Pleasant Beach, being surrounded in a rainbow of pastel-and-white and other two-tone cars. Shore vacations were special, and I always felt as if I was in a fantastic celebratory parade of rolling birthday cakes that would announce that two weeks at the beach was at hand. Pink-and-white was never a favorite, though, and seemed few and far between even back then. The vast expanse of Heather Rose dashboard in front of me took some getting used to. It might even be an affront to my sense of aesthetics under the cover of darkness. Thankfully, the black top of the dash did temper and tone down the color somewhat. The dash itself was classic Dodge, the instruments arranged in a purposeful "aircraft-inspired" manner across the fascia. Centered over the pink steering column (yes even the column was pink; I wonder what Freud would say?) is a large speedometer with attendant gauges to monitor all engine vitals spaced out on either side; a nice overall symmetry and balance. Down low to the right of the steering column is the small, protruding, knobbed-chrome lever, the "Flite Control" to operate the Powerflite automatic transmission. Radio and ventilation controls are spaced out along the bottom of the dash panel in their own tasteful fascia. To the right of the instrument panel, the simple glove box, finished in black carried down from the dash top, sported the gold "La Femme" logo plate on the lower right corner. Aside from the Heather Rose color, the dash layout was elegant and purposeful; in another color combination perhaps

Combination of chrome trim and Heather Rose "pinkish" color keeps driver readily alert.

Distinctive pointed nose and twin grilles were a one-year-only design for 1955 models.

one of the best dash layouts I've sat in front of from that era.

The seats are finished in vinyl edges with silvery pink fabric inserts. The same fabric is carried through in the door panels. Dodge press releases call the fabric "Cordagrain," and the pattern was small pink rosebuds on a pale pink background. The patterned tapestry-style fabric was made especially for "her majesty," and did not appear in any other Dodge or Chrysler product from the period. For the collector and restorer, the fabric did not hold up well, and deteriorated rapidly. Today, this fabric is virtually impossible to find. Spud is in the process of having the fabric specially made to repair a few problem areas on the back seat and door panels. "The maker will only deal in bulk, so I'll have more than I need. I've heard a rumor that a special hat box came in some of the La Femmes. I have so much of that material coming that we've decided to make up a hatbox using the excess material. "In letters to Dodge dealers announcing La Femme, it was stated that the "crowning touches which personalize the La Femme are its special feminine accessories in two special compartments." On the back of the passenger seat is a compartment shaped to hold the unique purse. The center of the compartment is open, no doubt, for rear seat passengers to view the purse with envy, perhaps, and be reminded of just how special the owner of this car is. In the back of the driver's seat is a similar compartment, slotted for each of the foul weather gear items.

The seats, in spite of their age, were still somewhat firm and comfortable...initially. Fore and aft adjustment allowed ample leg room for my six-

PARTS SUPPLIERS

Autosports
2410 W. Freeway Lane
Dept. SIA-186
Phoenix, Arizona 85021-4135
602-995-5311
Reproduction lenses.

Andy Bernbaum Auto Parts
315 Franklin St.
Dept. SIA-186
Newton, Massachusetts 02458
617-244-1118
Engine, suspension and body parts.

Antique Mopar Auto Sales
5758 McNicholl Dr.
Dept. SIA-186
Hale, Michigan 48739-8984
517-257-3123
Full line of parts for 1936 to 1969.

Arizona Parts
320 E. Pebble Beach

Dept. SIA-186
Tempe, Arizona 85282
602-966-6683
New and used parts and accessories.

Atlas Obsolete Chrysler Parts
10621 Bloomfield St. Unit 32
Dept. SIA-186
Los Alamitos, ?CA 90720
NOS & repro parts for 1936-74 models.

Mike Hershenfeld
3011 Susan Rd
Dept. SIA-186
Bellmore, New York 11710
516-781-7278
NOS mechanical and electrical parts.

MoreParts North
P.O. Box 345
Dept. SIA-186
Ornageville, Ontario, Canada L9W 2Z7
519-941-6331
Hard to find NOS parts 1930s to 1970s.

PRO Antique Auto
50 King Spring Rd
Dept. SIA-186
Windsor Locks, Connecticut 06096
860-623-8275
Body materials, carpet sets and weatherstripping.

Roberts Motor Parts
17 Prospect St.
Dept. SIA-186
West Newbury, MA 01985
New & NOS parts and literature.

Terrill Machine Inc.
Rout2 2, Box 61
Dept. SIA-186
DeLeon, Texas 76444
254-893-2610
New, used and rebuilt mechanical parts.

foot-three frame and, glancing back, adequate room still for rear-seat passengers. A turn of the key, and the 270-cu.in. V-8 awakened. Blipping the throttle proved the engine smooth and quiet. It was a reach to adjust the outside mirror; it was mounted forward on the door. After a fair amount of fiddling, it seemed I would have to be wary of a blind spot during lane changes. I reached down for the "Flite Control" lever and slipped the car into drive. We were off or, as Dodge proudly claimed, "in flite." Out on secondary roads at 40 mph, the car felt solid. There was a slight amount of rear-end wander, from the bias-ply tires perhaps, or maybe the suspension was just a bit tired after 45 years. Then, too, perhaps it was inherent in Dodge's suspension design of the period. Through sweeping curves, it exhibited its hefty weight of one and three quarter tons as the suspension loaded rapidly with each sweep of the turns. The handling, though lethargic, was predictable, and the tires whoomfed with a definite presence, in case you missed the signals emanating from your sliding posterior. La Femme was certainly not a real handful to control over such roads, and the car inspired more confidence the longer I was behind the wheel. The brakes seemed more than up to the task in routine driving and didn't appear to require a lead foot to engage them. "Her Majesty" would find them easy to operate, for sure. An overall slower response of the suspension and brakes required more attention to the task at hand: driving. As happens the more I drive Fifties cars, I wondered if drivers from that era were better skilled overall because of these shortcomings than the drivers of today's cars, where even an econ-o-box sedan has point-and-shoot handling and braking capabilities that require less on the part of the driver.

It was on the interstate that the Dodge exhibited the prowess that suspension designers of that period were becoming increasingly good at dialing in: "The Boulevard Ride." The Super Red Ram would never be mistaken for its sibling the Hemi as I nailed the accelerator to get up to the 65 mph posted speed down the on-ramp. The Powerflite kicked down a gear and held it there as long as I kept the pedal to the floor. Acceleration was smooth and adequate, considering the horsepower-versus-weight ratio; pretty much in line with other cars of the period that I've driven. Once up to 65, the Dodge felt solid and well built. Lane changes were a bit squirrely, however, as the bias-plies couldn't immediately decide which side of the road's center seam they wanted to run on. "I like this side...no this side...uhhh-hh...wait it was nice over there...uhh-hhh.... OK that's it!" There was a trace of gradual rear-end wander side to side,

Fed by a two-barrel Stromberg, the Super Red Ram Hemi V-8 makes 183hp at 4,400 rpm.

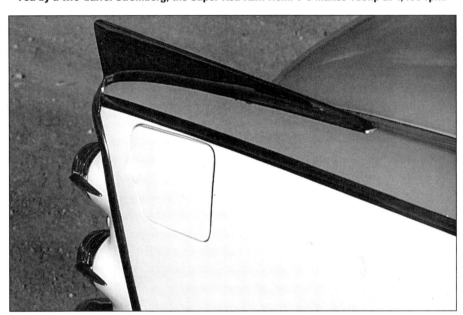

Unlike the larger fins of the later fifties, this "bolt-on" tailfin is a very tasteful design.

ever so slightly, but just enough to be mindful of. After 10 miles or so, it became borderline annoying, as course corrections were necessary at the wheel. The gauges on the dash were indeed very well placed, and once I oriented myself to each of them, a mere glance was all that was necessary to reveal that all was well under the hood. You get used to waves and thumbs-up driving Fifties cars on the interstate, and the color scheme screamed for attention. In La Femme I felt almost like a true celebrity, so encompassing was the positive response from each and every passing car and truck. Maybe it is just me and The Beave, after all, who have a real problem with "Heather Rose".

With dusk settling in, I headed off the interstate and back towards Spud's shop. The '55 Dodge has a six-volt electrical system; the more efficient 12-volt system was introduced in '56. Driving

CLUB SCENE

Chrysler Products Owners Club
809 Nelson St.
Rockville, MD 20850
Dues: $18/year; Membership: 350

National Chrysler Products Club
Walt Govern, Membership Director
5516 Silvercreek Dr.
Mechanicsburg, PA 17055-1961
Dues: $20/year; Membership: 707

Northeast Hemi Owners Association
74 Diller Ave.
New Holland, PA 17557
717-354-0502
Dues: $ 25/year; Membership: 235

Walter P. Chrysler Club
P.O. Box 3504
Kalamazoo, Michigan 49003-3504
Dues: $25/year; Membership: 5,000

Be it fashion, housing developments or two-tone cars, the '50s were unique.

Gold-trimmed compact case helped the "American Woman" always look her best.

WHAT TO PAY

Low	Avg.	High
$3,000	$12,000	$25,000

era bench seats, lumbar support was never ever a consideration. Maybe posture was just better in that postwar era, and back fatigue took longer to induce, but I wondered what toll a six-hour stint behind the wheel of La Femme or any Royal Lancer would exact on the back and sciatic nerve? Then, finally, it was time for the real "panic" brake test, as no test is complete unless you can stop swiftly. I nailed the brakes good approaching a stop sign. La Femme stopped in a dignified manner befitting her "majesty," with just a bit of sultry twitching in the rear end. There was a degree of…"come on, you can do this" coaxing as I pressed the brake pedal, but again, my feet know mostly of signals that emanate true from four-wheel discs. Four-wheel drums are another story indeed, and, again, I had to ask myself, were there better drivers on the road back when La Femme was new?

La Femme was fun to drive and a real window into 1955 engineering. Comparatively speaking, the Dodge La Femme offered the buyer a fine quality car combined with fantastic styling, as I assume all Royal Lancers of the period did. The oversized fins and chrome would arrive next year; in '55 Dodge had achieved an almost perfect balance of new design themes. Just enough chrome in just the right places, exciting new aircraft design themes tempered in harmony with overall shape. Too bad it lasted but one year. Unhappily, but certainly not surprisingly, in La Femme garb its meager sales record indicated that, "Her Majesty…The American Woman" was not about to be re-defined in Heather Rose with feminine accessories. No, the American Woman of 1955 was not even remotely close to Dodge's image of woman moderne. These women of the mid-fifties were women who just a short decade earlier attached wing spars to B-29 bombers, made up freight trains in frigid New England railroad yards, and wrestled millions of red-hot rivets into the sides of Liberty Ships. Yes, they had returned, many reluctantly, to the domestic lifestyle, but they had their own sense of what "feminine" was. When it came to automobiles, these "moderne" women wanted only what the men back then wanted: good cars, exciting new cars with fins and chrome, and cars with lots of power. La Femme was a dismal failure from a sales perspective. To see one today is not only special because of its rarity but because it is a reminder of a time when heady and limitless vision sometimes missed the mark entirely. ᔔ

ASKING PRICES

If you like the basic styling of the La Femme but can't seem to find one, perhaps you may want to consider the Custom Royal Lancer series, on which this rare option was based. We came across a few in *Hemmings Motor News* that are rather affordable examples. If you must have a La Femme, however, expect prices to be about 10 to 15 percent more than a standard Custom Royal Lancer, especially if all the original feminine accessories are included.

1955 Dodge Royal 2-dr hardtop, decent body, pink, black and white, $3,995

1955 Royal, V-8, pretty, $5,500.

1955 La Femme, perfect concours condition, complete with all accessories including luggage, cape and boots, $65,000

Stylish illustrations used in brochure.

over undulating back and secondary roads really illustrated the shortcomings of the meager, amp-challenged six-volt system. Over 30 mph the Dodge was clearly outrunning the paltry range of its dim bulbs. Nocturnal Javelinas and Coyotes, beware the approach of "Her Majesty…!" Oh, the seats; that familiar numbness in the lower back was there. Forty-five minutes behind the wheel told me yet again that, like most good fifties-

specifications

illustrations by Russell von Sauers, The Graphic Automobile Studio
© copyright 2001, Special Interest Autos

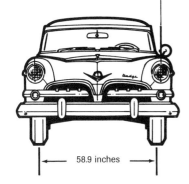

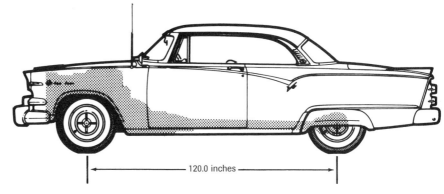

58.9 inches

120.0 inches

1955 Dodge La Femme

Price when new $2,518

Options Town & Country radio, heater, air-conditioning, PowerFlite, power steering, power brakes, power windows, power seat, D-500 custom wheel covers, whitewalls, windshield washers

ENGINE

Type Ohv V-8, cast-iron block, water-cooled, 5 mains, full pressure lubrication

Bore x stroke 3.63 inches x 3.25 inches

Displacement 270.0 cubic inches

Compression ratio 7.6:1

Bhp @ rpm 183 @ 4,400

Torque @ rpm 245 @ 2,400

Carburetor Two-barrel Stromberg

Exhaust system Cast-iron manifolds, single exhaust

Electrical system 6-volt battery/coil

TRANSMISSION

Type PowerFlite 2-speed automatic torque converter, planetary gears

Ratios 1.72/1.00

DIFFERENTIAL

Type Hypoid, open driveshaft

Ratio 3.54:1

Drive axles Semi-floating

STEERING

Type Power, recirculating ball nut

Turns lock-to-lock 3.5

Ratio 16.2

Turn circle 42 feet, 3 inches

BRAKES

Type Four-wheel hydraulic, power assisted

Drum diameter 11 inches

Total lining area 173.5 square inches

CHASSIS & BODY

Frame Double-dropped, channel and box section, steel, four crossmembers

Body construction All steel

Body style 6-passenger hardtop coupe

SUSPENSION

Front Independent, unequal A-arms, coil springs enclosing tubular hydraulic shocks, linkless stabilizer bar

Rear Solid rear axle, longitudinal semi-elliptic leaf springs, tubular shocks, stabilizer bar

Tires Tubeless type, 7.10 x 15

Wheels Drop-center rims, pressed steel discs, lug-bolted brake drums

WEIGHTS AND MEASURES

Wheelbase 120 inches

Overall length 212.1 inches

Overall width 74.5 inches

Overall height 60.6 inches

Front track 58.9 inches

Road clearance 5 inches (minimum)

Shipping weight 3,480 pounds

CAPACITIES

Crankcase 5 quarts

Cooling system 20 quarts

Fuel tank 17 gallons

FUEL CONSUMPTION

Best 21.3 mpg

Average 16.5 pounds

PERFORMANCE

0-30 4.95 seconds

0-60 13.8 seconds

Top speed 105.2 mph (fastest one-way)
103.2 mph (slowest one-way)

(from *Motor Life*, February 1955. V-8 sedan with PowerFlite)

"C" pillar trim same as Royal Lancer.

PARTS PRICES

Radiator	$270
Brake drum	$54
Water pump	$80
Stainless steel muffler	$70
Pressure plate/clutch assembly	$180
Ignition Switch	$33
Spark plug wires	$16
Rebuilt brake booster	$90
Master Cylinder, Rebuilt	$80
Timing Chain	$25
Shock Absorber Kit	$115
Engine Overhaul Kit	$95
Carburetor Rebuild kit	$45
Tune up kit	$19

Pocketbook slot on driver's seatback.

1959 DODGE CUSTOM ROYAL SUPER D-500 CONVERTIBLE

BARGAIN-BASEMENT CHRYSLER 300

By John Matras
Photos by the author

THE 1959 Custom Royal was the end of an era for Dodge. It was the division's last year for bigger and better fins, and although its corporate siblings would continue soaring to greater heights, 1960 would see diminished tailfin adornment at Dodge. What's more, the Custom Royal, top of the line for Dodge since 1955, would cease to exist in the following model year. On the other hand, 1959 saw the debut of the 383-cubic-inch V-8, an engine that would become Dodge's workhorse for the next decade.

The demise of the Custom Royal name would be more than just a change in nomenclature. First appearing in '55, the Custom Royal was the instant leader of a Dodge lineup totally restyled for that year. Six inches longer, the new Dodges were also lower and wider and definitely sleeker than their predecessors. Sales more than doubled—enough to inspire anyone—and from that point on, there was no turning back.

It was the hand of Virgil Exner, Chrysler Corporation's chief stylist, that would send Dodge (and the other divisions as well) styling into literal flights of fancy. Designs would be aggressively and unabashedly aeronautically inspired. Words such as Flightswept would describe designs with tailfins that grew year by year. Dodge for 1957 had the "Forward Look," and with fins that began just aft of the front seats and chrome-edged eyebrows over the head-

lamps, they marked the beginning of the design theme that would last through the 1959 model year.

If one were to seek the ultimate of this series of automobiles, hardly a better example could be found than the 1959 Dodge Custom Royal Super D-500 convertible. The Custom Royal, of course, because it was the top of the line. The Super D-500 because it was just the hottest Dodge engine available. And a convertible, naturally, because it's, well, who wouldn't rather have a convertible than a hardtop or, perish the thought, a sedan.

The Custom Royal shared its body and a 122-inch wheelbase with the lesser Royal and Coronet lines and the Sierra and Custom Sierra station wagons as well. They were big cars, stretching 217.4 inches bumper to bumper and 80

Originally published in Special Interest Autos #117, May-June 1990

Driving Impressions

Punch the throttle and the TorqueFlite drops a gear or two, the front end lifts as a gurgling roar rises under the hood. The line on the speedometer goes from green to yellow to red as it slides through the slot in the dash. Get a grip on that two-tone plastic oval, boy, because this two-lane highway's gettin' awful narrow.

They don't put performance in a package like this anymore. Truth is, they don't pack anything in something like this now. Eighty inches is a lot from side to side. Modern shapes have a lot less breadth and usually come nicely rounded in ways that hide their size. More often than not the driver can't even see the end of the hood.

You don't have to worry about that with a '59 Dodge. Those eyebrows arching outward emphasize the width. Of course, it's put to good use inside the car. There's room for six real people, three abreast front and rear. But put anyone in the middle and the dash-mounted rear-view mirror will give you nothing but grins. The fender-mounted mirrors won't be able to take up any slack, however, because first, they're too far away to give much of a field of view, and second, most of the field that's left is taken by those rear fins arching outwards to just the wrong place.

The swing-out seats seem to be an answer in search of a question. Tight skirts notwithstanding, how hard is it to slide onto a bench seat? The option's popularity showed in its staying power. Seen any on new cars lately?

Because we drove the car in daylight only, we didn't get to test the effectiveness of the automatic mirror and headlamp dimmer. Merv Afflerbach, of Quakertown, owner of our driveReport car, assures us that work they do.

The push-button transmission worked also, but it's another idea that time didn't prove. Not with imitators which included Edsel.

Contemporary reporters found that the suspension eliminated much of the sway and dive of non-torsion-bar-equipped Dodges, although that probably had as much to do with the anti-dive built into the upper control arm of the front suspension as with the springing medium. The flat cornering of 1959 looks very different to eyes 30 years older. All that weight leaning on skinny tires is less than confidence inspiring.

Dodge's "Constant-Control" full-time power steering gives full pressure at idle speed, which is good for parking, but the "finger-tip response" gave too light a feel for my taste. There's little feel and one steers by input and effect—do it and see what happens—rather than by touch. This, combined with the width of the car and good old squirmy bias-ply tires gave me some heart-in-the-throat experiences on some old, narrow eastern Pennsylvania roads. Merv says that it's simply a matter of getting used to it.

We met with unvarying enthusiasm while driving around. People just plain like the shape, some from memory and others, too young to have ever known it new, well, they just love it for what it is. My 11-year-old daughter Amanda, who accompanied me on this trip, was enthralled. What, I asked, did she like best? No hesitation: "The fins."

For me, well, of course, there are those lusty 345 horses. Stomp on the right side pedal and make the carburetors talk. The mufflers do their job all too well—some exhaust rumble would be appreciated—but sounds rolling out of those twin air cleaners are magnificent. The whistle of a turbocharger can never completely take the place of the throbbing ring of dual quads at full voice.

Dodge was the most aggressively styled of all the Chrysler Corporation cars for 1959, from the tip of its chromed tailfins to its thrusting headlamp eyebrows. **Bottom:** D-500's wheel covers have a little armored lancer in the centers.

1959 DODGE

inches side to side, weighing in excess of 3,800 pounds. It would be the last year for a full frame, with 1960 seeing the introduction of unit body construction with stub frames. Though Dodge used a perimeter frame, the convertible's frame added an X-shaped center brace for extra strength and rigidity. Torsion bar front suspension with rear leaf springs was already a Mopar tradition. Available on all Dodges—but selected for few— was Level-Flite Torsion-Aire, a pneumatic leveling device, basically air bags on the rear axle. It was an option that didn't last long, either on the car or on the order books.

Base engine in the Custom Royal was the 305-horsepower, 361-cubic-inch Super Ram Fire V-8 with wedge combustion chambers, introduced the year before as a replacement for Chrysler's famous but expensive-to-produce first Hemi series (which, incidentally, was still in use as the Coronet's V-8, and at 326 cubic inches and 255 horsepower still a long way from puny.) New for '59 was the 383-cubic-inch engine, larger by virtue of a bigger bore, and in Dodge guise it was called the D-500.

A conventional iron block, overhead-valve V-8, the D-500 had a compression ratio of 10.0:1 and produced 320 horsepower with a single four-barrel carburetor and dual exhausts. Add another carburetor and the engine became the Super D-500, the power peak rising from 4,600 rpm to 5,000 rpm and find-

ing another 25 ponies in the process. Maximum torque with either engine was 420 lb./ft., though at 2,800 rpm for the D-500 and 3,600 rpm for the Super D-500. Both the D-500 and Super D-500 were available as options for all models including station wagons, and the TorqueFlite transmission came with it as part of the package. The optional engines also conveyed bragging rights in the form of "500" badges on the fins, the left one on the gas filler door, presumably as a reminder of where all that gasoline went.

The Super D-500 engine cruised on two barrels of the rear carburetor. The secondary throats of the rear carb and the second carburetor were vacuum controlled. Each carburetor had its own small unsilenced air cleaner. The Super D-500 had a special high-lift cam, and heavy-duty valve springs enabled the engine to make use of the extra breath-

Above: Out back there's a goodly amount of trunk space. *Below:* The chromed lancer also shows up as front fender accents and on the tailfins as well as on the front name plate and trunk lid.

ing ability of dual carburetion. The Super D-500 was also equipped with a special dual-point distributor.

Incidentally, lest you believe this horsepower was for evil purposes, fear not. Dodge advised its salesmen that, "many times, the only way a driver can avoid danger is to accelerate away from it before a tight squeeze develops. The Dodge high-torque and high-horsepower V-8s have the *extra* muscle needed to deliver tremendous power whenever emergencies arise." Like emergencies where this other guy, see, comes up at

1959 Dodge Custom Royal Lancer Super D-500 Convertible

1959 Dodge Custom Royal convertible	$3,421.50
(includes factory retail price, distribution, excise and handling charge and dealer new car preparation)	
Solex glass (windshield only)	$18.55
Permanent anti-freeze $5.75	
Deluxe Radio-Heater Group	$221.65
(includes heater, backup lights, remote control outside mirror—left Mirror-Matic inside glareproof mirror, Music Master Radio)	
Convenience Group	$30.50
(includes variable speed electric wipers, windshield washer, handbrake warning light, map light, glove box light, visor vanity mirror, trunk light	
Deluxe Appearance Group with deluxe wheel covers	$58.90
(includes Two-Tone plastic padded steering wheel, deluxe wheel covers, stone shields, electric clock	
Ornamental Group	$26.25
(Fin end chrome inserts, license plate frame – rear dual aerials –rear	
Safety Group	$170.00
Power steering, power brakes, padded instrument panel, padded sun visors, speed warning device	
Automatic headlamp beam changer	49.70
70 amp heavy duty battery	$8.60
Super D-500 engine (383 cu. in.) - with dual	$414.95
4-barrel carburetors, and dual exhaust (aluminized), and TorqueFlite transmission	
Hood Ornament	$5.80
Quarter Panel Chevrons	$8.60
Power Seat Adjustment – 6 Way	$95.70
Power Window Lifts (4)	$102.30
Swivel seat	$70.95
Tires 8.00 x 14 nylon whitewall	$58.95
	$4,762.90

specifications

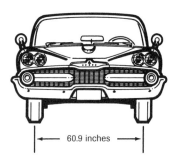

← 60.9 inches →

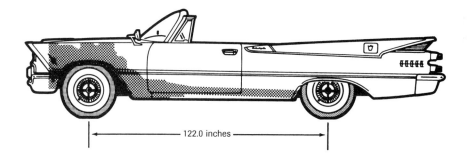

← 122.0 inches →

1959 Dodge Custom Royal Convertible

Original price	$4,768.65 with distribution, federal excise tax, handling charge and dealer new preparation included
Std. equipment	Carpet, foam rubber seat pad front and rear, fluted grille bombs, model specific trim and chrome moldings, 8.00 x 14 tires (partial list)
Options on dR car	Super D-500 engine, TorqueFlite transmission, power steering, power windows, tinted windshield, heater, radio, backup lamps, remote control left outside mirror, Mirror-Matic inside mirror, dual rear antennas, swivel seats, 6-way power seats, automatic headlamp beam changer (partial list)

ENGINE

Type	90-degree V-B
Bore x stroke	4.25 inches x 3.38 inches
Displacement	383 cubic inches
Compression ratio	10.0:1
Max bhp @ rpm	345 @ 5,000 (gross)
Max torque @ rpm	420 @ 3,600 (gross)
Taxable hp	57.8
Valves	Ohv in-line
Valve lifters	Hydraulic
Main bearings	5
Induction system	Two Carter 4-bbl downdraft carburetors
Exhaust system	Dual
Lubrication system	Pressure
Electrical system	12-volt

TRANSMISSION

Type	TorqueFlite 3-speed automatic
Ratios: 1st	2.45:1
2nd	1.45:1
Drive	1.00:1
Reverse	2.20:1

DIFFERENTIAL

Type	Hypoid
Ratio	3.31:1

STEERING

Type	Three tooth worm and roller, full-time power assisted
Turns lock to lock	3.5
Ratio	19.1:1
Turn circle	43.7 feet

BRAKES

Type	4-wheel hydraulic drum type, power assisted
Drum diameter	11 inches
Total swept area	230 square inches

CHASSIS & BODY

Frame	Channel siderail with X-member
Body construction	All steel
Body style	Convertible

SUSPENSION

Front	Independent, lateral non-parallel control arms with torsion bars
Rear	Conventional axle, semi-elliptic springs
Shock absorbers	Tube type
Tires	8.00 x 14
Wheels	Pressed steel

WEIGHTS AND MEASURES

Wheelbase	122 inches
Overall length	217.4 inches
Overall width	80.0 inches
Overall height	55.2 inches
Front track	60.9 inches
Rear track	59.8 inches
Ground clearance	5.2 inches
Shipping weight	3,820 pounds

CAPACITIES

Crankcase	6 quarts (w/filter)
Automatic trans.	17 pints
Cooling system	17 quarts (w/heater)
Fuel tank	20 gallons

CALCULATED DATA

Hp/c.i.d.	900
Pounds/hp	11.07
Pounds/cid.	9.97
Pounds/sq. in.	16.6

Flashy chromed model i.d. appears on the leading edge of each fin.

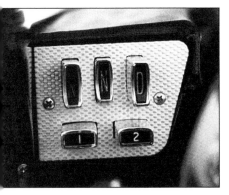

1959 DODGE

*Above left: Push buttons for tranny were a Mopar feature in the late fifties. **Above:** Dash has plenty of bright and shiny surfaces, too. **Below:** Peek-a-boo ashtray hides nicely in dashboard when not in use.*

the stop light and he, well, anyway....

Chrysler's three-speed TorqueFlite automatic transmission was standard on all Custom Royals, complete with pushbutton operation. Mounted on a pod to the left of the steering wheel—out of the reach of careless passengers—there were five buttons, requiring "less effort than dialing a telephone." Although there were "1" and "2" range buttons to hold the lower gears (second would shift up to direct drive if speed exceeded approximately 75 mph), there was no Park, Chrysler maintaining that an excellent parking brake made that position superfluous. Dodge put the parking brake on the drive shaft—"the most powerful in the industry." Perhaps a bit too much: *Motor Trend* tried to use it as an emergency brake, applying it at 30 mph, and dropped the drive shaft on the pavement.

Dodge touted the '59 models as being "the first all-pushbutton car." Pushbuttons were, of course, very much our future in 1959, but all it meant for Dodge cars was that heater controls (when the heater, still an option even on the Custom Royal, was included) were operated by pushbuttons—although heat was actually controlled by a lever. Air conditioning was still a rarity. Only 4.5 percent of Dodges came so equipped. The radio—AM band only, of course—was "transistorized." It was the first year for Dodge to go completely tubeless. A rear speaker was an available option, as was a pair of stylishly raked antennas just inside the rear fender fins.

Auto manufacturers never seem to be able to leave the speedometer alone, and for '59 Dodge had a "bar-type safety speedometer." This was a drum behind a slot that rolled color up past miles per hour markings as speed increased, the colors indicating a cool green to 30 mph, a cautionary amber to 50 mph, and a blazing red for the brave soul who ventured above 50. An optional clock was centered above the steering column, with an ammeter and fuel gauge to the left and an oil pressure and fuel gauge

Above: Fabric with anodized thread is used through the interior. *Below:* Swivel seats were a short-lived option on Chrysler-built cars of the time.

1959 DODGE

to the right. The dash itself was chrome on textured aluminum on painted metal, the latter padded as an option, for "greater peace of mind and protection in an accident." Good to have, that peace of mind in an accident.

Other options were power windows, six-way power seats, and new swing-out swivel seats. The swivel seat option was highlighted in factory sales literature. At the touch of a lever, either front seat would swivel out 40 degrees, making it easier for anyone, but especially a woman in a tight skirt, to get in. A speed control predecessor was the new-for-'59 "co-pilot speed warning signal." This self-imposed back seat driver would flash a red warning light at the driver

who exceeded a pre-set speed, and would do so up to approximately 15 mph above that. After that it apparently gave up in disgust.

High tech for '59 included a mechanical adjusting driver's side remote control outside mirror. Higher tech was the "Mirror-Matic" rearview mirror and the automatic beam changer. The mirror automatically adjusted itself to a nighttime setting when light from a following car hit a photo-electric cell. The automatic beam changer, contained in a pod on the instrument panel, dimmed the headlamps in response to approaching headlamps.

Dodge sales literature claimed, um, distinctive styling: "There is no mistaking this '59 Dodge. There is no mistaking the sweeping chrome hoods over the dual headlamps. The massive wraparound bumpers. The parking light pods. The fine grille. The flat, smooth

hood. Everything in the best of taste."

The question of taste aside, it was arguably the most extravagant Dodge ever made. From the "grille bombs"—the actual name for the parking lamp pods, really—to the "jet trail tail lamps"—yep, their name again—the '59 Dodge made a definite statement of fashion in the fifties. Those grille bombs by the way, were part of the bumper system, made of heavy stock and mounted to the frame. The taillamps were touted by Dodge as a safety feature, illuminating the car from the side. This benefit was probably more an after thought than anything else, as the tail lamps of '60 Dodges weren't visible from the side. In truth, the extended plastic lens proved to be quite vulnerable to passers-by, easily broken by an inadvertent bump of the knee.

The Custom Royal was outwardly distinguishable from lesser brethren by several trim clues. Most obvious was the gold colored "Custom Royal" script on the bright metal trim at the leading point of the fin. More restrained were wider chrome on the eyebrows, wider bodyside trim, "fin end chrome inserts on the "control surfaces" of the fins on Royals and Custom Royals, and, on the Custom Royal only, the grille bombs were fluted. A U-shaped chrome hood ornament (highly stylized wings?) appeared on various models up and down the line. If there was any rhyme or reason to this the factory literature failed to explain it. Deluxe wheel covers had spinners with the helmet, shield and lance motif in the center and white paint in the serrations. All '59 Dodges, for trivia enthusiasts, had grey painted—not body color—wheels.

The name "Lancer" was used in literature to designate a hardtop or convertible but did not appear anywhere on any 1959 Dodge. A badge consisting of a knight's helmet, shield and lance suggested the Lancer theme, but was used on Custom Royal sedans—which were not referred to as Lancers—and was not used on Coronet hardtops or convertibles, which were called Lancers. Go figure.

Incidentally, there was some limitation on body styles available in each line. Although four-door sedans and two-door and four-door hardtops (i.e. Lancers) could be had as Custom Royals, Royals, or in Coronet trim, convertibles came only as Custom Royals or Coronets, and two-door, or "club," sedans were available only as Coronets. The marketing guys must have worked hard on these distinctions.

The convertible was naturally the most glamorous model and also the one that, with the top down, arguably showed the tail fins to their best advantage. Putting the top down is simple though it does require climbing into the back seat to unzip the rear window. The

383 V-8 is rated at 345 bhp, with two four-barrel Carters supplying the go-juice.

top is power operated; it folds into a well behind the back seat and is covered by a boot that snaps around the edges. The top takes some of the room from the trunk, and the spare is relocated from the shelf over the axle to the left side of the trunk. Some stowage room is lost, but if you're going to complain about that you don't deserve a convertible in the first place.

Base price for a 1959 Dodge Custom Royal convertible was $3,125, only $100 more than a Custom Royal four-door hardtop but almost a thousand more than a base Coronet two-door sedan. Of course, no one ever drove out with a base price car. This was the era, remember, when even a heater was optional, and it was easy to spend thousands more on those optional extras. For example, the Super D-500 engine added $414.95 to the cost of a convertible; power seats, if not part of a package, $95.70; swivel seats, ditto, $70.95. Our driveReport car has a theoretical list price of $4,762.90, a hefty piece of change in 1959 (see sidebar, page 81).

The success of the '59 Dodges is subject to some question. Although sales jumped with the lower/longer/wider look introduced in 1955, they stayed relatively level through 1957 and then fell precipitously with the 1958 recession, from 281,359 in '57 to 133,953 in 1958. Sales recovered slightly in '59, up to 151,851. How much this was an effect of

the recession and how much can be attributed to America's new-found interest in compact cars (or how much it's a factor of both) is subject to speculation. However, over 353,000 Dodges were sold in 1960. Interest in convertibles saw 2,733 made, although there is no breakout of how many were Custom Royals and how many Coronets, much less how many were powered by D-500 or Super D-500 engines.

Regardless of the commercial success of the '59 Dodge Custom Royal Super D-500 convertible, it is undeniably a sensational expression of its time. Jet-plane styling died with the decade at Dodge. Future forms would be more conserva-

tive, more practical, smaller and sometimes faster. The stylist's pen, however, would never again display such undistilled optimism. ☜

Acknowledgments and Bibliography

Motor Trend, *July 1958, March 1959;* Standard Catalog of American Cars, 1946-1975, *John A. Gunnell, editor; 1959 Dodge Press Kit, Ross Roy Data Book and Confidential Bulletins: Dodge; 1959 Dodge Owners operating and maintenance manual; 1959 Dodge sales literature.*

Our special thanks to Mew Afflerbach for sharing his car and his library of 1959 Dodge literature.

1959 Dodge Silver Challenger

The special trim option has long been a staple of the auto sales game. The factory assembles a select group of options, slaps a special name on it and, with any luck, the little bell in the dealers' cash registers wears out. Usually this means a special top-of-the-line model that, if it doesn't sell, will draw showroom traffic that might just buy a lower cost model.

But in the spring of 1959, the competitive pressure was from below, so Dodge marketed a special low-cost model called the Silver Challenger. It was basically a Coronet, silver only, equipped with "luxury car features" consisting of white sidewalls, wheel covers, and special interior

trim of "black Coronet body cloth...silver vinyl bolsters...and rich-looking, black wall-to-wall carpeting!" And, of course, a "special jewel-like medallion" took the place of the Coronet script on the front fender,

And it sold for "less than many models of Ford, Chevrolet, and Rambler!" Total retail price: $2,530.50. Of course, that was with a six and three-in-the-tree, without radio or antifreeze.

Hey, she might not love you for your flashy car, but she'll respect you for your frugality. And which would you really rather have?

1960 DODGE POLARA
"YESTERDAY ONCE MORE"

Driving Impressions
by Richard Carpenter

by Arch Brown
photos by David Gooley

THE 1960 Dodge Polara has been one of my favorite cars since its introduction. It remains the forgotten Dodge, primarily due to the introduction of the highly successful Dodge Dart of that year. Granted, the "big" Dodge can be rightfully accused of stylistic overkill, due to the soaring, cantilevered fins (which were rapidly becoming passé), but overall it remains a sleek, well-balanced design, not awkward or ungainly from any angle.

My parents bought a little-used example in 1961, when I was fourteen. I remember vividly that day; while I was in the middle of a piano lesson, they pulled into the driveway with a black Polara. "A '60 Dodge!" I exclaimed, startling my teacher as I went running out the front door. My only disappointment was the

fact that the new family car was a four-door sedan, not a coupe, and did not possess the optional "shark's gill" stainless rear fender trim, though it was outfitted with the optional, outrageous

"Tarantula" wheel covers. Nonetheless, I was highly fond of it, loved the way it rode and performed and took great pleasure in the fact that a number of people thought it was an Imperial! I ultimately learned to drive and took my driver's test in it. When the family moved from Connecticut to Southern California in June 1963, the Dodge was the vehicle we used, and my Dad let me take it — and a date — to the senior Prom the following year.

For all of the reasons listed above, I just had to have a '60 Polara in my collection. The problem was locating one. Very few big Dodges were built in 1960, and the bulk of those were Matadors, not Polaras. Word of my interest had been around for quite a while in the collector community and the day finally came when an acquaintance let us know he had found one. It was definitely in need of considerable "TLC," but the important factors were: (a) it existed, (b) it

Originally published in Special Interest Autos #164, Mar.-Apr. 1998

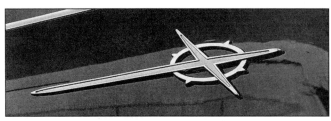

had never been hit, and was rust-free and original from its paint to the correct Holley carb on its 383.

The driveReport car had left the factory having been sprayed Cocoa Metallic with a contrasting Ivory top. Not my cup of tea. . . or cocoa. While we're usually quite strict in restoring the cars to as-new, in this case, concerning the colors, I couldn't do it. I like most cars in black and besides, our original had been black. Black it became with the contrasting top finished in Cocoa, which matches the interior. Paint and body work were done by the redoubtable Larry Leyk, who had performed similar magic on my '57 De Soto Adventurer and 300-F convertibles. Larry is quite particular and as a result the paint, fit and finish on these cars is closer to Mulliner Park-Ward than Detroit. Bill DiCicco and Robert Ludwig, who oversaw the restoration, did a marvelous job in procuring countless N.O.S. parts and interior and getting the car back together in relatively short time.

When the driver enters the Dodge and takes his place on the well-cushioned seat, he immediately has a close encounter with one of the most, shall we say, original instrument clusters ever designed. Chrysler was going through its "Buck Rogers" period at this time

and the Dodge was no exception. That being said, ergonomically it is very well executed, with the speedo, gauges, push buttons and clock all in front of the driver. With its panoramic windshield and optional oversize backlight, the cabin has a very airy feel about it. Whereas the rear quarters do not have the head room which we possessed in our four-door, there is still enough head room and leg room to make a comfortable trip for the rear-seat passengers. The upholstery lacks the panache of its GM counterpart, the Pontiac Bonneville. One

could order leather bucket seats in the Bonneville as well, but not in the Dodge, where the optional swivel seats were as sporty as anyone could order.

Performance, however, is a different matter; with its impressive flow of power from the venerable 383 to the crisp shifts of the Torqueflite, the Dodge is easily the Pontiac's equal and arguably its superior. (Send hate mail to Arch Brown.) As any *SIA* reader will know, Chrysler, with the exception of the Imperial, switched to unit-bodied construction in 1960; or "Unibody" as

1960 Dodge Polara

In terms of sheer audacious flashiness the Polara could give the '59 Cadillac Eldo some competition. Everywhere you look there's chrome, stainless or aluminum trim to dazzle the eye.

Madison Avenue termed it. This method of construction and sorely needed attention to quality control made these Mopars far superior to the 1957-59 offerings, though there was still room for improvement.

The ride, being a Chrysler product, is comfortable; firm but not harsh. The average American then still preferred the plusher "boulevard ride" offered in the contemporary Pontiac or Mercury. What the Dodge lacks in plushness it more than makes up for in handling, which is easily best in its class. For an automobile nearing two tons it has a remarkable fleetness of foot about it. Like all Mopars of this period, the Dodge has Chrysler's controversial "full-time" power steering. While it is welcomed when maneuvering into a tight parallel parking spot, it is just too lacking in "feel of the road" at other times. I am delighted they finally did away with it. Braking is on a par with other American offerings at that time, which is to say, barely adequate; certainly not up to the high performance of certain cars offered by the "Big Three."

All in all, for me the '60 Polara is impressive to look at and to drive; I'm highly pleased to finally own one. I wish my father were here to see it!

History & Background

There are some thirty automobiles in the collection of singer/songwriter Richard Carpenter, most of them Mopars and all of them meticulously and authentically restored. Ask Richard to name his favorite and he'll probably point to one of the high-stepping Chrysler "Letter" cars, perhaps the 300-F. But turn the question to his *sentimental* favorite and you might find some other candidates. Like the '67 Satellite that the family bought soon after Richard and his sister, Karen, broke into show business. Or the 1970 'Cuda 440 Six-Pack that was purchased from the proceeds of The Carpenters' first big engagement at one of the Reno clubs. Or maybe—and this may come as a surprise—the nod would go to the 1960 Dodge Polara hardtop, pictured here.

There's a good reason for this car's special status in the collection, and we'll get to that in a moment. But first, let's take an over-the-shoulder look at how things were at Dodge, back in 1960.

It was a pivotal year for the division, and for the Chrysler Corporation. Possibly more so than company executives realized at the time. The year's most conspicuous corporate event was, of course, the introduction of the Valiant. Not only did this stylish little junior edition propel Chrysler smartly into the Compact field, but along with it came the soon-to-be-legendary "slant six" engine. Not to mention the trend-setting alternator, which represented an enormous improvement over the ubiquitous generator.

During the immediate prewar years, Dodge seemed to have a lock on fourth place in the sales race, its popularity exceeded only by the "Low-Priced Three," Chevrolet, Ford and Plymouth. But after slipping to sixth rank in 1948, it stumbled badly in 1953, falling abruptly to eighth place behind Buick, Pontiac, Mercury and Oldsmobile, as well as the traditional "Big Three." So it can come as no surprise that the Dodge people saw the need for drastic changes.

Belatedly, we might add. In those days the late W. H. "Bud" Braley, a close personal friend of this writer and a veteran Dodge/Plymouth dealer, served on the Dodge Division Dealers' Council. According to Braley, the Council had for several years been stressing, in their negotiations with management, that it was long past time for something new, especially in terms of styling, to say nothing of the need for a fully automatic transmission to replace the "Gyro-Matic," Dodge's version of Chrysler's durable but clumsy semi-automatic. But the company turned a deaf ear to the Council, suggesting in effect that 'It's our job to build 'em; it's your job to sell 'em!"

So it wasn't until the coming of the 1955 models that Dodge really became style-conscious. For that matter, it wasn't until 1954 that Dodge had an automatic transmission, a popular option offered by Pontiac as early as 1948.

Eventually, of course, sweeping changes had been made. In 1953 there was the introduction of the "Red Ram" V-8 engine, a peppery little (241-c.i.d.) version of Chrysler's fabulous "hemi." Two years later there was dramatic new styling, the work of young Maury Baldwin of Virgil Exner's staff, transforming the dowdy Dodge into one of the best-looking cars on the market, regardless of price.

Dodge's output for 1955 was more than double the 1954 figure, though the division remained in eighth place. But if 1955's styling had been outstanding, as it surely was, 1957's — the work of Virgil Exner himself — had been downright sensational. This applied not only to Dodge, of course, but to the entire Chrysler Corporation line. "Suddenly it's 1960!" proclaimed the Plymouth ads. And overnight the entire line of cars from the Chrysler Corporation became the industry's undisputed style leaders.

But still, Dodge sales languished. After moving up to seventh place for 1957, the division slipped the following year to tenth rank. It was Dodge's worst showing since 1928, a year when the company's management had been in disarray, just before the firm's purchase by Walter Chrysler.

Nineteen fifty-nine wasn't much better, though Dodge did manage, that year, to elbow its way past Mercury and Cadillac to recapture eighth rank. The company's response to this dilemma was a dramatic one, as it obviously needed to be: Dodge entered a whole new price field. During recent years, Dodge had offered three lines of lower-medium-priced cars, priced against the likes of Pontiac and Mercury and the least costly Oldsmobile. But for 1960, while maintaining its presence in that particular market with two new series, the Matador and the Polara, Dodge

Left: Polara's "Tarantula" wheel covers are just as flamboyant as the rest of the car. *Right:* Even the seat controls have a space-age design.

1960 Dodge Prices and Weights

During 1960, Dodge offered an unusually wide array of cars — 35 different passenger cars in all, counting both six- and eight-cylinder models.

	Price	Weight
Dodge Series:		
Polara Sub-series, 122-inch wheelbase, 383-c.i.d.		
Sedan, 4-door	$3,141	3,735
Hardtop, 2-door	$3,186	3,740
Hardtop, 4-door	$3,275	3,815
Convertible coupe	$3,416	3,765
Station wagon, 6-passenger	$3,506	4,085
Station wagon, 9-passenger	$3,621	4,270
Matador Sub-series, 122-inch wheelbase, 361-c.i.d.		
Sedan, 4-door	$2,930	3,725
Hardtop, 2-door	$2,996	3,705
Hardtop, 4-door	$3,075	3,820
Station wagon, 6-passenger	$3,239	4,045
Station wagon, 9-passenger	$3,354	4,120
Dodge Dart Series:		
Seneca Six Sub-series, 118-inch wheelbase*, 225-c.i.d.		
Sedan, 2-door	$2,278	3,365
Sedan, 4-door	$2,330	3,420
Station wagon, 6-passenger	$2,695	3,805
Seneca Eight Sub-series, 118-inch wheelbase*, 318-c.i.d.		
Sedan, 2-door	$2,397	3,530
Sedan, 4-door	$2,449	3,600
Station wagon, 6-passenger	$2,815	3,975
Pioneer Six Sub-series, 118-inch wheelbase*, 225-c.i.d.		
Sedan, 2-door	$2,410	3,375
Sedan, 4-door	$2,459	3,430
Hardtop, 2-door	$2,488	3,410
Station wagon, 6-passenger	$2,787	3,820
Station wagon, 9-passenger	$2,892	3,875
Pioneer Eight Sub-series, 118-inch wheelbase*, 318-c.i.d.		
Sedan, 2-door	$2,530	3,540
Sedan, 4-door	$2,578	3,610
Hardtop, 2-door	$2,607	3,610
Station wagon, 6-passenger	$2,906	4,000
Station wagon, 9-passenger	$3,011	4,065
Phoenix Six Sub-series, 118-inch wheelbase*, 318-c.i.d.		
Sedan, 4-door	$2,595	3,420
Hardtop, 2-door	$2,618	3,410
Hardtop, 4-door	$2,677	3,460
Convertible coupe	$2,868	3,460
Phoenix Eight Sub-series, 118-inch wheelbase*, 318-c.i.d.		
Sedan, 4-door	$2,715	3,610
Hardtop, 2-door	$2,737	3,605
Hardtop, 4-door	$2,796	3,655
Convertible coupe	$2,988	3,690

*Station wagons used the 122-inch wheelbase of the senior Dodges.

specifications

© copyright 1998, Special Interest Autos

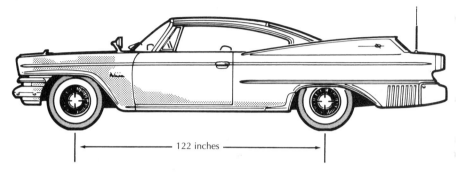

61.0 inches

122 inches

1960 Dodge Polara

Price	$3,196, federal taxes and handling charges included
Options on dR car	Torqueflite transmission, power steering, power brakes, radio, oversize backlight, swivel seats, special wheel covers, white sidewall tires, "shark's gill" aluminum fender trim, front bumper guards

ENGINE

Type	90-degree ohv V-8
Bore x stroke	4.25 inches x 3.38 inches
Displacement	383 cubic inches
Compression ratio	10.0:1
Horsepower @ rpm	325 @ 4,600
Torque @ rpm	425 @ 2,800
Taxable horsepower	54.3
Valve lifters	Hydraulic
Main bearings	5
Fuel system	Dual downdraft carburetor
Exhaust system	Dual
Electrical system	12-volt

TRANSMISSION

Type	Torqueflite 3-speed automatic with torque converter
Ratios: 1st	2.45:1
2nd	1.45:1
3rd	1.00:1
Reverse	2.00:1
Max. ratio at stall	2.20 @ 1,895

DIFFERENTIAL

Type	Hypoid
Ratio	2.93:1
Drive axles	Semi-floating
Torque medium	Rear springs

STEERING

Type	Rack and sector, power assisted
Turns lock-to-lock	3.5
Ratios	15.7:1 gear; 19.2:1 overall
Turning diameter	43 feet 9.5 inches (curb/curb)

BRAKES

Type	4-wheel hydraulic, drum type; power assisted
Drum diameter	11 inches
Effective area	230 square inches

CHASSIS & BODY

Construction	All-steel unitized, body-and-frame
Body type	6-passenger hardtop coupe

SUSPENSION

Front	Independent, torsion bars
Rear	Rigid axle, semi-elliptic springs

Shock absorbers	Direct-acting
Tires	8.00/14
Wheels	Pressed steel disc

WEIGHTS AND MEASURES

Wheelbase	122 inches
Overall length	212.6 inches
Overall width	78 inches
Overall height	54.8 inches
Front track	61 inches
Rear track	59.7 inches
Shipping weight	3,740 pounds

CAPACITIES

Crankcase	5 quarts
Automatic trans.	22 pints (refill)
Rear axle	3.5 pounds
Cooling system	17 quarts (with heater)
Fuel tank	20 gallons

CALCULATED DATA

Stroke/bore ratio	0.794:1
Horsepower per c.i.d.	0.849:1
Weight per hp	11.5
Weight per c.i.d.	9.77
Lb. per sq. in. (brakes)	16.26

MoPar 383 V-8 delivers 325 horses to propel Dodge down the road in very quick fashion. **Facing page, top:** *Engine puts out more brake horsepower than its competition in the mid-price range.* **Below:** *Is it a car or a spaceship? There's enough buttons on the dashboard to keep Buck Rogers happy.*

1960 Dodge Polara

staged an all-out invasion of territory previously occupied by Chevrolet, Ford and Plymouth.

They called the newcomer the Dodge Dart. This car was not to be confused with the compact Darts of later years. Rather, on close inspection it was revealed to be nothing more nor less than a re-badged Plymouth, built on the Plymouth's 118-inch wheelbase, four inches shorter than the traditional Dodge chassis. Engines, driveline and basic body shell were all pure Plymouth, although in the eyes of most people the 1960 Dodge Dart was a much better looking car than its intra-corporate rival. True, the Darts cost about $50 more than the corresponding Plymouth models. But to many people the prestige of the Dodge name was worth at least that much — not to mention buyer resistance to some of the 1960 Plymouth's styling excesses, notably the high-flying (and poorly integrated) rear fender fins.

As a result of the introduction of the Dart, Dodge jumped over Oldsmobile and Mercury to reclaim sixth place in the 1960 sales race. Calendar year production more than doubled, and dealers were ecstatic. (By way of comparison, Pontiac's output increased by a modest 16.8 percent that year.)

Inevitably, there were unintended consequences to all this, for the new Dodge Dart clearly robbed sales from the senior Dodges, as well as from Plymouth. (For that matter, it is also clear that the little Valiant ate away, to some extent, at the market for full-sized Plymouths.)

Consider the figures: During the 1959 season, Plymouth sold 458,281 cars, all

full-sized units, of course. The overall figure for 1960 sagged to 445,792, of which 192,362 were Valiants. In other words, sales of the full-sized Plymouths plummeted to 253,430 during the 1960 model year, a drop of 45 percent.

Meanwhile, at the Dodge Division, model year production skyrocketed from 151,851 passenger cars in 1959 to

349,120 the following season. But of that total, an astonishing 88 percent were Darts. Or to put a little finer point on the matter, output of the traditional 122-inch wheelbase Dodge plummeted, during the 1960 model run, from 151,851 to 42,317, a drop of 72 percent.

Dodge never really regained its earlier status as a leading lower-medium-

Dodge Polara versus the Competition

Here's how the 1960 Dodge Polara stacked up against some of its major competitors. (Prices shown are f.o.b. factory with standard engines, standard equipment.)

	Dodge Polara	Mercury Montclair	Oldsmobile Super 88	Pontiac Bonneville
Price, 2-door hardtop	$3,196	$3,331	$3,325	$3,255
Wheelbase	122 inches	126 inches	123 inches	124 inches
Overall length	212.6 inches	219.1 inches	217.5 inches	220.7 inches
Shipping weight	3,740	4,253	4,087	3,965
Construction	Unitized	Body/frame	Body/frame	Body/frame
Engine c.i.d.	383.0	430.0	394.0	389.0
Horsepower/rpm	325/4,600	310/4,100	315/4,600	303/4,600
Torque/rpm	425/2,800	460/2,200	435/2,800	435/2,800
Compr. ratio	10.00:1	10.00:1	9.75:1	10.25:1
Automatic trans?	Extra cost	Standard	Extra cost	Extra cost
Axle ratio*	2.93:1	2.71:1	3.07:1	3.08:1
Power steering?	Extra cost	Extra cost	Extra cost	Extra cost
Type	Rack/sector	Recirculating ball	Ball nut	Recirc ball
Turning diameter	43 feet 9.5 inches	43 feet 10.5 inches	46 feet 3 inches	46 feet 8.375 inches
Braking area (sq in)	230.0	204.0	156.8	173.7
Drum diameter	11 inches	11 inches	11 inches	11 inches
Tire size	8.00/14	8.50/14	8.50/14	8.00/14
Weight/horsepower	11.5	13.7	13.0	13.1

* With automatic transmission

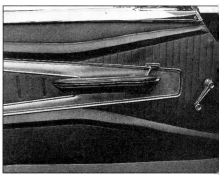

Above left: Wild styling extended to steering wheel. Top right: And to the inside door handles. Above right: Rear seat room is comfortable for most passengers. Below: Canted rear fins look especially dramatic from this angle.

1960 Dodge Polara

priced car. And not until 1970 was Plymouth able, thanks this time to the sporty compact Duster, to regain what had once been its traditional third place!

Still, 1960's full-sized Dodge Polara and Matador models must be regarded as among the industry's better buys. Apart from the upscale trim featured by the Polara, the two appeared nearly identical, the principal difference between them lying under the hood. There, standard power for the Matador came from the 361-cubic-inch, 295 horsepower engine first seen in the 1958 De Soto Firedome; while powering the Polara was a 383-c.i.d., 325 bhp mill, borrowed

from the '59 De Soto Fireflite. (That engine, due to be shared the following year with the Chrysler Windsor, was also available, at extra cost, in the Matador.)

Six body types were offered in the Polara line: Four-door sedan, two- and four-door hardtops, six- and nine-passenger station wagons and a convertible coupe. The Matador offered the same menu except that the ragtop was omitted. Prices began at $2,930 for the Matador sedan, and ranged no higher than $3,416 for the Polara convertible. Bargains, all!

Since the Matador/Polara's 122-inch wheelbase was identical to that of the Chrysler Windsor, and since most of the mechanical components were also shared between the two, it would not be out of line to suggest that these big Dodges could be thought of as the motorist's op-

portunity to buy a Chrysler on the cheap. And because of their excellent handling qualities and high speed (estimated by Dick Langworth in his *Illustrated Dodge Buyer's Guide* at 110-120 miles per hour with the "383" engine), these cars were highly popular with law enforcement.

It happens that it was in a 1960 Dodge Polara that Harold and Agnes Carpenter and their two talented youngsters Richard and Karen (who would come to fame, a few years later, as *The Carpenters*) made their move from Connecticut to California, in 1963. Tragically, Karen is gone now; but Richard is still active in the music world. And as most car buffs are aware, he has a collection of some 30 fine vintage cars. He calls the collection "Yesterday Once More," naming it for one of the Carpenters' platinum records. ᦉ

Acknowledgments and Bibliography

Automotive Industries, *March 1960; Langworth, Richard M.*, Encyclopedia of American Cars, 1940-1970; *Langworth, Richard M.*, Illustrated Dodge Buyer's Guide; *Lee, John (ed.),* Standard Catalog of Chrysler, 1924-1990; *McPherson, Thomas A.*, The Dodge Story.

Our thanks to David Gooley, Paramount, California; Robert Ludwig, Santa Fe Springs, California; Bill DiCicco, Santa Fe springs, California. Special thanks to Richard Carpenter, Downey, California.

Left: Swivel seats made a brief appearance as a feature on MoPars in the late fifties-early sixties. **Above:** *Power steering badge mimics steering wheel shape.* **Below left:** *Despite appearance, gauges are actually quite legible.* **Right:** *Trunk space galore for cross-country trips.*

1960

It was a time of tension and a time of change. In Greensboro, North Carolina, on February 1, a group of black students staged a sit-down demonstration at a variety store lunch counter. The movement spread quickly throughout the south, and even in New York there were sympathetic pickets. The Civil Rights movement was well and truly launched.

On May 1st a Soviet rocket shot down what was claimed to be a US weather research plane—a U-2—when its pilot, Francis Gary Powers, strayed into Soviet-Afghan territory. Insisting that in fact the plane had been on a spy mission, Soviet Premier Nikita Khrushchev angrily denounced the United States and President Eisenhower personally, rescinding his invitation for the latter to visit the USSR. Then five months later, while attending the United Nations General Assembly in New York, Khrushchev drew world-wide attention when, to signal his disapproval of remarks made by the Philippine delegate, he removed his shoe and pounded his desk with the heel.

The Soviet Premier's visit evidently wasn't confined to the business of state, however. Traveling to Hollywood, he visited the set of the musical production *Can Can,* with an all-star cast that included Shirley MacLaine, Frank Sinatra, Louis Jourdan and Maurice Chevalier. Unable to grasp the spirit of the comedy, he pronounced it "decadent." (Decadent or no, *Can Can* proved to be Hollywood's top money-maker for 1960.)

Other films that entertained us during 1960 included *The Apartment* (Shirley MacLaine and Jack Lemmon), *Butterfield 8* (Elizabeth Taylor), *Exodus* (Paul Newman, Eva Marie Saint), *G.I. Blues* (Elvis Presley), and *Please Don't Eat the Daisies* (Doris Day, David Niven.) Meanwhile, musicals running on Broadway included *Camelot, The Unsinkable Molly Brown,* and a revival of *West Side Story.*

It wasn't a particularly distinguished year for popular music, but 1960 had its share of bright spots. The television production *Mr. Lucky* featured superb music by Henry Mancini, while Alan J. Lerner and Frederick Loewe provided a marvelous score for *Camelot,* including "If Ever I Would Leave You" as well as the title song. "Never On Sunday," introduced in the film of the same name, was the Academy Award Winner for the year, and Chubby Checker (Ernest Evans) introduced a new dance craze with "The Twist."

Popular fiction included Elizabeth Goudge's *The Dean's Watch,* Marcia Davenport's *The Constant Image,* and Harper Lee's *To Kill a Mockingbird*—this last slated to receive a Pulitzer Prize during 1961. And in the realm of non-fiction there was William L. Shirer's *The Rise and Fall of the Third Reich,* Barry Goldwater's *The Conscience of a Conservative,* and Herman Wouk's moving statement of the Jewish faith, *This Is My God.*

Underscoring the chill of the Cold War, the nuclear-powered USS Triton, at 7,750 tons the world's largest submarine, circumnavigated the globe on a submerged voyage of 41,519 miles, pursuing in general the route followed by the sixteenth century Portuguese explorer, Ferdinand Magellan.

But in a great humanitarian undertaking, the SS Hope, a privately financed floating hospital and medical school, sailed from San Francisco on September 22nd on a year's mission to carry medical knowledge and treatment to the people of Indonesia and South Vietnam.

Here in the United States the political tide turned when, in the November elections, Democrat John F. Kennedy defeated Republican Richard M. Nixon for the presidency. During the campaign, the two men engaged in four precedent-setting, nationally televised debates, a new political technique to which some observers credited Kennedy's slim margin of victory.

Radio was rapidly losing its appeal, in favor of television. Signaling the change, *The Romance of Helen Trent,* a daytime soap opera whose run had commenced back in 1933, was terminated on June 24th with its 7,222nd episode.

Boxing, of course, was as popular as ever. Twenty-five-year-old Floyd Patterson became, on June 20th, the first (and youngest) man in boxing to regain the world's heavyweight championship, with a fifth round knockout of Sweden's Ingemar Johansson, to whom Patterson had lost the title in 1959.

Finned Flyer

Dodge's Distinctive 1961 Dart Phoenix

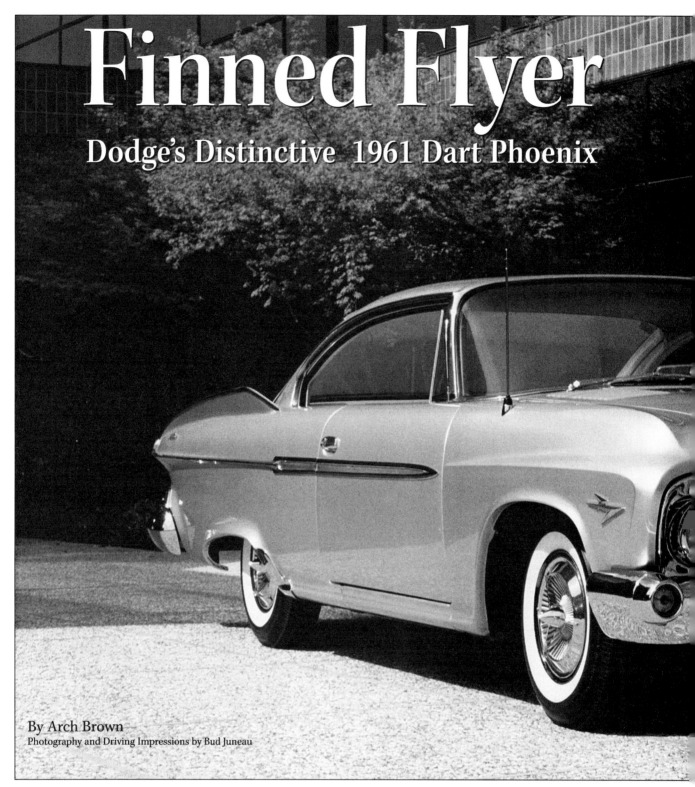

By Arch Brown
Photography and Driving Impressions by Bud Juneau

Y ou're sitting on what seems at first to be a typical bench seat when you slide into Mike Squires's 1961 Dodge Dart; yet it's a little unusual, having a one-third/two-thirds split in the backrest, with a sort of higher portion behind the driver. The steering wheel—round, not square like some of the senior Chrysler products—has two hand grips, one on either side. Facing the driver is a drum clock with a red line down the middle, with numbers rotating as a drum, like a Model "A" speedome-

ter. Numbers are easy to read. Oil and temperature gauges are kind of drum-shaped also.

There are two interesting push-button panels, sort of flared up on each side, rather like the quarter-panels on the car. The panel on the left contains the transmission buttons; Reverse on the left, then Neutral, then Drive, then Second and finally First. On the right are the heater/defroster fan, air (with temperature bar beneath). The mirror is mounted on the dash rather than hang-

ing from above the windshield. If you had your girlfriend sitting in the middle you wouldn't be able to see; she'd be right in the mirror.

The free-standing speedometer is interesting: It's frosted, located in a little see-through tunnel, illuminated from the back, by daylight. The four-way electric seat is rather shallow feeling, yet it is firm and comfortable. This is a well-equipped car, with power steering, power brakes, TorqueFlite automatic transmission, and the rare D-500 high-

performance engine with accompanying heavy-duty suspension.

The starter is on the key. You pull out and push down on the brake handle to release it. The engine starts right up, with a powerful sound. The exhaust system is strictly factory, but it sounds very much like a glass-pack. Press the Drive button and there's very little delay before the transmission takes hold. Acceleration is rapid. Upshifts occurred at 15 and 22 miles per hour, though if you stick your foot in it, it will remain in first

In defiance to its fairly large proportions and two-ton poundage, the Dart handles better and corners flatter than most cars its size.

gear almost as long as you want. Then you hit second, and get second-gear rubber. What a fun car!

We're driving down the freeway at about 60 when I punch it. The second two barrels cut in via mechanical linkage. Shifts are extremely tight and prompt, very nice. The TorqueFlite transmission was probably the best automatic of its time; and I can tell you, that engine surprised a lot of people on the street in the Sixties! There is one disadvantage to the early TorqueFlites, however: No parking sprag; no way to lock the transmission. That omission

"For those who wanted some extra punch, any 1961 Dodge Dart could be equipped with the 361-cu.in. V-8, putting out 305-hp."

Turbine-inspired wheel covers enhance the 7.50 x 14-inch whitewall tires.

was rectified when the 1962 model were introduced.

The Torsion-Aire suspension is ver even: comfortable, smooth, corners ver well with minimal lean; and there's ver little "nosedive," even on hard braking The power brakes are very effective pulling the car down nice and straight Probably the only drawback—if it reall is a drawback—has to do with the sus pension. It's firm, even a little choppy But this particular car's heavy-dut suspension is probably responsible fo that.

Perhaps the most unusual feature o this car (and other Chrysler products c its era) is the "full-time" power steering it's just so easy to steer.

Mention the Dodge Dart, and mos people will conjure up images of th highly successful "senior compact" tha Dodge marketed under that nam between 1963 and 1976. But that's no where it all began.

Back in 1960 there had been a majo re-alignment among the Chrysler Cor poration's dealerships. It was deter mined that Plymouth would no longe be simply a "companion" car, to be han dled by Chrysler, De Soto and Dodg dealers. Plymouth would thereafte stand alone with its own dealer bod (though in some cases it might b teamed with the Chrysler.) De Soto wa in its death throes by that time, s apparently nobody worried much abou the continued viability of its deale body. Dodge, however, was another mat

Turn signals incorporated into bumper.

Rear glass design similar to the Chevrolet and Pontiac "bubbletops" of the same year.

PROS & CONS

Pros
Plenty of power
Good parts supply
Extraordinary styling

Cons
Few available for sale
Overly firm suspension
Non-lockable transmission

ter entirely. For many years the Dodge had been America's fourth best-selling automobile, but by 1953 it had slipped to eighth rank. And there it had remained, overtaken by Buick, Pontiac, Mercury and Oldsmobile. This, despite the 1955 introduction of an extremely attractive new Dodge line, styled by young Maury Baldwin, a member of Virgil Exner's design team. And even that wasn't the end of the bad news, for between 1955 and 1959 sales tumbled another 68 percent. It was apparent that in a great many instances it had been the Plymouth franchise that had been keeping many Dodge dealers alive. So what to do now?

The solution to the dilemma seemed simple enough, although in at least two respects its consequences probably ran a good deal deeper than anyone expected. For 1960 saw the introduction of the original Dodge Dart, a full-sized car that was to all intents and purposes a rebadged Plymouth. Powertrains were identical between the Dart and the Plymouth. Both used a 118-inch wheelbase, four inches shorter than the traditional Polara and Matador series that remained as Dodge's premium models. Like the Plymouth, the Dodge Dart was offered in three trim levels, and prices of comparable models differed by only about $20.00.

The Dodge Dart differed from the Plymouth in two important respects. The first had to do with styling, for the '60 Plymouth had a rather odd grille; and its rear fenders took Virgil Exner's "fins" to the extreme, while those of the Dart

were much more subdued. So in the eyes of a good many of us the Dart was far better looking than the Plymouth. (In fact, it may well have been the best-looking car in the Chrysler Corporation's entire 1960 inventory!) All of this inevitably cut into Plymouth sales.

Then there was the Dodge name. Traditionally associated with the lower-medium price field, it carried with it a little extra measure of prestige that was attractive to many buyers of low-priced cars. Once again, the Dart stole sales from the Plymouth.

Pirating traditional Plymouth customers wasn't the only unintended consequence of the Dodge Dart's introduction. Sales of the larger Dodges, the Polara and Matador models, plummeted by a whopping 72 percent, compared to the previous year. Evidently Dodge buyers saw little reason to pay a premium, often more than $400, for the larger car. (Indeed, veteran Dodge dealer W. H. "Bud" Braley commented some years ago to this writer that, "Even my mother drove a Dart that year; and you know, she could have had any automobile she wanted!")

Perhaps we should explain at this point that the Polara represented the very top of the Dodge line in 1960. In addition to its substantially upgraded trim level, it differed from the Matador in its use of a 383-cu.in. V-8, in lieu of the less expensive car's 361-cu.in. V-8. Prices differed by a couple of hundred dollars on comparable models.

And then came

1961. The Dodge Dart's styling underwent a heavy facelift that year, "highlighted," in Thomas A. MacPherson's words, "by reverse slant tail fins and an overall curvaceous look." The effect wasn't too bad with respect to the coupes, as shown by our driveReport car, but it appears to have been disaster time as far as the sedans were concerned. Sales were down somewhat throughout the industry that year; but while Chevrolet suffered a 14 percent reduction in volume and Buick sales were off by five percent, Dodge plummeted from sixth to ninth rank on a sales reduction of 46 percent! Obviously, something was going on here that the public didn't like!

In a concession to reality, the traditional, larger Dodges were cut from two series to one. According to company advertisements, Matador was dropped while the Polara was retained in the line, but that's not really the way it worked. A comparison of both specifications and prices reveal the truth of what Dodge had done, which was simply this: The Matador name was dropped and

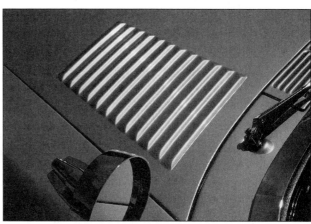
Decorative hood louvers were non-functional.

illustrations by Russell von Sauers, The Graphic Automobile Studio

© copyright 2000, Special Interest Autos

specifications

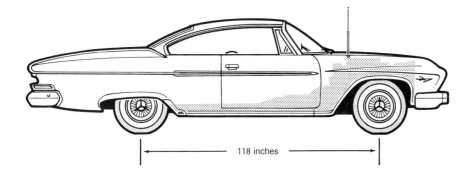

118 inches

61.5 inches

1961 Dodge Dart Phoenix

Original price	$2,737 f.o.b. factory, with standard equipment, federal excise tax included
Price as equipped	N/A
Options on dR car	D-500 engine, TorqueFlite transmission, power steering, power brakes, power seat, radio, remote left outside mirror, electric clock, backup lights, tinted glass, windshield washers, light package

ENGINE

Type	90-degree overhead-valve V-8
Bore x stroke	4.125 inches x 3.375 inches
Displacement	360.8 cubic inches
Compression ratio	9.0:1
Horsepower @ rpm	305 @ 4,800
Torque @ rpm	395 @ 3,000
Taxable horsepower	54.3
Valve lifters	Hydraulic
Main bearings	5
Fuel system	Carter AFB-3105S 4-barrel carburetor, mechanical pump
Cooling system	Centrifugal pump
Exhaust system	Dual
Electrical system	12-volt battery/coil

TRANSMISSION

Type	TorqueFlite 3-speed automatic planetary with torque converter
Ratios, 1st	2/45:1
2nd	1.45:1
3rd	1.00:1
Reverse	2.20:1
Torque converter	
Maximum ratio at stall	2.20:1

REAR AXLE

Type	Hypoid
Ratio	3.31:1
Drive axles	Semi-floating
Torque medium	Springs

STEERING

Type	Rack and sector, power assisted
Ratios	15.7+ gear, 19.2 overall
Turning diameter	42' 5" (curb/curb)
Turns, lock to lock	3.5

BRAKES

Type	4-wheel internal, drum-type, power assisted
Drum diameter	11 inches
Effective area	184 square inches

CHASSIS & BODY

Construction	All steel, unitized body and frame
Body type	2-door hardtop

SUSPENSION

Front	Independent, lateral non-parallel control arms, torsion bars
Rear	Rigid axle, 5-leaf semi-elliptic springs
Shock absorbers	Direct-acting
Tires	7.50/14
Wheels	Pressed steel, drop-center rims

WEIGHTS AND MEASURES

Wheelbase	118 inches
Overall length	209.4 inches
Overall width	78.7 inches
Overall height	56.7 inches
Front track	61.5 inches
Rear track	60.2 inches
Min. road clearance	5.1 inches
Curb weight	3,935 pounds

CAPACITIES

Crankcase	5 quarts
Cooling system	21 quarts (with heater)
Fuel tank	20 gallons
Transmission	19 pints (at refill)
Rear axle	4 pints

CALCULATED DATA

Stroke/bore ratio	.818:1
Hp per c.i.d.	.845
Curb weight per hp	12.9
Curb weight per c.i.d.	10.9
Lb. per sq. in. (brakes)	21.4

PERFORMANCE

Acceleration 0-30	2.9 seconds
0-50	6.4 seconds
0-60	8.1 seconds
40-60	3.9 seconds
Top speed	118.42 mph

PARTS PRICES

Carburetor kits	$45.00
Brake master cylinder	$79.50
Front-end rebuild kit	$180.00
Shock Absorbers (4)	$89.00
Trunk weatherstripping	$39.50
Wheel cylinders (front)	$29.50

Protruding fins have dramatic appearance.

Part of the Dart's intriguing style is its use of conflicting design elements.

the Polara title was transferred to the lower-priced big Dodge.

"Compact" cars had come into their own during 1960, with the introduction of the Falcon, the Corvair, and the Valiant. Naturally, Dodge dealers wanted a piece of the action, and for 1961 a Valiant clone called the Lancer appeared in Dodge showrooms across the nation. We mention the Lancer only in passing, since it is not really a part of our story here.

Once again in 1961, it was the Dart that accounted for the bulk of Dodge sales. It came again in three trim levels, known in ascending order as the Seneca, the Pioneer, and the Phoenix. There were three Seneca models, five Pioneers, and four in the upscale Phoenix line exemplified here. Standard power came, with one exception, from either the 225-cu.in. (actually 224.7) 'Slant Six," or the 318-cu.in. (317.6) V-8, rated respectively at 145 and 230 horsepower. (The one exception was the Phoenix ragtop, which was not available with the Six.)

For those who wanted some extra punch, any 1961 Dodge Dart could be equipped, at extra cost, with the 361-cu.in. (360.8) V-8 D-500 package, putting out 305-hp. It is that engine, essentially a high-performance version of the Polara mill, that powers our drive-Report car; and according to a road test by "Uncle Tom" McCahill, under the right conditions this sleeper of an automobile is good for a little better than 118 mph.

The 1957-59 models from Chrysler had been long on style but short on quality. Body construction was downright flimsy, the cars were subject to squeaks and rattles, the "dreaded tinworm" feasted on the under-side of the

headlamp brows, and the level of fit and finish left much to be desired. To a great extent this was remedied when the 1960 models came along, featuring unitized body-and-frame construction; and the '61s were at least as good.

In a couple of respects, Chrysler's engineering was unconventional during

TABLE OF PRICES AND WEIGHTS

	Price, 6/8 cyl.	Weight, 6/8 cyl.
Polara Series, 122" wheelbase		
Sedan, 4-door, 6-passenger	------- /$2,966	------ /3,700
Hardtop sedan, 4-door, 6-passenger	------- / 3,110	------ /3,740
Hardtop coupe, 2-door, 6-passenger	------- / 3,032	------ /3,690
Convertible coupe, 6-passenger	------- / 3,252	------ /3,765
Station wagon, 4-door, 6-passenger	------- / 3,294	------ /4,115
Station wagon, 4-door, 9-passenger	------- / 3,409	------ /4,125
Dart Series, 118" wheelbase*		
Phoenix Sub-series		
Sedan, 4-door, 6-passenger	2,595 / 2,715	3,350 / 3,535
Hardtop sedan, 4-door, 6-passenger	2,677 / 2,796	3,385 / 3,555
Hardtop coupe, 2-door, 6-passenger	2,618 / 2,737	3,325 / 3,520
Convertible coupe, 6-passenger	------/ 2,988	----- / 3,580
Pioneer Sub-series		
Sedan, 2-door, 6-passenger	2,410 / 2,530	3,290 / 3,460
Sedan, 4-door, 6-passenger	2,459 / 2,578	3,335 / 3,510
Hardtop coupe, 2-door, 6-passenger	2,488 / 2,607	3,335 / 3,500
Station wagon, 4-door, 6-passenger	2,787 / 2,906	3,740 / 3,940
Station wagon, 4-door, 9 passenger	2,892 / 3,011	3.825 / 4,005
Seneca Sub-series		
Sedan, 2-door, 6-passenger	2,278 / 2,397	3,290 / 3,470
Sedan, 4-door, 6-passenger	2,330 / 2,449	3,335 / 3,515
Station wagon, 4-door, 6-passenger	2,695 / 2,815	3,740 / 3,920
*Dart station wagons used 122" wheelbase		
Lancer Series, 106.5" wheelbase		
"170" Sub-series		
Sedan, 2-door, 6-passenger	2,007 /------	2,585 /------
Sedan, 4-door, 6-passenger	2,069 /------	2,595 /------
Station wagon, 4-door, 6-passenger	2.382 /------	2,760 /------
"770" Sub-Series		
Sport coupe, 2-door, 6-passenger	2,092 /------	n/a /------
Sedan, 4-door, 6-passenger	2,154 /------	2,605 /------
Hardtop coupe, 2-door, 6-passenger		
Station wagon, 4-door, 6-passenger		

Total 1961 model year production: 258,467
Total 1961 calendar year production: 220,779
Rank in industry: 9th

The Dart had power aplenty, thanks to its lively 360-cu.in. V-8 that produced 305 hp and a very usable 395-lbs.ft. of torque.

DODGE DART "PHOENIX" VS. THE COMPETITION

Here's how our driveReport car stacked up against three of its major competitors. Note that the Dodge, the Chevrolet, and the Ford all represent the top of their respective manufacturers' lines, while the Pontiac was the entry-level model.

	Dodge Dart Phoenix	Chevrolet Impala	Ford Galaxie	Pontiac Catalina
Base price, 2-door hardtop	$2,737	$2,704	$2,713	$2,766
Shipping weight (w/std. equip.)	3,520 lb.	3,480 lb.	3,643 lb.	3,680 lb.
Wheelbase	118"	119"	119"	119"
Overall length	209.4"	209.3"	209.9"	210.0"
Overall width	78.7"	78.4"	79.9"	78.2"
Overall height (unloaded)	56.7"	57.6"	57.0"	57.7"
Track, front/rear	61.5"/60.2"	60.3"/59.3"	61.0"/60.0"	62.5"/62.5"
Displacement, std. V-8 engine	318.2 cu. in.	283.0 cu. in.	291.6 cu. in.	388.9 cu. in.
Horsepower @ rpm	230/4,400	170/4,200	175/4,200	215/3,600
Torque @ rpm	340/2,400	275/2,200	279/2,200	390/2,000
Compression ratio	9.00:1	8.50:1	8.80:1	8.60:1
Carburetion	1 dual throat	1 dual throat	1 dual throat	1 dual throat
Automatic transmission	TorqueFlite	Powerglide	Ford-O-Matic	HydraMatic
Speeds	3	2	2	3
Torque converter ratio	2.20	2.10	2.60	1.20
Final drive ratio (w/automatic)	2.93	3.08	3.00	2.69
Front springs	Torsion bars	Coil	Coil	Coil
Rear springs	Leaf	Leaf	Coil	Coil
Steering ratio (power, over-all)	19.2	24.0	23.0	22.5
Turning diameter (curb/curb)	42'–5"	40'–10"	41'–0"	46'–0"
Braking area (sq. in.)	184.0	185.6	180.0	173.7
Drum diameter	11"	11"	11"	11"
Tire size (as original)	7.50/14	7.50/14	7.50/14	8.00/14

this period. Commencing with the 1957 models, the cars featured torsion bars in lieu of coil springs up front. The result was a slightly firmer ride than that of the competition, but handling was substantially improved. And those who specified the excellent three-speed TorqueFlite automatic transmission (as most buyers did) found it controlled by means of mechanical push-buttons rather than the customary lever. Personally, I always liked the push-buttons, but ultimately they were dropped in order that controls might be stan

WHAT'S IT WORTH?

Although the Dodge Phoenix was mass produced, we had to go back to the February 2000 edition of *Hemmings Motor News* to find a Phoenix for sale. The ad for this particular example read: 1961 Phoenix 2-door hardtop, ps, pb, air, new 318, red with red/white interior, $4,500.

A similar model, the Custom 880, but in four-door trim, featured 38,000 original miles, 361-cu.in. V-8, push-button automatic, ps, pb, and had an asking price of $6,000.

Drum-type secondary gauges include this very unusual, not-so-easy-to-read clock.

dardized throughout the industry, a legitimate safety concern.

Owner Mike Squires of Roseville, California, a long-time Mopar fancier, found his unusual Dodge Dart through an ad in a car magazine. He was attracted, first, by the fact that as a child he had visited a Dodge showroom with his father, where both of them had admired the 1961 models. So the acquisition was motivated partly by sentiment on his part. But beyond that, he was attracted by the car's performance potential, powered as it is by the D-500 engine and supported by heavier-than-standard suspension. No doubt his attention was also caught by the car's extensive list of optional equipment (see specification table).

A full restoration, both mechanical and cosmetic, was required in order to bring the car to its current condition. The hard part, Mike reports, was finding the correct parts, a task that sent him out combing the wrecking yards. Still, it was Squires's good fortune to find excellent restoration facilities in his hometown of Roseville, where the work was done by the Roseville Rod and Custom Shop and Jason's Hot Rod Shop. A complete mechanical overhaul was undertaken; nicks and dents were removed, and the car repainted in its original Silver Gray color; and with the exception of the headliner and the plastic door panels, the interior was completely redone.

Mike shows the car from time to time, and has taken several awards with it. But he really treats it as a driver, on both short and long hauls; for it is an excellent "road" car. 🕭

Could there be a more distinctive rear?

Deep bench seats are very comfortable.

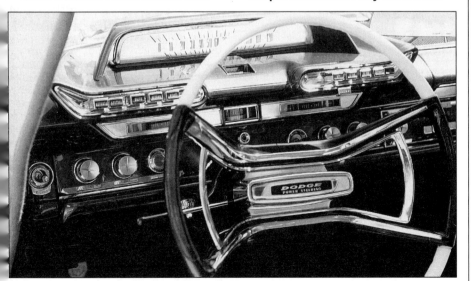

Push-button controls for the automatic transmission are located on left.

WHAT TO PAY

Low	Average	High
$3,200	$6,000	$9,000

SPECIALISTS

Andy Bernbaum
315 Franklin St.
Dept. SIA-180
Newton, MA 02458
617-244-1118
www.oldmoparparts.com

Kanter Auto Products
76 Monroe St.
Dept. SIA-180
Boonton, NJ 07005
973-334-9575
www.kanter.com

Original Auto Interiors
7869 Trumble Rd.
Dept. SIA-180
Columbus, MI 48063
810-727-2486

Pro Antique Auto Parts
50 King Spring Rd.
Dept. SIA-180
Windsor Locks, CT 06096
860-623-8275
www.proantiqueauto.com

Roberts Motor Parts
17 Prospect St.
Dept. SIA-180
West Newbury, MA 01985
978-363-5407
www.robertsmotorparts.com

CLUB SCENE

California Chrysler Products Club
P.O. Box 2660
Castro Valley, CA 94546
510-889-0533

Chrysler Product Owners Club
806 Winhall Way
Silver Spring, MD 20904
301-622-2962

National Chrysler Products Club
160 Joyce Drive
Fayetteville, PA 17222
717-352-7673

Slant 6 Club of America
P.O. Box 4414
Salem, OR 97302
503-581-2230

Walter P. Chrysler (WPC) Club
P.O. Box 3504
Kalamazoo, MI 49003
616-375-55350

1962 Dodge Lancer
A Valiant Effort?

By Arch Brown
Photos by Jim Tanji

IT was 1962, a great year for science and technology. In February that year Lieutenant Colonel John H. Glenn, Jr. became the first American in orbit when he circled the globe three times in the Friendship VII. Three months later Navy Lieutenant Commander Scott Carpenter duplicated the feat in the Aurora VII, and in October Navy Commander Walter Schirra shattered both previous records by making six orbits of the earth.

On July 10, meanwhile, "Telstar," an experimental communications satellite, revolutionized the communications industry by successfully transmitting—for the first time—trans-Atlantic television signals.

Small wonder, then, that when the Century 21 Exposition opened in Seattle on April 21—the first World's Fair to be held in the United States since 1940—its theme was the "Space Age."

The year marked a low point in the

career of former Vice President Richard Nixon. Defeated for the California governorship by incumbent "Pat" Brown, Nixon bitterly assailed the press for allegedly treating him unfairly, adding—in what was widely presumed to be his political swan song—"You won't have Nixon to kick around any more." He was, the pundits were certain, washed up.

It was an even worse year for screen star Marilyn Monroe. She died of an overdose of pills, evidently a suicide.

For the New York Yankees, however, 1962 was a year of triumph in which, in the seventh game, they edged out the San Francisco Giants to win the World Series.

The Cuban missile crisis found the world poised on the brink of war, as the

United States and the Soviet Union stood eyeball-to-eyeball in a confrontation over atomic missile sites then under construction in the Caribbean. In the end it was Premier Khrushchev who blinked, agreeing to remove the rocket bases in return for President John F. Kennedy's promise not to invade Cuba. But if 1962 was a good year for science and diplomacy—not to mention baseball—it was a terrible year for the Chrysler Corporation. Plymouth, which had occupied its traditional third place as recently as three years earlier, had plummeted to eighth position. Dodge, long (but not lately) the industry's number four nameplate, was reduced to ninth rank, garnering only 3.6 percent of the market—scarcely more than half its customary share. Overall, the corporation's market penetration came to 10.3 percent; traditionally it had been twice that figure.

There were a number of problems, not

the least of which was Chrysler's styling. Virgil Exner, the company's controversial chief stylist, had departed the previous year, his place taken by the more conservative Elwood Engel, but of course the 1962 designs had been laid down long before Engel's arrival. And while the Exner stylings of the midfifties had been the sensation of the industry, by the turn of the decade the master appeared—at least in terms of the corporation's full-sized cars—to have lost his touch.

Then, there was the matter of quality control. Under the leadership of Chrysler Corporation President Lester Lum "Tex" Colbert, a full year had been lopped off the development time of the 1957 models. The short-term result of this strategy, given the striking Exner designs that year, had been that Chrysler had displaced General Motors—for the nonce—as the industry's style leader.

But the long-range outcome of Colbert's speed-up had been pure catastrophe, for the quality of the corporation's 1957 cars was simply appalling. Doors rattled, windows leaked, body panels rusted. Even the traditional durability of Chrysler-built engines appeared, in some instances, to have been eroded. Chrysler's once-proud reputation was seriously damaged as owners of the new cars passed the word to their friends and neighbors. The automotive press picked up the scent, and by 1958 sales of Chrysler products were down by very nearly half, compared to the previous year's total. (Much of this was due to that year's recession, of course. But while the industry as a whole suffered a 30.6 percent drop in passenger car production, Chrysler was off by 47.4 percent.)

The restyled, unit-bodied 1960 models were much more solidly constructed than the 1957–59 cars, but quality control still wasn't all that it should have been. Labor problems, especially at the old Dodge main plant in Hamtramck, Michigan, were a scandal, with the inevitable result that workmanship often left much to be desired.

Meanwhile, a new element had been introduced into the automotive mix: small cars. Traditionally disdained by Detroit, the time had come when they could no longer be ignored. Imports, spearheaded by Germany's Volkswagen, were grabbing an ever-increasing share of the market. And American Motors' Rambler had zoomed from twelfth place in 1957 to seventh in 1958, then fourth in '59. When 1960 came along, it had elbowed Plymouth aside to become America's third most popular automobile. (The Rambler held that position through the following year, by the way. Some say it might have kept it longer had not George Romney, AMC's presi-

dent, heeded the siren call of politics, leaving his company in less capable hands.)

And so, for the 1960 season the Big Three fielded compact cars of their own. Ford had its Falcon, Chevrolet its Corvair and Plymouth the Valiant. And all of them were doing rather well for themselves.

All of which was cold comfort to the Dodge dealers. They wanted a compact car of their own. Chrysler happened to be strapped for cash at the time, thanks to Colbert's enthusiastic—if injudicious—investment policies; so there was no hope of developing anything really distinctive. But with comparatively minor modifications, the appearance of the Valiant was substantially altered, and thus for 1961 Dodge was able to present the Lancer.

In an effort to preserve at least a suggestion of the tradition that a Dodge represented a step up from a Plymouth, the newcomer was a few inches longer than its Valiant "parent." The difference was all in the sheet metal; both cars rode on the same 106.5-inch wheelbase, and power came from the same 101-horsepower "slant six" engine. A good many people thought the Lancer was the better-looking of the two, chiefly because it avoided the Valiant's fake

spare tire, outlined on the trunk lid—a styling excess that songwriter Richard Carpenter wryly refers to as the "toilet seat."

If the Lancer failed to set any sales records, at least it kept 1961 from being a complete rout for Dodge, whose senior vehicles that year—with their conch-shaped rear fenders—were almost painfully ugly. With model year sales of just under 75,000 cars, the Lancer accounted for about a third of Dodge's total, and probably represented the margin of solvency for many a dealer.

There was little change in the Lancer for 1962, And the most visible difference was not for the better. The attractive front-end treatment of the 1961 model, which had evidently been inspired by the bridgework of the 1960 Pontiac, was replaced by an unattractive convex grille, not unlike the head of a certain brand of electric shaver. At the same time, the Valiant traded the "toilet seat" for a smooth rear deck and tidied up its nose with a Chrysler-like grille. Result: Lancer sales for 1962 fell by almost exactly the same amount that Valiant's gained. Make no mistake about it, styling does sell automobiles.

In truth, the styling of both the Valiant and the Lancer had been controversial from the start. To some observers their

1962 Dodge Lancer

Above: *Fin or fender trim? Lancer helped distinguish itself from Valiant with special tail-lamp treatment.* *Below:* *These rear fender flashes were part of the dress-up package on the GT.*

long hood, short deck configuration gave them a smart, dashing, European flavor. To others the design was too "busy." But at least, nobody called it bland.

There is no controversy, however, when it comes to the engineering that went into these little cars. In that area they were outstanding.

• The "slant six" engine was easily the best-performing, and probably the most durable powerplant in its class.

• The optional automatic transmission was a new, lightweight version of the already famous Torqueflite, arguably the finest automatic on the market at that time.

• "Torsion-Aire" suspension, employing torsion bars at the front and traditional semi-elliptics to the rear, gave the Lancer/Valiant twins excellent handling characteristics and riding qualities that belied their short wheelbase and light weight.

Initially the Lancer came in two series, the base 170 and the upscale 770. These were retained for 1962, and a third, single-model series was added: the Lancer GT. Both two- and four-door sedans as well as a four-door station wagon could be had in either of the first two series, while the GT came only as a two-door hardtop.

Among the popular Lancer options was the larger, 225-c.i.d. version of the slant-six engine. This was the base engine for the full-sized Dodges and

Dodge Lancer GT versus the Competition

	Dodge Lancer	Chevy II Nova	Pontiac Tempest	Mercury Comet	Studebaker Lark VI
Body style	GT hardtop	Sport coupe	Sport coupe	S-22 sport coupe	Hardtop coupe
Base price, f.o.b. factory	$2,257	$2 ,264	$2,294	$2,368	$2,218
Standard engine	ohv 6	ohv 6	ohv 4	ohv 6	ohv 6
Displacement (cu. in.)	170.0	194.0	194.5	170.0	169.6
Hp @ rpm	101/4,400	120/4,400	110/3,800	101/4,400	112/4,500
Torque @ rpm	155/2,400	177/2,400	190/2,000	156/2,400	154/2,000
Compression ratio	8.2:1	8.5:1	8.6:1	8.7:1	8.25:1
Optional auto. trans.	3-speed	2-speed	2-speed	2-speed	3-speed
Axle ratio	3.23:1	3.08:1	3.08:1	3.20:1	3.73:1
Effective braking area	153.5	145.0	108.9	114.3	146.4 sq. in.
Brake drum diameter	9 in.	9 in.	9 in.	9 in.	10 in.
Front suspension	Torsion Bars	Coil Springs	Coil Springs	Coil springs	Coil springs
Rear springs	Semi-elliptic	Single leaf	Coil	Semi-elliptic	Semi-elliptic
Rear axle	Solid	Soli d	Swing	Solid	Solid
Steering ratio (overall, :l)*	28.7	25.4	23.6	27.0	28.0
Turning diameter (curb/curb)	36' 5"	38' 5"	37' 9"	39' 11"	39' 0"
Tire size	6.50 x 13	6.00 x 13	6.00 x 15	6.00 x 13	6.00 x 15
Wheelbase	106.5 in.	110 in.	112 in.	114 in.	109 in.
Overall length	188.8 in.	183.0 in.	189.3 in.	194.8 in.	188.0 in.
Overall width	72.3 in.	70.8 in.	72.2 in.	70.4 in.	71.3 in.
Overall height (unloaded)	55.7 in.	56.5 in.	55.2 in.	56.3 in.	N/a
Shipping weight (lb.)	2,560	2,530	2,800	2,458	2,765
Hp/c.i.d.	.644	.619	.566	.594	.660
Lb./c.i.d.	11.4	13.0	14.4	14.5	16.3
Lb./Hp	17.7	21.1	25.5	24.3	24.7

* Non-powered steering

Plymouths at that time, but as installed in the compact models it was often furnished with an aluminum block. The base 170-c.i.d. engine was a cast-iron unit, as was the 225 employed for the larger cars.

Not surprisingly, given the sporty hardtop's special appeal to the younger set, nearly all the GT models left the factory with the larger engine. For an extra $47—a reasonable figure, even in those days—the buyer had 145-horsepower on tap instead of the standard 101. A bargain it was, and the penalty in fuel mileage was minimal.

Even with the base 170 engine, however, the performance of the Lancer/ Valiant compacts was little short of astonishing. An independent test conducted by *Car Life* magazine produced a top speed of 95 miles an hour in a car equipped with the automatic transmission, and *Motor Trend* clocked zero-to-sixty in 16.1 seconds, using a similar car. Not enough to send anyone to the chiropractor with a dislocated neck, to be sure, but very respectable performance for an automobile of such modest horsepower.

The 225-c.i.d. engine, of course, gave an even better account of itself. An inch-longer stroke than that of the 170 mill resulted in an increase in torque from 155 foot-pounds at 2,400 to 215 at 2,800. It was capable of

moving the car from rest to 60 miles an hour in as little as 13.5 seconds, according to "Uncle Tom" McCahill, and its speed topped out at more than a hundred miles an hour. In his typically colorful way, McCahill called the Lancer "a helluva road car, as capable as a

gorilla in a saloon fight."

One Lancer owner, reporting to *Popular Mechanics* auto editor Jim Whipple, described the Lancer as "the poor man's Jaguar; the best handling car at high speeds that I've ever driven." There may have been some exaggeration on the part of this obviously proud owner, but Whipple added, "We could fill the rest of the report with such enthusiastic references to the Lancer's roadability. Despite its small size and light weight you can hurl the Lancer over rough roads at high speeds all day without undue discomfort or tension. In this respect, it is a real sports touring car."

Now, a recommendation like that from somebody like Jim Whipple is enough to pique one's interest.

Coincidentally, we received a telephone call from Mike Zampiceni, with whom we had become acquainted through the Nash Car Club. Mike had acquired, he said, a near-mint '62 Dodge Lancer GT, and he wondered whether we'd be interested in using it as a driveReport subject.

We asked for particulars, and as Mike described the car our interest level kept rising: A 36,000-mile automobile, purchased from the young man who had only recently inherited it from the estate of his great aunt, the Lancer's original owner. Sounds good! Original paint, with hardly a blemish on it.

Top: Unlike the early Valiants, Lancers avoided the false spare tire decoration embedded in the trunk lid. Above: GT was top of the line car among Lancers, but it was hardly a "Gran Turismo" in the Ferrari sense.

1962 Dodge Lancer Price List

	Price	Shipping Weight
Series 170	$1,951	2,495 pounds
Sedan, 2-door	$2,011	2,525 pounds
Sedan, 4-door	$2,306	2,685 pounds
Station Wagon, 2-seat	$2,306	2,685 pounds
Series 770		
Sedan, 2-door	$2,052	2,520 pounds
Sedan, 4-door	$2,114	2,540 pounds
Station Wagon, 2-seat	$2,306	2,705 pounds
"GT" Series		
Hardtop, 2-door	$2,257	2,560 pounds

specifications

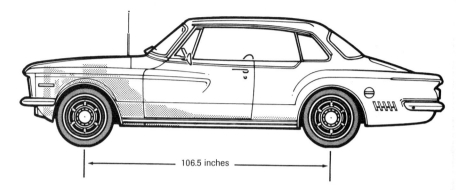

55.9 inches

106.5 inches

1962 Dodge Lancer

Price	$2,257 fob, factory with standard equipment, federal excise +tax and preparation charges included
Options on dR car	Torqueflite transmission, radio, wsw tires, undercoating

ENGINE

Type	Ohv "slant six"
Bore x stroke	3.40 inches x 3.125 inches
Displacement	170 cubic inches
Compression ratio	8.2:1
Max. bhp @ rpm	101 @ 4,400
Max. torque @ rpm	155 @ 2,400
Main bearings	4
Induction system	Carter BBS-3224S 1-bbl carburetor, mechanical fuel pump
Lubrication system	Full pressure
Electrical system	12-volt

TRANSMISSION

Type	Torqueflite 3-speed automatic with torque converter; push-button controls
Ratios: 1st	2.45:1
2nd	1.45:1
4th	1.00:1
Reverse	2.20:1
Maximum ratio at stall	2.20:1

DIFFERENTIAL

Type	Hypoid
Ratio	3.23:1

Drive axles	Semi-floating

STEERING

Type	Manual
Turns lock-to-lock	5.3
Ratios	24.0:1 gear; 28.7:1 overall
Turning circle	39 feet 7 inches wall-to-wall; 36 feet 5 inches curb-to-curb

BRAKES

Type	Hydraulic, drum type; bonded lining
Drum diameter	9 inches
Total effective area	153.5 square inches

CHASSIS & BODY

Construction	Unitized
Body style	GT hardtop

SUSPENSION

Front	Independent control arms with torsion bars
Rear	Semi-elliptic leaf springs, solid axle
Tires	6.50 x 1 3
Wheels	Steel disc

WEIGHTS AND MEASURES

Wheelbase	106.5 inches
Overall length	188.8 inches
Overall width	72.3 inches
Overall height	55.7 inches (unloaded)

Front track	55.9 inches
Rear track	55.6 inches
Min. road clearance	5.4 inches
Shipping weight	2,650 pounds

CAPACITIES

Crankcase	5 quarts (including filter)
Cooling system	12 quarts (including heater)
Fuel tank	14 gallons

PERFORMANCE

Top speed	95 mph*
Acceleration:**	
0-30	mph 5.5 seconds
0-45	mph 9.5 seconds
0-60	mph 16.1 seconds
Gas mileage	18-22 mpg**

* From a *Car Life* road test of a 1960 Plymouth Valiant equipped with 170-c.i.d. engine, Torqueflite transmission and 3.55:1 axle ratio.
** From a *Motor Trend* road test of a 1961 Plymouth Valiant hardtop equipped with 170-c.i.d. engine and Torqueflite transmission (ratio not specified).

PRODUCTION FIGURES (MODEL YEAR)

All Lancer series/ body styles	64,271
GT only	14,140

*Right: driveReport car is highly original, right down to its documents. **Facing page, top:** Torsion bar front suspension helps give Lancer taut, predictable handling. **Bottom:** Instrument layout is pleasant and logical. Pushbutton tranny controls are mounted on left.*

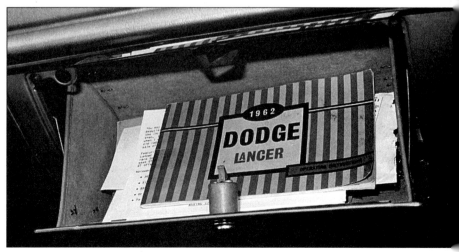

1962 Dodge Lancer

Even better! But when Mike told us that it was powered by a 170-c.i.d. engine we didn't believe him. So few GT's were equipped with the base engine that some sources actually list the 225 as standard equipment for that model. We knew that was incorrect, but we could hardly believe that we had actually stumbled upon the rarest of all Lancers: a 101-horsepower GT.

We had to go see for ourselves.

Of course, Mike was right. He was right about the car's condition, too. Except for a tear in the vinyl-upholstered driver's seat and a spot in the carpeting where the lady's heel had dug a hole, the Lancer looks brand new.

We learned that the smart little hardtop had been factory-ordered by Alice Osterheld, its original owner, to her own specifications. Hence the unusual combination of the base engine in a top-of-the-line car—not the sort of thing that a dealer might be expected to order for stock. That Mrs. Osterheld was well along in years was attested to by a well-weathered American Automobile Association bumper decal, proclaiming 50 years of membership.

The finish on this automobile is just as spotless as Zampiceni had described it. The color is known as "Coral Gray"—really a light beige with just a hint of rose in it. Very nice; and practical, too. The dark chocolate carpeting is deep and luxurious, but the vinyl upholstery—color-keyed to the Lancer's exterior—doesn't appear to be of equivalent quality. Thus, no doubt, the split in the driver's seat.

Nor are the individual front seats especially comfortable. They're not true "buckets," no matter what Dodge Division's hucksters called them. Their position is much too erect, and no provision is made for adjusting the angle of the backrests. Lateral support, as well as support to the lower back, is minimal.

On the other hand, leg room, both front and rear, is very good for a small car. Head room is fully adequate. Visibility is excellent in all directions. But unfortunately, the padding on the rear seat is too thin for comfort.

1962 Dodge Lancer

Above: *Upholstery quality isn't up to expectations.* **Below:** *Dash has unusual shape; radio and speaker can't be missed.*

The narrow-rimmed steering wheel is set at exactly the correct angle for our taste, and as we got under way we found the non-power steering to be delightfully light—though slower than we like. The Torqueflite transmission, like all Chrysler Corporation automatics from 1956 through 1964, is controlled by means of mechanical pushbuttons fitted to the dash on the driver's left. A parking sprag, taking the place of "park" position on most automatic shift quadrants, is activated by means of a small lever located beneath the dash panel.

Facing the driver, in addition to the speedometer, are factory-supplied fuel, temperature and ampere gauges, to which Mike has added an aftermarket oil pressure indicator. To the right of the instruments is another row of pushbuttons, matching the transmission controls on the other side. These activate the heater, an excellent fresh-air unit. And above the panel is a small hood, evidently for the purpose of preventing the reflection of the panel lights in the windshield. A simple enough idea, but a good one.

At center-dash there is the optional radio. It's a tube-type unit, slow to warm up, but its tone is good and selectivity is excellent. And the Lancer's dual horns have an impressive sound, suggesting a much larger car than this diminutive Dodge.

As we had anticipated, with the 101-horsepower engine, the Lancer's acceleration is no better than adequate. But even at 55 or 60, given just a little time

The Mouse That Roared: Slant Six

There are always those drivers who want a little extra punch. And there are those who want a *lot* of it. For the former group, the Lancer's optional 225-c.i.d. engine filled the bill very nicely. But for the all-out performance enthusiast it clearly didn't make it. By 1964 there would be a lightweight, 273-c.i.d. V-8 for those who wanted that "something extra" in their Mopar compacts. But in the meanwhile, what was a fellow to do?

Chrysler Corporation had the answer. Available as a dealer-installed option for either the 170- or the 225-cubic-inch engine was the "Hyper-Pack." For $403.30 plus labor—figure an extra hundred, there—the Lancer/Valiant owner got:
- A larger-capacity carburetor, with intake manifold to match;
- A freer-flowing exhaust system; and
- A camshaft designed to shove the peak torque point upward, from 2,800 to 4,200 rpm.

Displacement and compression ratio remained unaltered, but the package resulted in some startling differences in power output. Horsepower of the little 170 mill was boosted from 101 to 148, though it had to turn 5,200 rpm in order to produce that figure. Correspondingly, the 225 engine's 145 horsepower was transformed all the way to 196—again at 5,200 rpm. That's more power than a number of good-sized V-8's developed in those days

Translated into performance terms, the Hyper-Pack cut about one-third off the Lancer's zero-to-sixty time—and even more off the zero-to-eighty. Fifteen miles an hour was added to the top speed, and elapsed time for the standing quarter-mile was chopped (in the case of the 225-c.i.d. engine) from 19.0 to 16.4 seconds—while speed at the end of that run was increased from 70.5 miles an hour to an even 80.

Of course, the Hyper-Pack exacted its price. And not only in initial cost, though the extra 20 percent added to the window-sticker figure was hardly insignificant. Nor was the price measured entirely in dollars and cents, though a five-mile-per-gallon

loss in fuel mileage wasn't to be sneezed at, either! But, perhaps most importantly, with the Hyper-Pack fitted, the "slant six" was no longer the smooth, docile powerplant that had become an instant favorite with just about everyone who had driven it. Because of the changes in the torque curve brought about by that sizzling camshaft, the engine had to be run at very high rpms in order to tap its power potential. *Car Life* explained the difference this way: "The Lancer engine, after having been hyper-packed, is neither smooth nor unobtrusive. The radical valve-timing of the substitute camshaft takes care of smoothness with dispatch, while the fact that the 4-barrel carburetor of the package is so huge that no room remains under the hood for an air cleaner takes care of the unobtrusiveness...."

Did the high performance make the ragged edges worthwhile? Not many buyers thought so, evidently. So, for most of us, the hotshot Mopar compacts had to wait for the coming, later in the decade, of the new V-8.

it will pick up plenty of speed for passing. The car cruises smoothly and quietly at 65. That little engine is a gem, and evidently Dodge did a good job with the sound insulation, for it's very quiet in the passengers' quarters. We don't make a practice of piloting our driveReport cars flat-out, for obvious reasons, and we didn't try to do so in this instance. But it's easy for us to believe that in proper tune these little cars will readily top 90 miles an hour.

There were owners' complaints, when this Lancer was new, of squeaks and rattles in the body. We didn't hear any; Mike's car is tight and solid. We have no doubt that the quality control at Chrysler's Los Angeles assembly plant, where this unit was built, was superior to that at the main plant in Hamtramck.

The Lancer provides a surprisingly comfortable ride, one that would do credit to a much larger, heavier car. This is an automobile that, apart from its mediocre seating, would make an excellent long-distance traveler, as well as a handy little number for in-town use.

At the same time, the Lancer's torsion bar suspension is firm enough to give the car excellent cornering characteristics. It stays flat, is easy to control, and does just about exactly what the driver tells it to do. Whatever the assembly-line problems may have been (and they're manifested in this car by such annoyances as window cranks that are stiff and balky), the engineering that went into the design of Chrysler Corporation's compacts was outstanding.

Chrysler advertising made much of the corporation's "Total Contact" brakes in 1962. Bonded, rather than riveted, lining was what they were talking about. We found that the binders do their work well. No swerve, no fade, no excessive pedal pressure required. Power brakes were an available option, but we can't imagine why anyone would need them. The Lancer, though it was among the lightest cars in its class, provided more effective braking area than any of its competitors (see sidebar, page 104), and the effect of this is readily apparent to the driver.

When we stopped for gas we noted that the fuel tank is located well forward. This is an excellent feature from a safety standpoint, of course; no Pinto-esque pyrotechnics in the event of a rear-ender. It also makes possible a flat floor in the trunk, with the spare tire recessed beneath. The 13.5 cubic feet of storage space is thus arranged for maximum utility and convenience. But the gasoline filler pipe has a tendency to spit back and spill the fuel down the side of the car.

The trunk on this car, by the way, looks as though it has never been used. The same is true of the immaculate ashtray. This is one of the nicest unre-

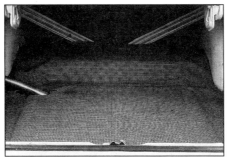

*Top left: GT offered little extras like dual ashtrays in back. **Above left:** There's a generous amount of trunk space for a compact, thanks in large part to hiding the spare, **above right**, under the trunk floor.*

stored, original automobiles that we've encountered in our travels.

If it were possible for us to move back through the dimension of time and find ourselves once more in 1962, it would be relatively easy for a Dodge salesman to interest us in a Lancer—and especially in a smart little GT, though we'd be happy to pop the extra $47 for the optional engine. For a conveniently sized, good-performing, comfortable yet economical automobile—and one that's fun to drive—it would be hard to beat! ᐅᐅ

The Remarkable Slant Six

It was apparent, by the time development got under way in 1957 on Chrysler Corporation's first overhead-valve six, that styling trends would dictate lower hood lines for future models. Since an overhead-valve engine, by the very nature of things, is taller than the L-head configuration that had characterized all of Chrysler's previous six-cylinder engines, this posed something of a dilemma.

The solution was as simple as it was ingenious: Chrysler engineers canted the engine 30 degrees to the right of vertical. At the same time, incidentally, the manual transmission on cars so equipped was inclined 30 degrees to the left, providing a more convenient location for the shift lever and permitting the use of a lower tunnel down the center of the passenger compartment.

But the lower hood line wasn't the only advantage gained by tipping the engine. Not even the most important one, in fact. For the tilt permitted the use of a long intake manifold, likened by one contemporary writer to "a bunch of bananas." This improved the engine's breathing capacity—Dodge called it a "semi-ram effect"—providing better performance, greater fuel economy and, according to the company's claims, extended engine life. High-turbulence, wedge-shaped combustion chambers further increased the

powerplant's efficiency, and six low-restriction, gradually curved exhaust pipes effectively removed the burned gases. Altogether, the "slant six" was (and remains to this day) a remarkably efficient design.

There were other superior features to the new "six," in both its 170- and 225-c.i.d. dimensions. An extra rigid crankshaft was cradled in larger bearings than Chrysler's 318- and 383-c.i.d. V-8's—the same size, in fact, as those of the Imperial's huge, 413-c.i.d. powerplant. Even the crankpin journals were bigger than those of the 318.

And there was one more under-the-hood feature, as significant as any Chrysler engineering coup in a number of years: With the "slant six," upon its introduction in 1960, came the alternator. Instantly, the old-style generator became obsolete, and it wasn't long before the rest of the industry followed the Chrysler Corporation's lead. For the alternator—really an alternating-current generator—supplied far more current at low engine speeds than the traditional direct-current generator. And it was far lighter than the generator, besides.

From the start, the Chrysler Corporation had prided itself its engineering prowess. The "slant six" gave it one claim to fame.

Senior Compact

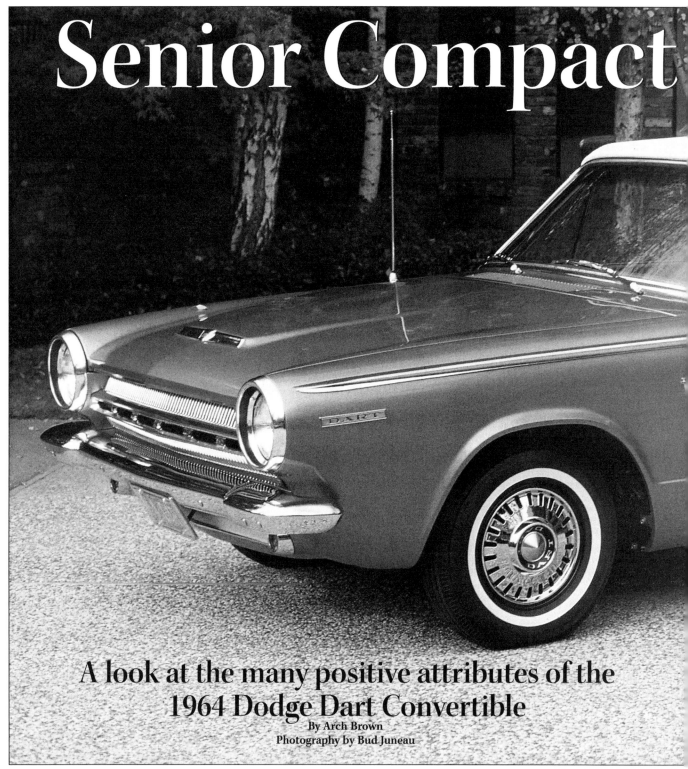

A look at the many positive attributes of the 1964 Dodge Dart Convertible

By Arch Brown
Photography by Bud Juneau

The Dodge Dart that my wife and I owned and put nearly 100,000 miles on over a period of eight years was a bottom-of-the-line Series 170 sedan, equipped with the 273-cubic-inch V-8 engine, TorqueFlite transmission, factory air, foam-padded seat (a $7 option, as I recall) and very little else. Our driveReport Dart, on the other hand, is a middle-trim-line Series 270 convertible. It has power steering, and although it lacks the factory air with which our sedan was fitted, it has been provided with heavy-duty torsion

bars, normally reserved by Dodge in those days for air-conditioned models.

The bench seat is nothing to write home about, as far as lumbar support, in today's terms, according to photographer Bud Juneau who drove Cliff Fales' beautifully restored convertible. There's not much padding, and you're not very far off the floor. It's certainly no worse than what most manufacturers were offering at this time, but it's no more than barely adequate, in my estimation.

Of interest is the transmission, con-

trolled by push-buttons to the far left of the instrument panel. There's a parking sprag, controlled by a lever that you push up in order to release the transmission lock. Buttons are labeled, top-to-bottom, R-N-D-2-1. Farther left are the wiper/washer control and the light switch. Instruments include gauges for gasoline, temperature and alternator, while a red light signals any trouble with oil pressure. The speedometer reads to 110 mph, and the odometer shows 112.6 miles. This represents how far the car has been

driven since its restoration was completed. Total mileage, its owner estimates, is about 165K.

To the right are heater controls above the radio, then the glove box. Of special interest is a card hanging from the heater button, giving instructions on how to use the heater. Most people would throw this item away the first week. This one is original, and a nice item to have. The horn button at the center of the steering wheel says "Dodge Golden Anniversary, 1914-1964," a rare and interesting, if minor, feature.

The engine starts with the key, with the transmission in either neutral or park. The double-reduction starter, typical of Chrysler products of that era, has a distinctive, powerful sound. The engine is quiet, despite the absence of hydraulic valve lifters. Press the "D" button and the car gets under way.

The Chrysler full-time power steering might be criticized for permitting too little road feel, but one gets accustomed to that characteristic. I like the slender steering wheel rim, which feels good to the hands.

The power steering mechanism, rebuilt by an Ohio outfit, has a firmer feel than a standard unit and is in superb condition—as is the entire car.

The shocks feel good; and the brakes stop the car nice and even, in an absolutely straight line, with very little nosedive. The transmission, personally rebuilt by owner Cliff Fales, shifts very nicely, responding promptly to whatever push-button is punched. TorqueFlite was probably the best automatic on the market in 1964.

The car corners without much plow, in

111

ASKING PRICES

With more than 180,000 Dodge Darts built in 1964, you'd think that more would have been ordered with the V-8 than only 20,000. According to our findings in *Hemmings Motor News*, we found only one convertible advertised for sale during the last year that was V-8 equipped. While they aren't as easy to come by as a six-cylinder model, they are very affordable even if in excellent condition. We've also included two Dart GT coupes for comparison, just in case you prefer having a roof over your head.

Dart 1964 GT convertible, anniversary edition, 273 V-8, AT, bucket seats, rust-free black-plate California Dodge, $7,500.

Dart 1964 GT coupe, 38,000 rust-free Colorado miles, 273 V-8, push-button automatic, cold factory air, nice white original paint, near mint blue bucket seat interior, manuals, records, beautiful, $6,500.

Dart 1964 GT coupe, original 273 V-8, complete car, straight body, excellent drive train, some rust but minimal amounts, needs restoration, $3,200.

CLUB SCENE

National Chrysler Products Club
5844 West Eddy Street
Chicago, IL 60634
773-685-4980
Dues: $20/year; Membership: 700

Chrysler Products Owners Club
7004 Vancouver Road
Springfield, VA 22152
703-451-6012
Dues: $18/year; Membership: 350

Walter P. Chrysler Club
P.O. Box 3504
Kalamazoo, MI 49003
616-375-5535
Dues: $25/year; Membership: 5,500

WHAT TO PAY

Low	Average	High
$3,000	$6,000	$9,000

PROS & CONS

Pros
Ruggedly reliable
Affordable drop-top fun
Powerful and torquey V-8

Cons
Poor braking ability
Styling is a little lackluster
Difficult to find in good shape

Fine details abound, such as protruding bumper end and frenched-in headlamp design.

Emblem fitted atop each interior door.

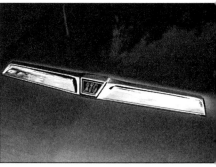

Fake hood scoop trimmed in chrome.

part no doubt because Cliff has equipped it with heavy-duty torsion bars, taken from a later car equipped with air conditioning. (Probably our old sedan was also fitted with heavy-duty bars as well, for it came with factory air, and for the most part it cornered better than most of the cars we've owned over the years.)

In summarizing his experience with the Dart, Bud says, "It's a pretty decent handling car. I'm impressed with it. I like it. It feels to me like it would be very good on the highway. It's a nice size. You could park it easily and feel very comfortable driving it. And when I got on it a little bit, it felt fairly peppy. You could have a good time racing with certain people, if you were a teenager!"

There's not a lot that I can add to Bud's comments, but perhaps I can elaborate on a point or two, based on having owned a similar car. We drove ours from 1964 to '72, then passed it on to our son, who squeezed another year or so out of it. We always liked that car; and although it had a couple of conspicuous faults, of which I'll have more to say presently, on the whole it served us exceptionally well.

When the compact Dart (as differentiated from the heavier 1960-62 models bearing that name) was first introduced in 1963, its standard engine was the 170 cu.in., 101hp slant six. Performance was better than one might have expected given such a modest displacement, but most buyers opted for the 225-cu.in. 145hp version—a bargain at $47 extra.

The 1964 Darts were little changed apart from an attractive new grille and a different rear window treatment on the sedans. But early in that model year the V-8 became available, priced just $61 higher than the Series 225-equipped models. Needless to say, with 180 horsepower on tap, the Dart V-8 was a lively, responsive car; I once saw 100 on the speedometer! It also offered a remarkably comfortable pleasantly firm ride, thanks in part to its 111-inch wheelbase, the longest chassis of any compact then on the market.

I mentioned two drawbacks to these otherwise excellent little cars. The first of these has to do with balance. The Dart V-8 outweighed the Six by about 180 pounds, a difference of nearly seven percent. Since virtually all of the extra heft is located

With the coming of the boxy Dart in '67, the last remnants of Fifties-era fins are clearly evident in the 270's rear-end design.

13-inch wheels feature full wheelcovers.

over the front wheels, handling qualities are obviously affected. In a sense, this is not entirely a negative characteristic, for it is easy and fun to throw a Dart V-8 into a controlled skid—and equally easy to correct its direction with a slight turn of the wheel. And that's fine, when it's done intentionally and under the right conditions. Once in a while, however, the driver receives an unpleasant surprise.

The other downside to the early Dart V-8s has to do with the brakes. Not to put too fine a point on the matter, they aren't very good. Our son, who is an excellent driver, once ended up in the ditch during an emergency stop. Drums are only nine inches in diameter, and although the 153.5 square inches of lining should be adequate for a comparatively light car, it is my personal guess, though I'm unable to prove it, that the binders don't receive adequate ventilation.

In any case, in restoring our driveReport Dart, Cliff replaced the brakes with ten-inch drums, borrowed from a 1965 model,

SPECIALISTS AND RESTORERS

David Curtis Parts
21002 44th Ave. West
Dept. SIA-188
Lynnwood, WA 98036
425-640-8038
Body, chassis and powertrain components

Golden Oldies Automotive
2728 Hatalla Rd.
Dept. SIA-188
Munnsville, NY 13409
315-843-4657
Used and reproduction Dodge body parts

Hydro-E-Lectric
5475 Williamsburg Dr., Unit 8
Dept. SIA-188
Punta Gorda, FL 33982
800-343-4261
Convertible top motors, switches, latches and hardware

Jim's Auto Parts
40 Lowell Road, Route 38
Dept. SIA-188
Salem, NH 03079
603-898-0535
New, used and reproduction Mopar parts supplier

Jim's Classic Auto
3010 Shue Rd.
Dept. SIA-188
Salisbury, NC 28147
704-857-8647
Body, interior and engine parts

Layson's Restorations
26164 126th Ave. S.E.
Dept. SIA-188
Kent, WA 98031

253-630-4088
Reproduction parts and accessories

Legendary Auto Interiors
121 West Shore Blvd.
Dept. SIA-188
Newark, NY 14513
800-363-8804
www.legendaryautointeriors.com
Original-style repro upholstery kits

Mega Parts
201 Roosevelt St.
PO Box 249
Dept. SIA-188
Coon Valley, WI 54623
608-452-2045
New, used and rebuilt Dodge parts

PRO Antique Auto Parts
50 King Spring Road
Dept. SIA-188
Windsor Locks, CT 06096
860-623-8275
www.proantiqueautoparts.com
New trim parts, carpet sets, wiring and accessories

SMS Auto Fabrics
2325 SE 10th Avenue
Dept. SIA-188
Portland, OR 97214
503-234-1175
Original Dodge upholstery

Wittenborn Auto
133 Woodside Ave.
Dept. SIA-188
Briarcliff Manor, NY 10510
914-941-2744
New and used body parts

Snugly fitting convertible top, whose proportions are just right, operates electronically.

Cast emblem denotes Dart 270 series.

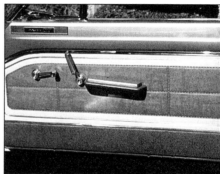

Upholstered door panels are very stylish.

TABLE OF PRICES AND WEIGHTS

Seemingly, for 1964 Dodge offered something for everyone, with a broad array of models at a wide range of prices. Here's the roster:

	Price, 6/8 cylinder	Weight, 6/8 cylinder
Dart 170, 111-inch w/b		
Sedan, 2-door	$1,988/$2,096	2,585/2,765
Sedan, 4-door	$2,053/$2,161	2,620/2,800
Station Wagon (106 w/b)	$2,315/$2,423	2,730/2,910
Dart 270, 111-inch w/b		
Sedan, 2-door	$2,094/$2,202	2,595/2,775
Sedan, 4-door	$2,160/$2,268	2,630/2,810
Hardtop Coupe	$2,182/$2,290	2,640/2,820
Station Wagon (106 w/b)	$2,414/$2,522	2,740/2,920
Convertible Coupe	$2,389/$2,49	2,710/2,890
Dart GT, 111-inch w/b		
Hardtop Coupe	$2,318/$2,426	2,650/2,830
Convertible Coupe	$2,536/$2,644	2,740/2,920
TOTAL PRODUCTION, ALL DART MODELS:		**181,300**
Dodge 330, 119-inch w/b		
Sedan, 2-door	$2,264/$2,372	3,075/3,270
Sedan, 4-door	$2,327/$2,424	3,105/3,300
Station Wagon, 6-pass.	$2,654/$2,762	3,375/3,555
Station Wagon, 9-pass.	$2,755/$2,863	3,445/3,560
Dodge 440, 119-inch w/b		
Sedan, 2-door	$2,401/$2,508	3,085/3,280
Sedan, 4-door	$2,454/$2,562	3,115/3,310
Hardtop Coupe	$2,483/$2,590	3,090/3,285
Station Wagon, 6-pass.	---------/$2,861	-------/3,615
Station Wagon, 9-pass.	---------/$2,962	-------/3,620
Dodge Polara, 119-inch w/b		
Sedan, 4-door	$2,615/$2,722	3,150/3,310
Hardtop Coupe`	$2,637/$2,745	3,115/3,310
Hardtop Sedan	---------/$2,794	-------/3,390
Convertible Coupe	---------/$2,976	-------/3,415
TOTAL PRODUCTION, STANDARD DODGE:		**200,000**
Dodge 880, 122-inch w/b		
Sedan, 4-door	---------/$2.826	-------/3,790
Station Wagon, 6-pass.	---------/$3.155	-------/4,135
Station Wagon, 9-pass.	---------/$3.270	-------/4,195
Custom Sedan	---------/$2,977	-------/3,800
Custom Hardtop Coupe	---------/$3,043	-------/3,785
Custom Hardtop Sedan	---------/$3,122	-------/3,820
Custom Convertible Cpe.	---------/$3,264	-------/3,845
Custom Sta Wag, 6-pass	---------/$3,305	-------/4,135
Custom Sta Wag, 9-pass	---------/$3,420	-------/4,230
TOTAL PRODUCTION, DODGE 880 LINE:		**31,800**

Note: All production figures are rounded off.

where ten-inchers were standard issue in combination with the V-8. The effective area was thus increased only marginally, but the braking action is considerably improved.

Our own Dart did not have power steering, and except in parking maneuvers we liked it that way, although we'd have preferred a slightly faster ratio. Surely manual steering would at least be light enough when fitted to a six-cylinder car.

Let me summarize it this way, taking into account both the Dart that we owned years ago and the beautifully restored and modestly updated hardtop pictured here: If it were 1964 again, and we were once more in the market for an inexpensive car, I would opt for a Dodge Dart without hesitation. But, knowing what I know now, I would specify the 225 slant-six engine (which offered plenty of power, and literally more main bearing surface than Chrysler's famed 383-cu.in. V-8); and I would make every effort to find larger brakes to fit it.

The Chrysler Corporation's first foray into the compact car field was the Valiant. Not the Plymouth Valiant at first, for initially the little car was marketed as an independent marque and was handled exclusively by Chrysler dealers. By 1961 it had become the Plymouth Valiant, though it was still to be found only in Chrysler showrooms. This left the Dodge dealers out in the cold at a time when compacts were becoming increasingly popular. So a Valiant clone, bearing the familiar Lancer name, was devised.

Mopar magic resides in the form of a 180hp, 273-cu.in. V-8 that develops 260-lbs.ft. of peak torque at only 1,600 rpm.

The Lancer was continued through the 1962 season, but it never sold particularly well. Since the Dodge had traditionally been aimed at a market one notch above the Plymouth, there is a certain logic to what happened next. The wheelbase of the smallest Dodge was stretched by five inches, weight was increased by a little over a hundred pounds and styling was attractively modified. Dodge then had a senior compact with a little more leg room than the Valiant and a base price only about $50 above that of the Plymouth compact.

The Dart, during 1963-64 and beyond, came in three trim levels. The entry series, known as the 170, came in three body types: two- and four-door sedans and a station wagon. All were neatly trimmed, in better quality materials than one might expect. In fact, time was to demonstrate that the 170 sedan's upholstery was more durable than that of the 270, next up in the Dart hierarchy! The latter came in the same three body styles, plus the smart convertible coupe displayed on these pages. And at the top of the line was the Dart GT, available as either a hardtop or a ragtop, each equipped with bucket seats, and each featuring a superior quality of vinyl trim.

Cliff, whose immaculately restored 1960 Valiant appeared in *SIA* #144, found his '64 Dodge Dart 270 in the early 1980s. It was sitting by the roadside with a "For

Gear selection on the TorqueFlite transmission operates via push buttons on dash.

Asymmetrical instrument layout may look odd, but all the gauges are easy to read.

Well-appointed and stylish rear features shapely armrests and durable upholstery.

Integrated taillamp looks right, yet horizontal reverse lamp looks like an afterthought.

Trunk is very spacious for a compact.

Sale" sign in its window; and after some dickering, Cliff drove it home.

For the next five years the little ragtop served as a family car, during which time, according to Cliff, "My kids drove it into the ground." Finally, in 1985, with some 165,000 miles on its clock, the Dart was retired. A year later, Cliff started the painstaking job of restoring it to his own high standards. He built a rotisserie for it, took it down completely and sandblasted it down to the bare metal, removing even the factory undercoating. He then applied fresh undercoat to the fenders.

The car received a complete mechanical overhaul, with Chris doing the entire job himself except for the machine work, which was farmed out to experts. Also referred to specialists were the paint, top and upholstery—other than the door panels, which Cliff also did, using the old panels for patterns. New carpeting, ordered from an eastern outfit, didn't fit properly at first; but eventually that problem was resolved.

We caught up with the Dart during its first time out on the show circuit, at the 2000 Chico Concours d'Elegance, a remarkably good small show, held each September on the Chico State University campus in Northern California. There, it took second behind a prize-winning Continental convertible. The little ragtop could hardly have looked any better, or run any smoother, on the day it first rolled off the showroom floor! And you can bet that its brakes didn't work as well! ᐁᐁ

TWO SPORTY COMPACT RAGTOPS

The Dodge Dart, as we've noted elsewhere in this issue, offered two smart compact convertibles for 1964, the 270 series that serves as our principal subject, and the fancier GT, featuring bucket seats. At the time, there was just one other comparably equipped compact convertible on the market: the Ford Falcon Sprint. In order to assure comparability in equipment, this time we're comparing the Dart GT, rather than the 270, with the Falcon Sprint. Here's how they stacked up:

	Dodge Dart GT	Ford Falcon Sprint
Base price	$2,644	$2,660
Wheelbase	111 inches	109.5 inches
Length	195.0	181.1
Track, front/rear	55.9/56.6	56.6/58.0
Shipping weight	2,920 pounds	3,008 pounds
Engine c.i.d.	273.5	260.0
Horsepower @ rpm	180 @ 4,200	164 @ 4,400
Torque @ rpm	260 @ 1,600	258 @ 2,200
Compression ratio	8.80:1	8.70:1
Automatic transmission (opt.)	3-speed	2-speed
Final drive ratio	2.93:1	3.25;1
Turning diameter	38' 8"	38' 10"
Braking area	153.5 square inches	127.8 square inches
Brake drum diameter	9 inches	10 inches
Front suspension	Torsion bars	Coil springs
Tire size	7.00 x 13	6.50 x 13

PARTS PRICES

Carpet set	$314
Front suspension rebuild kit	$180
Front brake drums	$104
Front windshield seal	$90
Pitman arm	$75
Piston ring set	$68
Overhaul gasket set	$60
Motor mount set	$50
Water pump	$40
Oil pump	$35
Trunk weatherstripping	$30
Timing chain	$25

specifications

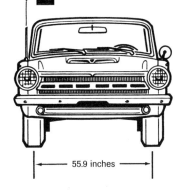

← 55.9 inches →

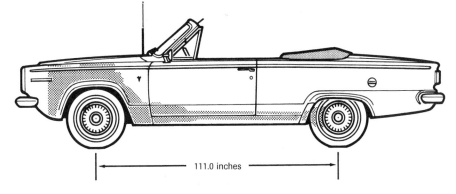

← 111.0 inches →

1964 Dodge Dart 270

Base price	$2,497 f.o.b. factory, federal excise tax included
Options on dR car	TorqueFlite transmission, power steering, radio, white sidewall tires

ENGINE

Type	90-degree OHV V-8
Bore x stroke	3.625 inches x 3.125 inches
Displacement	273.5 cubic inches
Compression ratio	8.8:1
Horsepower @ rpm	180 @ 4,200
Torque @ rpm	260 @ 1,600
Taxable horsepower	42.2
Valve lifters	Mechanical
Main bearings	5
Fuel system	One 2-bbl carburetor, mechanical pump
Lubrication system	Pressure
Exhaust system	Single

TRANSMISSION

Type	TorqueFlite Six 3-speed automatic with torque converter
Ratios: 1st	2.45:1
2nd	1.45:1
3rd	1.00:1
Reverse	2.20:1
Torque converter max. ratio at stall	2.20:1

DIFFERENTIAL

Type	Hypoid
Ratio	2.93:1
Drive axles	Semi-floating

STEERING

Type	Chrysler integral power-assisted
Ratios	15.7 gear; 18.8 overall
Turning diameter	38' 8" curb/curb
Turns lock-to-lock	3.5

BRAKES

Type	4-wheel hydraulic, drum type
Drum diameter	9" originally, now 10"
Effective area	153.5 square inches originally; now 156.2 square inches

CHASSIS & BODY

Construction	All-steel unitized body and frame
Body style	Convertible coupe, seats five
Layout	Front engine, rear-wheel drive

SUSPENSION

Front	Independent, torsion bars
Rear	Rigid axle, longitudinal leaf springs
Shock absorbers	Direct-acting, telescopic
Tires	7.00 x 13

WEIGHTS AND MEASURES

Wheelbase	111 inches
Overall length	196.3 inches
Overall width	69.8 inches
Overall height	53.5 inches (loaded)
Front track	55.9 inches
Rear track	55.6 inches
Road clearance	5.5 inches

Shipping weight	2,890 pounds

CAPACITIES

Crankcase	4 quarts (less filter)
Cooling system	18 quarts (with heater)
Fuel tank	18 gallons
Auto. transmission	17 pints
Rear axle	2 pints

CALCULATED DATA

Engine revs per mile	2,450
Stroke/bore ratio	.914:1
Hp per c.i.d.	.658
Weight per hp	16.1 pounds
Weight per c.i.d.	10.6 pounds
Lb. per sq. in. (brakes)	18.5 (as modified)

PERFORMANCE

Top speed	105 mph
Standing 1/4 mile	17.8 sec./72 mph
Acceleration: 0-30	4.5 seconds
0-40	6.7 seconds
0-50	9.5 seconds
0-60	12.9 seconds
0-70	17.0 seconds
0-80	22.2
0-100	39.0 seconds

(from a July 1964 *Car Life* road test of an identically powered Plymouth Barracuda)

Note: The test crew's Barracuda, while employing the same driveline as our Dodge Dart, was 150 pounds lighter, which could affect performance somewhat.

Dodge Model Year Production, 1914–1975

Year	Units
1914-1915	45,000[1]
1916	71,400[2]
1917	90,000[2]
1918	62,000[2]
1919	106,000[2]
1920	141,000[2]
1921	81,000[2]
1922	152,673
1923	171,421
1924	207,687
1925	201,000[2]
1926	249,869
1927	146,001
1928	N/A
1929	121,457
1930	90,755
1931	52,364
1932	27,555
1933	106,103
1934	95,011
1935	158,999
1936	263,647
1937	295,047
1938	114,529
1939	179,300
1940	195,505
1941	236,999
1942	68,522[3]
1943	0
1944	0
1945	0
1946-1948	649,695[4]
1949	260,000
1950	350,000
1951	292,000
1952	206,000
1953	304,000
1954	150,930
1955	273,286
1956	233,686
1957	281,359
1958	133,953
1959	151,851
1960	400,720
1961	230,805
1962	165,861
1963	363,762
1964	388,800
1965	550,795
1966	526,800
1967	497,380
1968	527,500
1969	552,852
1970	503,392
1971	584,946
1972	593,181
1973	**675,161[5]**
1974	N/A[6]
1975	315,021

[1] Dodge Brothers organized 7/14/14
[2] Calendar Year Production
[3] Production stopped 2/1/42
[4] Year Breakouts Unavailable
[5] **Highest Production Total from 1914-1975**
[5] Exact figures not available

Dodge Engines, 1914–1975

Year	Cylinders	Displacement	Bore & Stroke	Compression Ratio	Output (Gross HP)
1914	I-4	212.3-Cu.in.	3-7/8 X 4-1/2 in.	4.0:1	35
1915	I-4	212.3-Cu.in.	3-7/8 X 4-1/2 in.	4.0:1	35
1916	I-4	212.3-Cu.in.	3-7/8 X 4-1/2 in.	4.0:1	35
1917	I-4	212.3-Cu.in.	3-7/8 X 4-1/2 in.	4.0:1	35
1918	I-4	212.3-Cu.in.	3-7/8 X 4-1/2 in.	4.0:1	35
1919	I-4	212.3-Cu.in.	3-7/8 X 4-1/2 in.	4.0:1	35
1920	I-4	212.3-Cu.in.	3-7/8 X 4-1/2 in.	4.0:1	35
1921	I-4	212.3-Cu.in.	3-7/8 X 4-1/2 in.	4.0:1	35
1922	I-4	212.3-Cu.in.	3-7/8 X 4-1/2 in.	4.0:1	35
1923	I-4	212.3-Cu.in.	3-7/8 X 4-1/2 in.	4.0:1	35
1924	I-4	212.3-Cu.in.	3-7/8 X 4-1/2 in.	4.0:1	35
1925	I-4	212.3-Cu.in.	3-7/8 X 4-1/2 in.	4.0:1	35
1926	I-4	212.3-Cu.in.	3-7/8 X 4-1/2 in.	4.0:1	35
1927	I-4	212.3-Cu.in.	3-7/8 X 4-1/2 in.	4.0:1	35
1927	I-4	212.3-Cu.in.	3-7/8 X 4-1/2 in.	4.1:1	44
1927	I-6	224.3-Cu.in.	3-1/4 X 4-1/2 in.	5.3:1	60
1928	I-6	208-Cu.in.	3-3/8 X 3-7/8 in.	5.2:1	58
1928	I-6	224-Cu.in.	3-1/4 X 4-1/2 in.	N/A	68
1928	I-6	241.6-Cu.in.	3-3/8 X 4-1/2 in.	5.2:1	78
1929	I-6	208-Cu.in.	3-3/8 X 3-7/8 in.	5.2:1	63
1930	I-6	189.8-Cu.in.	3-1/8 X 4-1/8 in.	5.2:1	60
1930	I-8	220.7-Cu.in.	2-7/8 X 4-1/2 in.	5.4:1	75
1931	I-6	211.5-Cu.in.	3-1/4 X 4-1/4 in.	5.2:1	68
1931	I-6	211.5-Cu.in.	3-1/4 X 4-1/4 in.	5.4:1	74
1931	I-8	240.3-Cu.in.	3 X 4-1/4 in.	5.2:1	84
1932	I-4	196.1-Cu.in.	3-5/8 X 4-3/4 in.	N/A	65
1932	I-6	217.8-Cu.in.	3-1/4 X 4-3/8 in.	5.35:1(std) 6.35:1(opt.)	79
1932	I-8	282.1-Cu.in.	3-1/4 X 4-1/4 in.	5.2:1(std) 6.2:1(opt.)	90, 100
1933	I-6	189.8-Cu.in.	3-1/8 X 4-1/8 in.	N/A	70
1933	I-6	201.3-Cu.in.	3-1/8 X 4-3/8 in.	5.5:1(std) 6.2:1(opt.)	75, 81
1933	I-8	282.1-Cu.in.	3-1/4 X 4-1/4 in.	6.5:1(std) 5.2:1(opt.)	100, 94
1934	I-6	201-Cu.in.	3-1/8 X 4-3/8 in.	N/A	77
1934	I-6	217.8-Cu.in.	3-1/4 X 4-3/8 in.	5.6:1(std) 6.5:1(opt.)	82, 87
1935	I-6	201-Cu.in.	3-1/8 X 4-3/8 in.	N/A	82
1935	I-6	217.8-Cu.in.	3-1/4 X 4-3/8 in.	6.5:1	87
1936	I-6	201-Cu.in.	3-1/8 X 4-1/8 in.	N/A	82
1936	I-6	217.8-Cu.in.	3-1/4 X 4-3/8 in.	6.5:1	87
1937	I-6	201-Cu.in.	3-1/8 X 4-1/8 in.	N/A	82

Year	Cylinders	Displacement	Bore & Stroke	Compression Ratio	Output (Gross HP)
1937	I-6	217.8-Cu.in.	3-1/4 X 4-3/8 in.	6.5:1	87
1938	I-6	201-Cu.in.	3-1/8 X 4-3/4 in.	N/A	82
1938	I-6	217.8-Cu.in.	3-1/4 X 4-3/8 in.	6.5:1	87
1939	I-6	201-Cu.in.	3-1/8 X 4-3/4 in.	N/A	82
1939	I-6	217.8-Cu.in.	3-1/4 X 4-3/8 in.	6.5:1	87
1940	I-6	217.8-Cu.in.	3-1/4 X 4-3/8 in.	6.5:1	87
1940	I-6	218-Cu.in.	3-1/4 X 4-3/8 in.	N/A	84
1941	I-6	217.8-Cu.in.	3-1/4 X 4-3/8 in.	6.5:1	91
1941	I-6	218-Cu.in.	3-3/8 X 4-1/6 in.	N/A	88
1942	I-6	230.2-Cu.in.	3-1/4 X 4-5/8 in.	6.7:1	105
1946	I-6	230-Cu.in.	3.25 X 4.38 in.	6.6:1	102
1947	I-6	230-Cu.in.	3.25 X 4.38 in.	6.6:1	102
1948	I-6	230-Cu.in.	3.25 X 4.38 in.	6.6:1	102
1949	I-6	230-Cu.in.	3.25 X 4.38 in.	7.1:1	103
1950	I-6	230-Cu.in.	3.25 X 4.38 in.	7.1:1	103
1951	I-6	230-Cu.in.	3.25 X 4.38 in.	7.1:1	103
1952	I-6	230-Cu.in.	3.25 X 4.27 in.	7.0:1	103
1953	I-6	230-Cu.in.	3.25 X 4.27 in.	7.1:1	103
1953	V-8	241-Cu.in.	3.44 X 3.25 in.	7.0:1	140
1954	I-6	230-Cu.in.	3.25 X 4.27 in.	7.25:1	110
1954	V-8	241-Cu.in.	3.312 X 3.25 in.	7.5:1 or 7.1:1(Meadowbrook)	150, 140
1955	I-6	230-Cu.in.	3.25 X 4.63 in.	7.4:1	123
1955	V-8	270-Cu.in.	3.63 X 3.26 in.	7.6:1	175
1955	V-8	270-Cu.in.	3.63 X 3.26 in.	7.6:1	183(std.), 193(opt.)
1956	I-6	230-Cu.in.	3.25 X 4.63 in.	7.6:1	131
1956	V-8	270-Cu.in.	3.63 X 3.26 in.	7.6:1	189
1956	V-8	315-Cu.in.	3.63 X 3.80 in.	8.0:1	218, 230
1956	V-8	315-Cu.in.	3.63 X 3.80 in.	9.25:1	260, 295
1957	I-6	230-Cu.in.	3.25 X 4.63 in.	8.0:1	138
1957	V-8	325-Cu.in.	3.69 X 3.80 in.	8.5:1	260
1957	V-8	325-Cu.in.	3.69 X 3.80 in.	10.0:1	285, 310
1957	V-8	354-Cu.in.	3.94 X 3.63 in.	10.0:1	340
1958	I-6	230-Cu.in.	3.25 X 4.83 in.	8.0:1	138
1958	V-8	325-Cu.in.	3.69 X 3.80 in.	8.0:1	245
1958	V-8	350-Cu.in.	4.05 X 3.38 in.	10.0:1	295
1958	V-8	361-Cu.in.	4.12 X 3.38 in.	10.0:1	305, 320
1958	V-8	361-Cu.in.	4.12 X 3.38 in.	10.0:1	333
1959	I-6	230-Cu.in.	3.25 X 4.38 in.	8.0:1	135
1959	V-8	326-Cu.in.	3.95 X 3.31 in.	9.2:1	255
1959	V-8	361-Cu.in.	4.12 X 3.38 in.	10.1:1	295
1959	V-8	383-Cu.in.	4.25 X 3.38 in.	10.0:1	320, 345
1960	I-6	225-Cu.in.	3.41 X 4.13 in.	8.5:1	145
1960	V-8	318-Cu.in.	3.91 X 3.31 in.	9.0:1	230
1960	V-8	361-Cu.in.	4.12 X 3.38 in.	10.0:1	295
1960	V-8	381-Cu.in.	4.12 X 3.38 in.	10.0:1	330
1960	V-8	383-Cu.in.	4.25 X 3.38 in.	10.0:1	325
1961	Slant-6	170-Cu.in.	3.40 X 3.13 in.	8.2:1	101
1961	Slant-6	225-Cu.in.	3.41 X 4.13 in.	8.2:1	145, 195
1961	V-8	318-Cu.in.	3.91 X 3.31 in.	9.0:1	265
1961	V-8	361-Cu.in.	4.12 X 3.38 in.	9.0:1	265, 305
1961	V-8	361-Cu.in.	4.25 X 3.38 in.	10.0:1	325, 330
1961	V-8	383-Cu.in.	4.19 X 3.75 in.	10.0:1	350, 375
1962	Slant-6	170-Cu.in.	3.40 X 3.13 in.	8.2:1	101
1962	Slant-6	225-Cu.in.	3.41 X 4.13 in.	8.2:1	145, 195
1962	V-8	318-Cu.in.	3.91 X 3.31 in.	9.0:1	230, 260
1962	V-8	361-Cu.in.	4.12 X 3.38 in.	9.0:1	305
1962	V-8	413-Cu.in.	4.19 X 3.75 in.	11.0:1	410
1962	V-8	413-Cu.in.	4.19 X 3.75 in.	13.5:1	420
1963	Slant-6	170-Cu.in.	3.40 X 3.13 in.	8.2:1	101
1963	Slant-6	225-Cu.in.	3.41 X 4.13 in.	8.2:1	145
1963	V-8	318-Cu.in.	3.91 X 3.31 in.	9.0:1	230
1963	V-8	361-Cu.in.	4.12 X 3.38 in.	9.0:1	265
1963	V-8	383-Cu.in.	4.25 X 3.38 in.	10.1:1	330
1963	V-8	413.2-Cu.in.	4.188 X 3.75 in.	10.0:1	330, 360, 390
1963	V-8	426-Cu.in.	4.25 X 3.75 in.	11.0:1 or 13.5:1	415, 425
1964	Slant-6	170-Cu.in.	3.40 X 3.13 in.	8.2:1	101
1964	Slant-6	225-Cu.in.	3.41 X 4.13 in.	8.4:1	145
1964	V-8	273-Cu.in.	3.63 X 3.31 in.	8.8:1	180
1964	V-8	318-Cu.in.	3.91 X 3.31 in.	9.0:1	230
1964	V-8	361-Cu.in.	4.12 X 3.38 in.	9.0:1	265
1964	V-8	383-Cu.in.	4.25 X 3.38 in.	10.0:1	305, 330
1964	V-8	426-Cu.in.	4.25 X 3.75 in.	10.3:1 or 11.0:1 or 12.5:1	415, 425, 400
1965	Slant-6	170-Cu.in.	3.40 X 3.13 in.	8.4:1	101
1965	Slant-6	225-Cu.in.	3.41 X 4.13 in.	8.4:1	145
1965	V-8	273-Cu.in.	3.63 X 3.31 in.	8.8:1	180
1965	V-8	318-Cu.in.	3.91 X 3.31 in.	9.0:1	230
1965	V-8	361-Cu.in.	4.12 X 3.38 in.	9.0:1	265
1965	V-8	383-Cu.in.	4.25 X 3.38 in.	10.0:1	330
1965	V-8	413-Cu.in.	4.19 X 3.75 in.	10.1:1	340
1965	V-8	426-Cu.in.	4.25 X 3.75 in.	10.1:1 or 11.0:1 or 12.0:1	365, 415, 425
1966	Slant-6	170-Cu.in.	3.40 X 3.13 in.	8.5:1	101
1966	Slant-6	225-Cu.in.	3.41 X 4.13 in.	8.5:1	145
1966	V-8	273-Cu.in.	3.63 X 3.31 in.	8.8:1 or 10.5:1	180, 235
1966	V-8	318-Cu.in.	3.91 X 3.31 in.	9.0:1	230
1966	V-8	361-Cu.in.	4.12 X 3.38 in.	9.0:1	265
1966	V-8	383-Cu.in.	4.25 X 3.38 in.	9.2:1 or 10.0:1	270, 325
1966	V-8	426-Cu.in.	4.25 X 3.75 in.	12.0:1 or 10.25:1	425
1966	V-8	440-Cu.in.	4.32 X 3.75 in.	10.0:1	365
1967	Slant-6	170-Cu.in.	3.40 X 3.13 in.	8.5:1	101
1967	Slant-6	225-Cu.in.	3.41 X 4.13 in.	8.4:1	145
1967	V-8	273-Cu.in.	3.63 X 3.31 in.	8.6:1 or 10.5:1	180, 235
1967	V-8	318-Cu.in.	3.91 X 3.31 in.	9.0:1	230
1967	V-8	383-Cu.in.	4.25 X 3.38 in.	9.2:1 or 10.0:1	270, 325
1967	V-8	426-Cu.in.	4.25 X 3.75 in.	10.25:1	425
1967	V-8	440-Cu.in.	4.32 X 3.75 in.	10.0:1	375
1968	Slant-6	170-Cu.in.	3.40 X 3.13 in.	8.5:1	101
1968	Slant-6	225-Cu.in.	3.41 X 4.13 in.	8.4:1	145
1968	V-8	273-Cu.in.	3.63 X 3.31 in.	8.6:1 or 10.5:1	180, 235
1968	V-8	318-Cu.in.	3.91 X 3.31 in.	9.0:1	230
1968	V-8	340-Cu.in.	4.04 X 3.31 in.	10.5:1	275
1968	V-8	383-Cu.in.	4.25 X 3.38 in.	9.2:1 or 10.0:1	290, 300
1968	V-8	426-Cu.in.	4.25 X 3.75 in.	10.25:1	425
1968	V-8	440-Cu.in.	4.32 X 3.75 in.	10.0:1	375
1969	Slant-6	170-Cu.in.	3.40 X 3.13 in.	8.5:1	115
1969	Slant-6	225-Cu.in.	3.41 X 4.13 in.	8.4:1	145
1969	V-8	273-Cu.in.	3.63 X 3.31 in.	8.6:1 or 10.5:1	180, 235
1969	V-8	318-Cu.in.	3.91 X 3.31 in.	9.0:1	230
1969	V-8	340-Cu.in.	4.04 X 3.31 in.	10.5:1	275
1969	V-8	383-Cu.in.	4.25 X 3.38 in.	10.0:1	335
1969	V-8	426-Cu.in.	4.25 X 3.75 in.	10.25:1	425
1969	V-8	440-Cu.in.	4.32 X 3.75 in.	10.0:1	375
1970	Slant-6	198-Cu.in.	3.40 X 3.64 in.	8.4:1	125
1970	Slant-6	225-Cu.in.	3.41 X 4.13 in.	8.4:1	145
1970	V-8	318-Cu.in.	3.91 X 3.31 in.	9.0:1	230
1970	V-8	340-Cu.in.	4.04 X 3.31 in.	10.0:1	275, 290
1970	V-8	383-Cu.in.	4.25 X 3.38 in.	9.2:1 or 10.0:1	290, 330, 335
1970	V-8	426-Cu.in.	4.25 X 3.75 in.	10.25:1	425
1970	V-8	440-Cu.in.	4.32 X 3.75 in.	10.0:1 or 10.1:1	350, 375, 390
1971	Colt-4	97.5-Cu.in.	3.03 X 3.39 in.	N/A	100
1971	Slant-6	198-Cu.in.	3.40 X 3.64 in.	8.4:1	125
1971	Slant-6	225-Cu.in.	3.41 X 4.13 in.	8.4:1	145
1971	V-8	318-Cu.in.	3.91 X 3.31 in.	9.0:1	230
1971	V-8	340-Cu.in.	4.04 X 3.31 in.	10.0:1	275
1971	V-8	360-Cu.in.	4.00 X 3.58 in.	8.7:1	255
1971	V-8	383-Cu.in.	4.25 X 3.38 in.	9.2:1 or 9.5:1	275, 300
1971	V-8	426-Cu.in.	4.25 X 3.75 in.	10.25:1	425
1971	V-8	440-Cu.in.	4.32 X 3.75 in.	9.7:1 or 10.5:1	370, 385

Net Rating System was used to determine Gross HP

Year	Cylinders	Displacement	Bore & Stroke	Compression Ratio	Output (Gross HP)
1972	Slant-6	198-Cu.in.	3.40 X 3.84 in.	8.4:1	100
1972	Slant-6	225-Cu.in.	3.41 X 4.13 in.	8.4:1	110
1972	V-8	318-Cu.in.	3.91 X 3.31 in.	8.6:1	150
1972	V-8	340-Cu.in.	4.04 X 3.31 in.	8.5:1	240
1972	V-8	360-Cu.in.	4.00 X 3.58 in.	8.8:1	175
1972	V-8	400-Cu.in.	4.34 X 3.38 in.	8.2:1	190, 255
1972	V-8	440-Cu.in.	4.32 X 3.75 in.	8.2:1 or 10.3:1	280, 330
1973	Slant-6	198-Cu.in.	3.40 X 3.84 in.	8.4:1	95
1973	Slant-6	225-Cu.in.	3.41 X 4.13 in.	8.4:1	105
1973	V-8	318-Cu.in.	3.91 X 3.31 in.	8.6:1	150
1973	V-8	340-Cu.in.	4.04 X 3.31 in.	8.5:1	240
1973	V-8	360-Cu.in.	4.00 X 3.58 in.	8.4:1	170
1973	V-8	400-Cu.in.	4.34 X 3.38 in.	8.2:1	175, 260
1973	V-8	440-Cu.in.	4.32 X 3.75 in.	8.2:1	280
1974	Slant-6	198-Cu.in.	3.40 X 3.84 in.	8.4:1	95
1974	Slant-6	225-Cu.in.	3.41 X 4.13 in.	8.4:1	105
1974	V-8	318-Cu.in.	3.91 X 3.31 in.	8.6:1	150
1974	V-8	360-Cu.in.	4.00 X 3.58 in.	8.4:1	200, 245
1974	V-8	400-Cu.in.	4.34 X 3.38 in.	8.2:1	205, 250
1974	V-8	440-Cu.in.	4.32 X 3.75 in.	8.2:1	230, 275
1975	I-6	225-Cu.in.	3.40 X 4.12 in.	8.4:1	95
1975	V-8	318-Cu.in.	3.91 X 3.31 in.	8.5:1	145
1975	V-8	360-Cu.in.	4.00 X 3.58 in.	8.4:1	180, 200
1975	V-8	400-Cu.in.	4.34 X 3.38 in.	8.2:1	175, 190
1975	V-8	440-Cu.in.	4.32 X 3.75 in.	8.2:1	215

Dodge Clubs & Specialists

For a complete list of all regional Dodge clubs and national clubs' chapters, visit **Car Club Central** at **www.hemmings.com**. With nearly 10,000 car clubs listed, it's the largest car club site in the world! Not wired? For the most up-to-date information, consult the latest issue of *Hemmings Motor News* and/or *Hemmings Collector Car Almanac*. Call toll free, 1-800-CAR-HERE, Ext. 550.

DODGE CLUBS

Dodge Brothers Club
P.O. Box 292
Eastpointe, MI 48021-0292
313-884-4327
Dues: $20/year
Membership: 1,100

Challenger T/A Registry
912 Louella Drive
Windber, PA 15963
814-467-5515
1970 Dodge Challenger T/A
Dues: must own one
Membership: 720

The Dodge Charger Registry
P.O. Box 184
Green Bay, VA 23942
804-223-1305
Dues: $25/year
Membership: 500

Walter P. Chrysler Club
P.O. Box 3504
Kalamazoo, MI 49003-3504
clubs.hemmings.com/wpc/
Dues: $28/year
Members: 5,000

DODGE SPECIALISTS AND RESTORERS

SMS Auto Fabrics
2325 SE 10th Ave.
Portland, OR 97214
503-234-1175
1940–80 Dodge upholstery

Phoenix Graphix
5861 S. Kyrene Rd., Suite #10
Tempe, AZ 85283
800-941-4550
Dodge decal kits

Roberts Motor Parts
17 Prospect St.
West Newbury, MA 01985
978-363-5407
Dodge passenger and truck parts

Andy Bernbaum Auto Parts
315 Franklin St.
Newton, MA 02458
617-244-1118
1930–60 Dodge parts

Paul Slater Auto Parts
9496 85th St. N.
Stillwater, MN 55082
651-429-4235
Dodge muscle car parts

Legendary Auto Interiors Ltd.
121 W. Shore Blvd.
Newark, NY 14513
800-363-8804
Dodge car and truck interiors

Kramer Automotive Specialties
P.O. Box 5
Herman, PA 16039
724-285-5566
1960–70s Dodge muscle parts

Vintage Power Wagons, Inc.
302 S. 7th St.
Fairfield, IA 52556
515-472-4665
1939–70 Dodge Power Wagon specialists

Power Play, Bob Walker
276 Walkers Hollow Tr.
Lowgap, NC 27024
336-352-4866
1953–57 Dodge Hemi engines

Original Auto Interiors
7869 Trumble Rd.
Columbus, MI 48063
586-727-2486
Upholstery fabrics for Dodge 1950–80s